Understanding the Art of Sound Organization

Understanding the Art of Sound Organization

Leigh Landy

The MIT Press
Cambridge, Massachusetts
London, England

MIT Press books may be purchased at special quantity discounts for business or sales promotional use. For information, please email special_sales@mitpress.mit.edu or write to Special Sales Department, The MIT Press, 55 Hayward Street, Cambridge, MA 02142.

This book was set in Sabon by SNP Best-set Typesetter Ltd., Hong Kong, and was printed and bound in the United States of America.

Library of Congress Cataloging-in-Publication Data

Landy, Leigh, 1951–.
Understanding the art of sound organization / Leigh Landy.
    p.   cm.
Includes bibliographical references and index.
ISBN 978-0-262-12292-4 (hardcover : alk. paper)
1. Electronic music—History and criticism. 2. Computer music—History and criticism. 3. Electro-acoustics. I. Title.
ML1380.L28   2007
786.7′11—dc22

2006034588

Contents

Preface

The twentieth century was one that celebrated artistic innovation of all sorts. In music an extremely radical innovation was undoubtedly the introduction of any sound as potential material. This broadening of material accompanied the equally radical developments in music technology allowing, for example, individual sounds to be generated *ex nihilo* or recorded and then manipulated and subsequently placed into an audio or audiovisual musical context. The emancipation of the sound in music is the climax of a list of developments that includes the earlier freeing of dissonance, pitch (including tuning systems), dynamics, structure, timbre, and space from traditional practices and restrictions.

Of course, replacing the note with the sound as unit measure of a work did not imply that artists using new materials were obligated to ignore the rich diversity of music history. All notes are sounds, after all. Still, the rapid and diverse developments of sound-based artistic work have been remarkable, comprising creative manifestations currently ranging from electroacoustic art music to turntable composition, music in club culture, microsound, both acoustic and digital sound installations, and computer games. New means of composition, listening, presentation, and participation have all come into existence.

Yet as with other forms of liberation in society, a move forward raises all sorts of questions and will not be found acceptable or appreciable by everyone. One reason that this book has been written is to suggest a means to make at least some of this work more accessible to those who might have difficulty finding it and also appreciating it. Its key goal, however, is to create a framework for this body of music's field of studies. These two areas, access (or accessibility)[1] and scholarship, might be seen as better subjects for two separate publications. But it is my view that scholarship in the arts, in particular the innovative arts, serves both understanding as well as more fundamental functions such as facilitating access for potentially interested inexperienced participants and audiences.

Two issues that will appear and reappear in the following chapters are the categorization of works of organized sound and terminology associated with categorization. Clear classification systems are an obvious aid in terms of accessibility. Do artistic works of organized sound all belong to specific traditional categories of music such as art or popular music? If not, where do they belong, in new musical categories or eventually even nonmusical ones? Must there always be but one answer to these questions? Are the terms we use currently to assist in their placement commonly accepted and accurate? Established categorization systems will act as our point of departure but will also be challenged; suggestions for renewal will be made and current terminology will be found to be responsible for a good deal of confusion.

Scholarship has to deal with the quantum leap that works of organized sound represent. Fortunately there has been a great deal written on this, including a number of very important theses. This book offers the view, however, that the research so far is fragmentary and that far too little foundational work has been done. It is proposed that one needs to build a foundation in a given architecture before the diversity of upper floor rooms and suites can be fully valued. The foundation should also be of use in terms of facilitating and developing appreciation. It is for this reason that I attempt to create a general framework for the study of works of organized sound. It is intended to complement historical and technical surveys that are generally available. Consequently some basic knowledge of the relevant repertoire, pioneers, and theorists as well as of the associated technology is assumed.

Understanding the Art of Sound Organization is structured as follows. The remainder of the preface introduces the ElectroAcoustic Resource Site (EARS). EARS serves as a glossary, bibliographic and general information reference within the field of studies that this book represents. The structure of the book has been designed to parallel the site's architecture, which in turn has been created to serve as the foundational framework for sound-based music's field of studies. As the site is updated regularly, it offers bibliographic and other relevant information that will remain up to date after the publication of this volume. EARS is therefore the book's dynamic annotated bibliographic presence.

The introduction begins by investigating one of the many opportunities that have arisen through the growth of the sound-based musical repertoire, namely the ability to make clear links with our day-to-day experience, something a good deal of music, in particular contemporary art music, has often avoided. It continues by introducing the two returning subjects, classification and terminology.

Chapter 1 focuses primarily on questions of accessibility related to sound-based music, in particular those genres of music involving sound organization that have been relatively marginalized. Accessibility can be enhanced using basic tools such as a concept called the "something to hold on to" factor in timbral composition that will form a starting point for the discussion. This particular notion is based on the listening experience. Another aspect relevant to accessibility that can be something to hold on to is extrinsic to the listening experience, namely the dramaturgy of sound-based works. Musical dramaturgy concerns the "why" and the context of a given work more than the traditional aspects of the "what" and the "how." The investigation of a work's dramaturgy is where the subject of artistic intention is introduced.

A tendency in the artistic scholarship of the latter half of the twentieth century concerns the step away from the study of an artwork's construction and, where articulated, an art maker's intention toward the experience of the recipient, that is, from *poiesis* to *aesthesis* (to follow Jean Molino; see, e.g., Nattiez 1990). The source of this radical, much needed development can be found in both reception theory and critical theory. In a sense this step represents a move from Hegelian thesis to antithesis. The final subsection of chapter 1's section B, on communication, focuses on the third of Hegel's triad, the synthesis involving the ideal of triangulating artists' intentions and listener reception, where artists' visions meet up with the listening experience. Through the introduction of the Intention/Reception project, an example of recent research involving sound-based works is offered in which data have been collected that demonstrate that the potential audience for certain works of sound organization is much larger than one might imagine. This chapter is distinctly different from the following two owing to its rather specific focus. It combines more of my own research with personal comments than found elsewhere in order to contextualize access-based research and support its importance. Chapter 1 is thus potentially more provocative than the following two chapters, which are more general and offer the character of musical and scholarly surveys.

Chapter 2 delineates the types of works that are relevant to this study. It also introduces several existent theories pertinent to the proposed delineation. This is done as an attempt to commence the creation of cohesion between thought and deed. It is therefore the lengthiest of the three chapters. It is here where a first step is made toward the discovery of how major theoretical contributions might fit within a greater structure, where the framework proposed in chapter 3 begins to take shape. Chapter 2 also touches upon some of the means of construction of works; it investigates how difficult it is to place many sonic artworks into genres and how (in)consistently these works are categorized.

This book seeks to discover some sense of coherence among works and, similarly, among theoretical treatments of works of organized sound. It will be demonstrated in chapter 2 that some pieces will fit comfortably into more than one particular category. This part of the delineation is intended to allow for further studies to be written investigating aesthetic cohesion, something that is by no means necessarily genre-dependent. Studies focusing on aesthetics are a bit of a rarity currently, as most scholarship tends to focus on technical or technological cohesion more than content and valorization.

One of the subjects investigated in chapter 2, namely the decades-old split between works that end up recorded in a fixed medium (such as tape, CD, hard disk, and the like) and works involving technology that are presented live, represents a typical area that has contributed both to ongoing terminology problems as well as placement issues. It will be demonstrated that this is one of many areas in which convergence has been taking place in recent years, and thus that presentation may be a less important factor in terms of seeking musical cohesion than the aural reception of works. The chapter concludes with another look at the subject of placement, this time from a specific angle. It is here where current classifications are questioned and a potential new paradigm is proposed. The word *paradigm* is sometimes criticized as an overused, somewhat unclear term. It has been found to be appropriate in this book when used in the sense of a "supergenre," that is, a class bringing together a cluster of genres and categories often considered as being separate that have been converging in recent years owing to their use of materials and the knowledge concerning the artistic use of those materials.

Chapter 3 involves processing all of the information presented thus far and defining patterns that have emerged leading toward the introduction of the framework for the scholarly area of research that is being proposed for the field. It begins by placing the studies of sound-based music into interdisciplinary contexts, that is, contexts involving musical study in combination with the other arts as well as with other subject areas ranging from acoustics and acoustic ecology to semiotics; furthermore, a holistic approach to research is proposed concerning the interconnectedness of a given work's history, theory, technological aspects, and social impact.

The chapter's heart is its proposal of a framework for the study of sound-based music. This is presented in such a way as to suggest an architecture where the theories introduced in chapter 2 find a logical place in the structure of this new domain. It is interesting to note how the further down chapter 3's subject list one goes, the more interrelated theory, practice, and technology become. Section B of chapter 3, the subject list, relates this framework to the architecture of the EARS site.

The short closing word at the end of chapter 3 has a dual purpose. It commences by tying together the main ideas proposed in the book and then moves on to consider what the study of musicianship might consist of that best serves this artistic corpus. It is intended to leave the reader with food for thought and, ideally, the desire to help fill in one or more of the many gaps within the field's framework proposed in this final chapter. It is therefore an invitation for others to pick up where the current volume leaves off.

Introducing the EARS Project

One of the great advances in the publishing world in recent years is the availability of dynamic websites that support an increasing number of new books. This allows not only for supplementary information, but also any relevant corrections or addenda that may become available. This book is related to a website, albeit in a manner slightly different from the one just described.

The ElectroAcoustic Resource Site (EARS—http://www.ears.dmu.ac.uk)[2] offers pertinent information and useful pointers in any given area of the field to its growing community. To achieve this, a glossary of terms relevant to works of sound-based music has been created.[3] All glossary entries can be found on the EARS index to help users find scholarly work related to their subject of interest, whether published, posted on the Internet, or available by any other means.

The EARS project is clearly rather ambitious; yet we are realists. It is not our goal to provide site visitors with every definition ever written for each glossary item or to have sound, image, or movie files to illustrate all relevant listed terms. EARS is particularly focused on the arts and humanities—as opposed to the audio engineering–based technological development—aspects of the field. There are sufficient ways of finding out about the more technical subjects through reference publications and numerous users groups.

What the site offers is as complete a list of relevant terms as we have been able to compile with information that we discover or that our international users provide us with.[4] Therefore the bibliography of this book forms a modest subset of the one that can be discovered by working one's way through the website.

Currently there are six main categories within the EARS project:

1. Disciplines of Study (primarily chapter 3)
2. Genres and Categories of Electroacoustic Music (chapter 2)
3. Musicology of Electroacoustic Music (all chapters)
4. Performance Practice and Presentation (primarily chapter 3)
5. Sound Production and Manipulation (primarily chapter 3)
6. Structure, Musical (primarily chapter 3)

Granted the fourth to sixth categories usually concern processes of composition and dissemination more than theoretical studies concerning the artworks themselves. Still, the link between some of these practices and the analysis of new tendencies in music making are clear; a modest number of publications reflect this. As these subject areas are often treated in technology-based publications in the field, they will only be called upon here to support the top three categories.

The category of the musicology of electroacoustic music receives the greatest amount of attention throughout the book. This is because it forms the heart of the field of studies presented here.[5] The EARS team's hope is to support the creation of scholarly cohesion in this area by offering those interested a chance to discover who has been working in the subjects of their choice and what has been achieved, thereby permitting new networks and communities to be formed. The remainder of this book is not subservient to the EARS project. It is therefore not intended to act as "the EARS book"; the book is certainly influenced by the site's structure and uses this as a basis for discussions which culminate in the description of that architectural foundation which has thus far been missing in terms of the study of works of organized sound.

I would like to acknowledge EARS codirector Simon Atkinson's support. He worked closely with me to create the EARS architecture and has kindly helped me keep to the task during the later stages of writing this book. His advice (not to mention his pestering me about my "Dutchified" English) has been invaluable. The subject of collaboration appears from time to time in the book. I have thoroughly enjoyed this collaboration, in which each of us has always been able to offer the other useful criticism since the project's early days. I would also like to thank my colleague Simon Emmerson for his invaluable feedback during the book's preparation and after the completion of the draft as well as contributing his thoughts on the Varèse–Cage distinction presented in the introduction and on current usage of the word "paradigm." Finally, I would like to thank MIT Press editor Doug Sery and copy editor Judy Feldmann for all of their suggestions during the final preparation of the book for publication.

Introduction

(A) Art Meets Daily Life: Listening to Real-World Sounds in an Artistic Context

[M]usic, classical music as we know it, European classical music that we have today, will not survive unless we make a radical effort to change our attitude to it and unless we take it away from a specialised niche that it has become, unrelated to the rest of the world, and make it something that is essential to our lives: not something ornamental, not only something enjoyable, not only something exciting, but something essential. Some of us are more fanatic about music, more interested than others, but I think we should all have the possibility to learn not only about it but to learn from it. It is perfectly acceptable throughout the world that you have to have acquired a lot of life experience in order to then bring it out in your music making, but there's so many things that you can learn from the music towards understanding the world, if you think of music as something essential.

—Daniel Barenboim (2006)

Issues associated with access to and accessibility of innovative contemporary art have always been of major interest to me. One of the themes I have focused on in terms of barriers to accessibility is the dissociation of art from life. I have often wondered why we have separated much of our artistic work from our daily lives to such an extent, at least in most of what has traditionally been called the "high arts."[1] In traditional societies, art often seems to have been integrated into aspects of daily routines, or at least refer to these routines in their content. In many societies, music has been known to provide the rhythm to one's work. In western Africa, the griot sings the history of his community to his fellow villagers. Visual artwork in such cultures is often functional. In today's society, in contrast, most popular culture is consumed. Popular music does continue to relate to life through its dance culture and associated rituals and, naturally, through its lyrics. Art music, on the other hand, is often more abstract. It does not have to be about anything, regardless of whether we are discussing a string quartet or a work of sound organization. The twentieth-century drive toward novel forms of abstraction, as deeply profound as they may be, has tended to alienate many people or at least keep them at a proper distance, in particular in terms of contemporary art music, as many listeners find such works fairly inaccessible. They often have difficulty linking the listening experience of such works to things they have heard before. Little has been done to combat this abyss[2] and as a result contemporary music has, to a large extent, been marginalized from society in general.

Yet it did not have to have worked out this way. My view, and a premise that will play a major role in this book, is that most people, in particular nonspecialists, enjoy the discovery of meaning in some form when appreciating art. They want to connect with it on any level, whether in terms of content or in terms of something else linked with experience. Nattiez has offered a useful definition of meaning for our purposes: "An object of any kind takes on meaning for an individual apprehending that object, as soon as the individual places the object in relation to areas of his [or her] lived experience—that is, in relation to a collection of other objects that belong to his or her experience of the world" (Nattiez 1990, 9). This definition is particularly useful as meaning can be as specific as one desires or, alternatively, related to other types of shared experience such as specific emotional reactions. It therefore allows us to find meaning in, for example, abstract artistic work.

It is my belief that if means toward the discovery of meaning in contemporary art music works had been offered more often during recent decades, whether directly by way of musical content or by way of supporting information, the marginalization of much music may not have become so extreme. People would have been better able to access and appreciate contemporary works, and artists might have been better informed about what had been perceived as successful in their work and what was perceived to be less successful. Briefly, to borrow terms from phenomenology concerning the reception of music: there is a form of experienced listening, *noema*, based on a person's previous experience. The inexperienced listener, however, has no previous experience of a given type of music to rely on; thus in this case there is no learned form of noema. The listener relies, therefore, on what is called experiencing listening, *noesis* (terms borrowed from Lochhead 1989, 124–125). Through the provision of tools aiding the experience of meaning, that which we will call the "something to hold on to" factor later on, the interplay between noesis and noema becomes less independent.

Every story has two sides, of course. There also seems to have been a strong societal embargo against most contemporary art music works— through media avoidance: think of how little radio play and television coverage contemporary art music has received; and through an education embargo: contemporary music in primary or secondary schools has been the exception, not the rule, to put it mildly. Most musicians, themselves, however, have hardly come to their own rescue, allowing their works to be marginalized, quite a feat in the information society we enjoy these days. Many works have been found to be too complex for a public beyond a select few. Artists in general have also done too little to engage with society at large, most composers passively accepting little media exposure, few performances, and so on. This might be the legacy of modernism: one simply relies on an avant-garde status. It may also simply be the result of a situation whereby artists do not feel that it is their role to be involved with attempts to support access to their arts. In either case, there is room for improvement.

Some (although by no means all) works of sound-based composition offer a return to the connection of art and life, not in the sense of the listener's working to the rhythms of these works, but instead because the specific content creates experiential associations linked with meaning by listeners. Naturally, a sound-based work with real-world sound references can still be abstract; and a large percentage of sound-based works do not use such sounds, so we are only focusing on a distinct subset for the present discussion. The point is that one of the diverse things a listener can latch on to in works that use perceived real-world sounds are the references these sounds provide, either through identifying the references directly or, alternatively, through experiencing the context the artist(s) creates in which these sounds appear. What is being described is of course the use of mimesis in works of sound organization. David Hahn has provided this type of use of sounds from the real world with an intriguing descriptive term, *audio vérité* (Hahn 2002, 57). Associated with this, Luke Windsor has borrowed a term from James Gibson, "affordances," to signify a notion concerning "the relationship between a perceiving, acting organism [e.g., the listener] and the environment [e.g., what is perceived as belonging to a real-world environment in an artistic work]" (Windsor 1994, 87). An affordance can provide a common ground between composer and listener, which in turn allows such artworks to come closer to daily life as that common ground relates to the diversity of personal experiences concerning the particular element(s) from the environment.[3]

One of the key theorists in the field, Pierre Schaeffer, preferred that "sound objects"[4] in his works be appreciated on the basis of their abstract timbral characteristics as opposed to their own specific nature such as source, cause, or context. I have some difficulty with this goal, in particular as it relates to less experienced listeners, as I believe that most people prefer to latch on to a sound's perceived origin, whether created by the artist or simply recorded and placed in an artistic context. Any visually impaired person will confirm this. Schaeffer's goal is perhaps one to aspire to after listening repeatedly to a work, but in itself it is not an obvious tool in terms of finding experiential access to sonic works. Ambrose Field, in questioning the extreme nature of Schaeffer's ideal form of listening, has suggested: "It is now evident that we need to develop a discourse which can encompass the compositional use of real-world sounds that includes the possibility for extra-musical signification in addition to timbral manipulation" (Field 2000, 36). He demonstrates his reserve concerning the Schaefferian approach by adding, "by compartmentalising real-world sounds into objects and suggesting that listeners might focus their attention solely on the timbral activity within a sound, Schaeffer had effectively invented the electroacoustic equivalent of the note" (ibid., 37). His point is that in general a musical note bears no specific meaning, but a real-world sound can be seen to be a sound event or object (like a note) as well as possessing signification.

Although there are many other things to hold on to in terms of finding a means to appreciate an unknown sound-based work, this particular aspect—source recognition—offers a unique opportunity, potentially bringing a good deal of sound-based artworks out of their currently marginal position. It may not signal a return of the tradition of art being part of life, but instead may indicate parts of life being part of art. One of the key goals in chapter 1 will be to demonstrate that owing to such experiential links, much sound-based work is potentially accessible to a substantial audience.

To achieve greater acceptance, the placement of these works within music and, eventually, other art forms needs to be looked into as well as, more specifically, what such works should be called. These are the subjects of the following two sections.

(B) Commencing the Classification Debate: Is Sound Art Music?

Let's look at the question of whether all works involving sound organization belong to specific traditional categories of music and/or possibly those of the other arts. Ever since Edgard Varèse daringly introduced the notion of "organized sound,"[5] the broadening of potential source material within music became an entrenched part of music. His view was essentially that the term *music* was becoming too restrictive; organized sound allowed him to avoid the eternal question of how to define music, in particular his own works. Today few question whether his instrumental works are musical compositions. Yet many people still have difficulty associating a large portion of sound-based works, perhaps even Varèse's few electroacoustic works, with the art form called music. Why is this so? Is it a question of a lack of debate concerning the placement of artworks, the nature of the works in question, or merely the lack of open-mindedness of those members of the public?

We will investigate this question of placement through four hypothetical examples.

(1) The first concerns an interactive sound installation. A bicycle-like object is situated in a public space. The movement of the public within the space controls the sounds produced by the installation. All sounds heard are easily associated with bicycle riding. Normally there is no

audible beat, nor are there any particular sounds that could be called notes with the exception of two bicycle horn sounds which are occasionally triggered. This is a digital work using recorded and triggered acoustic sounds. So where does it fit? Using today's parlance, most people would place this work under the banners of sound art (please refer to the definitions section below) and of installations, both of which have at least some of their roots in the fine arts. But might it also fit under the banner of music, as similar in certain ways to a film or a piece of musical theater that contains music and/or a sound design?

(2) The second example involves a piece of electroacoustic art music that is clearly more sound- than note-based. In this case, structure, time layout, and the application of other traditional parameters of music are all rather esoteric. Occasionally broadcast on the radio, such music finds its key venue in the university or conservatoire recital space, not to mention the CD. Most involved in making electroacoustic works of this kind see themselves as clearly influenced by musical developments of the latter half of the twentieth century.

(3) The third example involves electroacoustic processes and an overtly sound-based introduction. However, once the piece commences it becomes a pitch- and more importantly beat-driven piece employing sampled sounds that belong to today's club culture. No one doubts whether what he or she is hearing is music; but to what extent do DJs' performances have anything to do with the first two examples?

(4) A fourth example possesses a much shorter duration, but it also reaches a mass public: the sound design for a television advertisement. People clearly hear the sound design but normally do not listen to it actively and thus are quite likely to be unaware of its content or detail to any extent.

Where do these last three pieces fit? Is it sufficient to classify them solely as belonging to art music, pop music, and sound design, respectively? Do the first and last examples fit under music at all?

We can obviously relate these works to known genres or art forms. That is what most of us are used to anyway. However, chapter 2 will pose the question of whether a new paradigm, as defined in the preface, has come into existence, one where the common aspects of these four examples could be bound together. With this in mind I shall attempt to demonstrate that the question raised earlier—"Is there but one answer to these questions?"—should often be answered in the negative. The premise behind this thought is that many people, regardless of age and background, might be open to a wider variety of sound-based works than one might think. Children are introduced to organized sound works by way of their video game consoles and the like. Most of them probably would not hesitate in calling the sound used in these games a form of music, as such concepts are more fluid at that age; they are also usually open to new experiences, including artistic ones. Adults who have enjoyed sound installations often react with more than some reserve when offered the opportunity to attend an electroacoustic concert. They might discover if they did attend such an event that other sound-based genres are often a natural extension of an aesthetic that they have already appreciated.

If works like the four described above were found to possess a common ground in terms of their artistic classification, regardless of their very diverse approaches to discourse, a natural evolution would take place. This implies our culture developing to a point where finding access to these repertoires is not only relatively easy, but also a natural thing to do, as is already the case in examples (3) and (4) owing to our consumer culture, as well as (1), albeit to a much lesser extent. The current reality is, however, that most people are often left to accidental discovery in at least two of the four cases, as there is no obvious means for them to know about the existence of such artistic activities. Given the exciting revolution that led to the development of organized sound works, and given, too, the copious and rich repertoire which has grown during recent decades, shouldn't those involved in the field in any capacity be investigating how to increase the appreciation of works belonging to the more marginalized areas of sonic artistic endeavor?

This discussion therefore not only concerns classifying works; it also involves the cultural placement of this artistic corpus. I myself have no problem calling any of the four examples "music," but I feel equally at home using some of the other terms that will be introduced in the next section in which the word "music" is absent. Edgard Varèse did make his radical statement about *organized sound*, after all. However, he clearly intended that works of organized sound should be placed within a musical (e.g., a concert, or in the exceptional case of *Poème électronique*, an audiovisual performance) context. Decades later, John Cage would use the same two words, "organized sound," to refer to any experience of sound organization. In Cage's view, music is available anywhere, at any time, as long as people are willing to listen. Although he presented his work in musical and other contexts, his definition of music was much more emancipatory than Varèse's. Today, many are willing to hear sounds that have been organized in any circumstance as musical. There are also many who are open to organized sound works as music only when such works are clearly related to the rituals associated with the musical art. Works such as the above-mentioned interactive sound installation, or sounds emanating from a computer game, both of which create user-controlled sound organizations, may not be seen as music, as their associated rituals (audiovisual artistic presentation, game playing) are not necessarily directly related to traditional musical practice. Supporting the former "Varèsian" view, Christopher Small has added a word to our music vocabulary, *musicking*: "I [use] . . . the verb 'to music' . . . and especially its present participle, 'musicking,' to express the act of taking part in a musical performance" (Small 1987, 50). He includes not only composing and performance but also listening and dancing as pertaining to the musicking experience. Yet, is it not true that the installation and the computer game also form new ways of musicking?

This distinction is of enormous importance to the remainder of this book, as I shall now make a very conscious choice to honor the Cage view over the less broad one that Varèse exemplified. This choice implies that the sound installation in a gallery or placed at a public square and my daughter's algorithmically generated sequence on her computer game are both examples of music. However, I do not intend to force this view on anyone, in particular the readers of this book. What I am suggesting is that I consider all examples discussed in these pages to be music. I also support the view that some of these sound organizations may be given other designations as well, such as sound installations, that represent another form of today's fine arts. Those of a non-Cageian persuasion, that is, people who associate music only with those varieties that are presented in traditional musical situations, may disagree with this, but they should nevertheless understand my view and make their own choices throughout the book based on our difference of opinion. When "sound-based music" appears, they may need to replace the word "music" with "art works" or even something else.

Debating our means of classification more often would do this body of work a world of good. It is important that people recognize that these questions of placement are as urgent today as they were in the 1950s when sound-based works came rapidly to the fore; that is, one might investigate why after so many years this question seems to have been left unattended as if the relevant genres are all still new, rather unknown. I have yet to discover a discussion concerning genre theory that focuses specifically on issues related to works of sound organization; for the sake of achieving more appropriate classification systems for, and thereby, greater accessibility of the artworks, a collaborative effort to achieve better genre terminology would be very much worth the effort. With these issues in mind we can now take a look at a few of the most-often employed terms and see why there is still more than some terminological confusion in the early twenty-first century. During this final section of the introduction, the key choices concerning which terms we will retain throughout the book will be made.

(C) The Terminology Debate: Defining the Main Terms

It is perhaps not totally unexpected that a field of study which is missing parts of its foundation is also one whose main umbrella terms are at best somewhat useful, at worst confusing. However one looks at them, there is no single significant term for which a universally accepted definition is known; furthermore, it seems that no designator currently exists that is commonly used to define broad ranges of works of organized sound or to identify the field of its study.

The term "the art of sound organization" has been chosen in the title to describe this area, thus ignoring the state of current technology. "Sound organization" is related to its cousin, "organized sound," a term to which I have always been partial. I was part of the team (along with my former coeditors) who named the journal *Organised Sound: An International Journal of Music Technology*. However, a new term will be launched below as an alternative to "organized sound" and all other current terms in the hope that it best represents the area of our focus and is least ambiguous. The following list investigates several terms associated with the entirety or broad areas of artwork within the field. Some entries include more than one interpretation, demonstrating the lack of universal acceptance of definitions. Working definitions for the purposes of this volume are provided. Through this list, a delineation of the field will be begun. All of the following definitions have been taken from the EARS site. There has also been some commentary added in places.

Organized sound   This is the term adopted by the composer Edgard Varèse to describe his music. His use of this term reflects in particular his insistence on the musical potential of an expanding "palette" of possible sounds for use in the concert hall, in particular, new kinds of percussion, electronically generated sounds, and recorded sounds. The term is often cited in attempts to define music and anticipates the notion of music as a "plastic" art form.

Sonic art   This term generally designates the art form in which the sound is its basic unit. A liberal view of sonic art would take it to be a subset of music.[6] It is also used in its plural form.

In Germanic languages, the term *Klangkunst* and equivalents could be synonymous, but in fact this is not a literal translation of the term; instead it is a literal translation of the next term, sound art, and tends to be used as such most of the time. In Mediterranean languages, the term *art sonore*, a literal translation of sonic art, and its equivalents are not used often. Some romance language specialists have used the term as a synonym for both sonic and sound art. Complicating matters further, *les arts sonores* (and equivalents, not to mention *Tonkunst* in German) is an older term that simply differentiates the art of music from *les arts scèniques* (performing or stage arts) and *les arts plastiques* (plastic or fine arts). It is perhaps for this reason that the term *art sonore* is used relatively uncommonly in these countries. A small number of people use the term *audio art* as a synonym for sonic art, although in some countries, including the Netherlands, this term has often been associated with radiophonic work. It does imply that a work is not audiovisual, which limits the genres it might cover.

It is worthwhile to note that people involved in sonic art (and sound art as well) not only call themselves composers, but also sonic artists, sound artists, sound designers, and audio designers (see, for example, Heiniger 1999). This reinforces the ambiguity concerning to which art form(s) sonic art belongs. And then there are people who have simplified the term audio art even further, stating that the art they make is simply *audio*. For example, Markus Popp of Oval has suggested, "I usually don't use the term [music] too much. I just say 'audio'" (Weidenbaum, cited in Cox and Warner 2004, 363–364).

Sound art This term has been used inconsistently throughout the years. Currently it is typically used to designate sound installations (associated with art galleries, museums, and public spaces), sound sculptures, public sonic artifacts, and site-specific sonic art events. It is often used to include radiophonic works (see below) as well. Its German equivalent, *Klangkunst*, is in greater use than this English language term (see, e.g., de la Motte-Haber 1995).[7] Sound art has traditionally been largely associated with fine and new media artists, but has also been associated with some musicians' works.

Radiophonic art/radio art Radio art is the use of radio as a medium of art. Sound quality here is secondary to conceptual originality. Radio art's history demonstrates an evolution from radio play through *musique concrète* and documentary radio to any manifestation of sonic art through the radio medium. Interestingly, its German name, *Hörspiel*, means radio play (or, more literally, play in order to be heard) but refers to a well-established (experimental) medium. Michel Chion's term *cinéma pour l'oreille* (cinema for the ear) is often apropos.

Electronic music Originally, this referred to music in which the sound material is not pre-recorded, but instead uniquely generated electronically, historically through oscillators and noise generators, currently digitally. There are some, particularly in the United States, who use this term today as a synonym for electroacoustic music (see below).

The German equivalent, *elektronische Musik*, has more precise historical connotations, referring to electronically generated postserial composition that originated in the early 1950s in the broadcast studios of Cologne.

Computer music   This term covers a broad range of music created through the use of one or more computers. The computer may function as (assistant) composer; in this case one speaks of algorithmic composition. Alternatively the computer can be used as an instrument; that is, the computer generates the sounds themselves. Here one speaks of sound synthesis. The computer can also record and transform existent sounds. The computer is sometimes brought on stage to create and manipulate sounds made during performance. Finally, the computer may analyze incoming performance information and "reply" in what is known as interactive composition. The former two possibilities sometimes necessitate a good deal of compilation time; the latter two belong to the category of real time. More recently, music making has witnessed extensive use of the networked computer.[8]

Electroacoustic music, electroacoustics   The somewhat elusive meaning of the term electroacoustic has evolved since the late 1950s, and attempts to define it have provoked much heated debate among academics and practitioners. The term has a specific meaning in audio engineering, which is problematic (see 2 below). Separate from this, a rather too simplistic explanation is that it was adopted as an inclusive and umbrella-like term for the activities of musique concrète, tape music, and electronic music composers, activities that saw almost immediate cross-fertilization which continued through the 1960s and 1970s.

The term saw early usage in the United Kingdom and Canada, and during the 1970s it tended (among other terms) to be used in the French language (*électroacoustique*) in place of musique concrète. The term was never in wide use in the United States, where electronic music, tape music, and computer music predominated, but recent years have seen an increased usage there too. The term is currently widely used in several European and South American languages, including Spanish and Portuguese.

More recently, some, particularly in Canada, have adopted the term *electroacoustics*, which seems to incorporate electroacoustic music making and electroacoustic music studies in its definition, and has the advantage of emphasizing the interdisciplinary nature of the field in its plural nuance. (See definition 4 below.)

Some argue that the term electroacoustic music is so elusive as to be unhelpful, and should therefore be abandoned. Others opt for the most general possible use of the word as an umbrella term (see 1 below). The English language has seen increased recent usage of the terms sonic art (and sonic arts) and electroacoustics in place of electroacoustic music. The French language has several nuanced alternatives, including *l'art des sons fixés* ("the art of sounds recorded on a fixed medium"—Michel Chion) and *musique acousmatique* ("acousmatic music," proposed by François Bayle in the early 1970s as a replacement for musique concrète, and a means of delineating his aesthetic concerns within the broader field of electroacoustic music), not to mention the more recent *électro*.

In an attempt to illustrate the various nuances of the term "electroacoustic music," the following four established definitions are offered.

1. Electroacoustic music refers to any music in which electricity has had some involvement in sound registration and/or production other than that of simple microphone recording or amplification (Landy 1999, 61).[9]

2. An adjective describing any process involving the transfer of a signal from acoustic to electrical form, or vice versa. Most commonly transducers, such as the microphone or loudspeaker are examples of this process.

Although the term most precisely refers to a signal transfer from electrical to acoustic form or vice versa, it also is often used more loosely to refer to any process for the electronic generation and/or manipulation of sound signals, including techniques of sound synthesis for the electronic or digital generation of such signals. When the purpose of such manipulation is artistic, the result is commonly called electroacoustic music (Truax 1999).

3. Music in which electronic technology, now primarily computer-based, is used to access, generate, explore and configure sound materials, and in which loudspeakers are the prime medium of transmission. There are

two main genres. Acousmatic music is intended for loudspeaker listening and exists only in recorded tape form (tape, compact disk, computer storage). In live electronic music the technology is used to generate, transform or trigger sounds (or a combination of these) in the act of performance; this may include generating sound with voices and traditional instruments, electroacoustic instruments, or other devices and controls linked to computer-based systems. Both genres depend on loudspeaker transmission, and an electroacoustic work can combine acousmatic and live elements (Emmerson and Smalley 2001).

4. (Electroacoustics) The use of electricity for the conception, ideation, creation, storage, production, interpretation, distribution, reproduction, perception, cognition, visualization, analysis, comprehension and/or conceptualization of sound (K. Austin 2001, with an acknowledgment to Michael Century).

It should be noted that there is no consistent spelling for the term electroacoustic. Many hyphenate the word, spelling it "electro-acoustic." Furthermore, there are also definitions which deviate from the four above, such as those that restrict electroacoustic music to contemporary art music, or even more narrowly, as Anne Veitl states, to "the repertoire of works composed for and diffused by way of a fixed medium (record, tape, or any other medium whether analog or digital)" (Veitl 2001, 341 ftn.), thus suggesting that live electronic performance does not belong to this category.[10] Immodestly, I shall use my own definition (number 1 above) from now on.

Electronica Electronica is a particularly interesting term in current use, as its definitions 1 and 3 demonstrate little to no overlap. The second definition is more inclusive, but most favor the first one.

1. An umbrella term for innovative forms of popular electroacoustic music created in the studio, on one's personal computer, or in live performance. Typically, although influenced by current forms of dance music, the music is often designed for a non-dance-oriented listening situation.

2. The unlikely meeting of several genealogical strands of music: the sonic and intellectual concerns of classic electronic music; the do-it-

yourself and bruitist attitudes of punk and industrial music; and beat-driven dance floor sounds from disco through house and techno (Cox and Warner 2004, 365).

3. Real-time improvised (networked) laptop performance approaches (although fixed medium works also exist). A number of musicians have used this term in recent years in this way. Many such works are based on the structuring and manipulation of small audio arti-facts traditionally considered as defects, such as "clicks." Noise is a common characteristic. Here the term implies a celebratory lo-fi aes-thetic that is not directly influenced by either popular or art music traditions.

If one were to attempt to create a Venn diagram of all the above terms, it would look extremely messy, especially when taking the various sig-nifications of certain terms into account. Words will have to do.

Organized sound vs. sonic art   As Varèse found his works of the late-1920s and '30s as belonging to the category of organized sound, it is clear that the notion of sound organization here includes an emancipated approach to the sounds of instruments as well as to musical works incorporating sounds. Therefore, sonic art forms a subset of works of organized sound.

Sound art vs. sonic art   Sound art as defined here is a subset of sonic art. The type of artwork involved and the venue where it is exposed determines whether a work is both a sound art and a sonic artwork or simply the latter.

Radiophonic art vs. sonic art   In principle, radiophonic productions are also a subset of sonic art. That said, a good deal of radiophonic art includes more traditional musical elements which could be said to fall outside the large space of sonic art, but that leads us into a gray area of to what extent note-based music should be allowed within a sonic art context, an area better left to the discretion of the reader.

Electronic music vs. electroacoustic music   As electronic music is described in three ways above, it is only the most general that is of rel-evance here. Suffice it to say that those who use the term in a general manner, a great many of them in the United States, would probably be using the term electroacoustic music or electroacoustics elsewhere. For those using the term in the sense of electronically generated work, it becomes a subset of electroacoustic composition.

Computer music vs. electroacoustic music   First of all, some older works of electroacoustic music are analog and therefore do not fit into the computer music category. More importantly, the world of computer music is, as can be seen in its definition, a very broad church. For simplicity's sake, suffice it to say that, for example, computer-based algorithmic composition for instruments and computer pattern recognition in jazz improvization form two of many areas that have nothing to do with electroacoustic music.

Electronica and electroacoustic music   Although there are too many definitions of both available currently, works falling under the electronica definition represent a subset of definition 1 of electroacoustic music cited above. Ironically, there are some people working within the worlds of popular music, some of whom are not acquainted with the term electroacoustic, who use the term electronica as a synonym. Some of these people are not using electronica in the sense associated with, say, laptop performance and the like.

Electroacoustic music and sonic art   The time has come for a showdown as far as these two most pertinent terms are concerned. I tend to use the former more often as is evident from the "EA" in the EARS abbreviation, owing to its inclusion of the word, music. I also tend to use the terms interchangeably. However, for the purposes of this book, I have chosen neither, which may come as a bit of a surprise. I have opted against sonic art because it allows critics to claim, "So it isn't music after all." There is also the problem of translation into Mediterranean languages where the term sonic arts has a much more general meaning. The term electroacoustic music is awkward as there are pieces made solely from acoustic sounds that are relevant to our discussion; none of the definitions of electroacoustic music would include these works. Furthermore, "electroacoustic" is a compound word, one currently used in too many different ways within music and the sciences. It was probably born of a compromise. Time will tell how long the term will retain its importance. Another of my concerns about using this term here is that there are more than a few electroacoustic pieces that lean heavily on note-based composition, elegantly applying sound manipulation and timbre-based techniques to move a piece from the instrumental to the electroacoustic universe. Such works are borderline cases and fall into that gray area in terms of the organized sound works that this book is investigating. The definition of "sonic art," in contrast, was not only short, it was clear and it covers the pertinent area.

This leaves me in the awkward situation that I have a reasonably satisfactory definition, but an unsatisfactory term. I have to decide between adding certain nuances to an existent term in the hope that this nuance gains support and taking the more neutral stance of using an unambiguous term that is not currently in circulation.

I have chosen the latter path and will use the term *sound-based music* for the purposes of this book.[11] To paraphrase and slightly refocus the sonic art definition above: the term *sound-based music* typically designates the art form in which the sound, that is, not the musical note, is its basic unit. A liberal view of sound-based artworks would indicate it to be a subset of music.

Returning to the four examples cited above, the work of sound art with the sampled bicycle sounds is clearly sound-based art and, in my view, sound-based music by implication. The electroacoustic piece is most likely to fall within this category as well. The club piece is a borderline case that does not fit comfortably based on the usually minor role sound and sound manipulation play in terms of its material. If almost all samples are taken from pop instruments and remain relatively untreated, if the piece utilizes traditional pitch to a large extent, the work is then most likely to rely on note-based procedures more than sound-based ones and by implication will be less relevant to our study. The advertisement sound design can be described in the same manner. Listening to radio and television advertisements, one discovers how ubiquitous the electroacoustic treatment of organized sounds has become these days.

If sound-based music is the ideal (or least worst) choice for the corpus of artistic works that we are investigating, what then should its field of study be called? The choice is between the musicology of sound-based music (or one of the other terms) and the studies of sound-based music (or one of the other terms). Both have their drawbacks. Barry Truax once told me that one should avoid calling an area of study "X studies" as the latter word indicates that it does not know what it is about yet, which may be seen as cause for embarrassment. In one of his own fields he has seen his Communication Studies Department renamed Communication, allegedly once it got its act together. "Musicology" provides other problems. It is not a terribly trendy word at present for people in Anglophone countries interested in sound-based works owing to the general lack of engagement of most musicologists with sound as opposed to note organization. Perhaps one day the musicology of sound-based music will become a commonplace term. Relevant musicological areas will be identified (as is the case on the EARS site) and in turn will form fields of investigation of the chosen subject area that does, indeed, include that word "studies."

One point deserves to be emphasized here: most studies that concern sound-based music are technological ones. In 1984, Truax wrote, "From a quick look at the major professional journal in the field, namely the *Computer Music Journal*, one will see that research in computer music is currently more dominated by technical matters, than philosophical ones, as is probably inevitable at this stage of a field which is being rapidly propelled by technological forces that are not confined to music alone" (Truax 1984, 221). Have things progressed over the last two decades? Fortunately, they have, but given the foundation issue on which this book is focused, there remains a better balance between technological and musical discussion yet to be achieved.

So which name might be most appropriate? To start with a potential obvious choice, and with respect to my many Canadian colleagues, I cannot choose "electroacoustics." It does have an emancipatory sense (it includes music making alongside scholarship), but, as stated, it excludes acoustic sound-based work and has gained relatively little support outside of Canada in recent years. Similarly "electroacoustic music studies" cannot be chosen here regardless of its usage on the EARS site for reasons stated above.[12] For consistency's sake, the area of studies related to the art of sound organization proposed in this volume will be called *studies of sound-based music.*

It has taken a long time to come to these choices, and in fact my decision changed more than once in recent months. I have attempted to identify a valuable term in the marshland of terminology and to delineate our principal area of concern. The next step will be to identify important patterns related to sound-based music and its studies. This process of identification in terms of the artworks will be found in chapter 2, and in terms of subfields of the studies of sound-based music in both chapters 2 and 3. First, however, our concentration will be focused on aspects of access and appreciation in chapter 1.

1

From Intention to Reception to Appreciation: Offering Listeners Some Things to Hold On To

(A)   How Accessible Are Works of Organized Sound?

This chapter is founded on the premise that artworks are normally created for an audience greater than a select few. Granted, there are exceptions, including certain works of sound-based music. The chapter starts on a rather pessimistic note; however, its conclusion is in fact highly optimistic, so the gloom of the next few paragraphs exists solely to create a context.

About five years ago I toyed with the idea of writing a book with the title *Why Much of Twentieth-Century Music Was Doomed to Marginalization*. It would have been a natural follow-up to my first book, entitled *What's the Matter with Today's Experimental Music?* The unwritten book would have investigated patterns of behavior, such as the enormous increase of commercial music against the loss of much folk music activity in certain societies and, more relevantly, the decrease of relative interest in contemporary art music as a general phenomenon. In other words, "doomed" has to do first with societal interest and second with content. It really is a sad tale when regarded from a distance; and there is much to be said. Some have already taken on the subject, such as Benoît Duteutre in his *Requiem pour une avant-garde*. In *What's the Matter* I cited the late ethnomusicologist John Blacking (Landy 1991, 102–103), who once told me informally that he considered twentieth-century art music to be a "hiccup in music history."[1]

However, the thought of writing a book on the destiny of much of contemporary art music proved to be too depressing. Furthermore, no matter how diplomatic my intentions were, there seemed no way of avoiding personal preference, something clearly evident in Duteutre's book and similar publications I have encountered throughout the years.

But then again, how does one separate any discussion concerning music appreciation from some form of valorization and, consequently, how does one separate any discussion of valorization from personal preference? The word "valorization" has crept into musical vocabulary in recent decades, but it is still in its infancy, that is, it is a term without associated methodologies. The avoidance of valorization discussions surrounding contemporary music in general, and the art of sound organization in particular, might well have contributed to a good deal of the music's relative obscurity. Most writings about music are about a work's construction, not the listening experience or related appreciation issues. Investigations into aesthetic response must surely be at least as significant as the discovery of a composer's working methods. Such investigations are at the heart of this chapter.

The situation that is being sketched here is partially influenced by a twentieth-century development of music's becoming one of the main "cultural industries." I, for one, do not see musical consumption, an important by-product of the music industry, as being completely synonymous with appreciation. Given the particular means applied to achieve sales, a dissimilar type of valorization system contributes to people's popular music listening behaviors, including repeated exposure and peer pressure. Of course listeners do appreciate certain musical products they consume; yet many do not actively listen to them a good deal of the time, often turning the musical product into a *musique d'ameublement* (*pace* Erik Satie) or background music. Music becomes a pacing device, a screen to block out noises of the environment. In a world in which passive listening is often the norm, the success of any music made intenionally to be listened to actively is endangered.

So why start out this chapter with this particular tale of woe in a book concerning the art of sound organization? The answer is quite simple. Similar to most contemporary art music, a great deal of today's sound-based music is of marginal relevance to today's society in terms of its appreciation. As I took the decision not to write at length about why some musical works were doomed to marginalization, although I shall briefly summarize my view now, it is more important to investigate the positive and demonstrate how certain works and, in consequence, certain genres deserve a better lot in terms of appreciation than the one they currently achieve. It is against this background that chapter 1 has been included.

German critics seem to have truly understood what was taking place within the twentieth-century arts when they coined the frequently used terms *E-Musik* and *U-Musik*. The "E" stands for *Ernst* (or serious, i.e., high art) and the "U" for *Unterhaltung* (or entertainment, i.e., popular). The graph of appreciation during roughly the last 100 years would have to demonstrate an ever-increasing line for "U" consumption and an ever-decreasing one for the "E" listeners regardless of the fact that Germany's highly subsidized *E-Kultur* forms a special exception at the global level.[2]

Returning to our microhistory, one of the more obvious things to state about much of twentieth-century art music's being appreciated by a very small audience concerns a side effect of the "art for art's sake" movement dating from the century's early years: many composers chose to ignore the interests, desires, and perceptual abilities of the public, focusing particularly on whatever new protocol(s) they were involved with at the time, a manifestation of the modernist epoch. Another consequence of art for art's sake was the conscious separation of art from life, as was presented in the introduction. This separation is by no means new. Certain forms of art music of ages past could be similarly described, music that was so new or complex that listeners might have difficulty linking such work to their own experience. What makes this separation more troublesome in terms of certain aspects of twentieth-century music is the fact that a number of these composers took little account of what most people were able to process in terms of musical content. This, to me, is a critical issue. I have often written of one's perception "fuse box" blowing during works that are simply too complex for most listeners, sometimes including those "in the know." Composers such as de Vitry, who wrote choral works in which several languages were heard simultaneously, seemed equally ignorant of this fuse box. I would suggest that this music, too, would never share the success of, for example, later baroque or classical composers' work, which always contained elements people could relate to their own previous musical experiences.

One of the more curious aspects of certain works of twentieth-century music is that, when they did reach a larger public, this was the result of the work's being used in audiovisual contexts often unrelated to the original narrative or intention of the works on their own. For example, the use of György Ligeti's *Lux Aeterna* in Stanley Kubrick's film, *2001—A Space Odyssey* typifies this change of meaning. The association with science fiction or horror films arising from otherwise intended works of the last century occurred rather often, in fact. This illustrates how certain composers' intentions have been replaced by other forms of dramaturgy by visual artists. Kubrick, of course, chose well; the eerie qualities of Ligeti's textural fields in no way challenge the listener's perceptual boundaries as the work offers a clear homogeneous sound.[3]

As the century evolved, high or *E*-culture tended to grow on university campuses where elitism was respected. My experience as a student in New York City exemplifies this evolution rather clearly. Although I thoroughly enjoyed my years as a student at Columbia University, I could never adopt the focus on esoteric neo- or postserial music with which most staff composers were associated at the time. Even when working in the Columbia-Princeton Electronic Music Studios, I was trained in a quasi-serial approach to tape composition. This resulting school of electronic music composers, which produced true masterpieces of the genre, would rarely reach a broad public. That fuse box inevitably got in the way. As far as works that cause the mind's fuse box to blow, the English literature scholar Gary Day's sarcastic yet humorous words come to mind.

Under the double aspect of reciprocal determination and complete determination, however, it appears as if the limit coincides with the power itself. . . . The job of academics should be to clarify things, not to make them impenetrable, which is what they did in the 1980s and 1990s. And how! The prose in literary theory was so glutinous the pages were practically stuck together. Derridean devotees stretched language on a rack, but couldn't force it to yield any sense. . . . Believe me when I say that if it wasn't for the likes of Roland Barthes, we in Britain would still be oppressed by the idea that literature had something to do with life. . . . [I]t wasn't long before we (Brits) were looking at books as signifying systems of combinations of codes. (Day 2004, 15)[4]

Moving from the "uptown" to the "downtown scene," even the master of experimentalism, John Cage, is currently running the risk of being remembered more as a philosopher than as a composer. More poignantly, his early, less experimental works seem to be the most often performed, as they appear to be his most accessible ones. I would suggest, therefore, that musicians consider the fuse box and thus, borrowing a term from Day's title, think about at what point their art turns into gobbledygook for nonspecialists.

Another way to look at the issues being raised here is to focus on the combination of challenge or innovation on the one hand and appreciation on the other. I remember a wonderful story told to me by the renowned music scholar Charles Seeger. In his younger days he had known both Igor Stravinsky and Arnold Schoenberg. He, too, was a composer at the time. He said to me that he liked the works by Stravinsky and was more interested in those by Schoenberg and could not fully understand why he could not make the two attitudes meet. He claimed that he stopped composing at the time and decided to remain so until he found an answer to this dilemma and, at least until our meeting in the 1970s, had not composed for some fifty years.

A similar version of the same story came from the pioneer music technology developer, Giuseppe Di Giugno. He once told me of a particular frustration after years of working with both Pierre Boulez and Luciano Berio. He confessed to me that his frustration was simply that, in his view, Boulez composed too much from the mind and Berio, more concerned with being appreciated, from the heart. Although we were both aware of the slight exaggeration, the point was taken. He heard the Cornelius Cardew Ensemble in 1995 and told me that the concert combining instrumental with mixed electroacoustic works that he had attended was the first concert in which both heart and brain were touched during many of the works performed. The balancing act between communication and applying tools of innovation was a focus of this ensemble, one that worked for Di Giugno. I would contend that sound-based music offers an obvious means toward achieving this balance through its inherent innovative nature, at least in these early years of its history, and the relationship with people's life experience in its potential material.

Returning to the premise that most artworks are made to be appreciated by more than a select few, Rajmil Fischman has noted: "Electroacoustic music seems to attract small audiences which, at best, are regarded by some as specialist and, at worst, as elitist and non-representative of society" (Fischman 1994, 245).[5] Granted, any emerging practice or genre will likely limit itself to a specialist audience in its early years. It is the seemingly permanent state of affairs that is being questioned here. Fischman's goal as stated in his essay is that he would like not necessarily to reach a mass audience, but at least to discover "an optimal" one (ibid., 253), a community of interest as it were beyond the makers themselves. He goes on to claim that this can only be achieved through the avoidance of overcomplexity (ibid., 253). Fischman is here acknowledging the need for composers to consider how to create an audience that is larger than one's group of peers.

Supporting this praiseworthy goal, I intend to demonstrate in the rest of this chapter that the appreciation a large percentage of sound-based works might achieve is much higher than is currently the case. Furthermore, the following pages will establish that "it takes two to tango": when sound-based artists take the trouble to offer listeners some things to hold on to as a means of entering their works, appreciation can and will be heightened.

The "Something to Hold On To" Factor

In 1993 I started a project to demonstrate that a substantial number of Serious sound-based works, primarily recorded works, possessed characteristics that could provide listeners with a listening strategy that would allow them to find a way into these works. Supporting this goal, a framework was proposed that listed things to hold on to that I had discovered in commercially available recorded works at the time. Most of these items concern sonic behavior, as will be introduced below.[6] One aspect that goes beyond the listening experience and is related to a composer's intention, the dramaturgy of sound-based works, will be treated separately after this subsection. Accessibility can occur spontaneously; it can also be triggered by offering listeners some form of tips, stated or simply by implication, concerning how to find their way through a piece.

Let's look at the situation from the musician's point of view for a moment before identifying some of these things to hold on to. One of the key revolutions in the birth of sound-based music was that virtually every parameter of sound traditionally used in a musical context is thrown open. What used to be applied in discrete measure: C, C#, D, or half note, quarter note, eighth note, or *p*, *mp*, *mf*, *f*, and so on can now be found in continua: in hertz, in microseconds (ms), in decibels (db), and so on. And then there is the revolution in timbre, not to mention discursive principles. There was little or no tradition on which to lean.

All of this freedom is simultaneously a luxury, both in terms of potential content, structure, and appreciation, and a burden, in terms of too much choice and the omnipresent potential of too many musical languages to learn. In such circumstances, what types of musical means are there which allow a new listener, particularly a less experienced one, to enter into the world of a sound-based musical work? In other words, the goal here is the identification of useful musical devices that support the listening experience.

This question formed the basis for the "something to hold on to" project. Reading postgraduate theses, programs, and liner notes, one tends to discover the formulae, often obscure and in most cases inaudible, that lead to the construction of a piece, or, one or more aspects that inspire a work, but which are, again, not necessarily to be discovered by listening. Why this happens so often in these situations has always puzzled me. What is missing is the articulation of musical content and structuring devices that can be shared or discovered that would thus aid willing listeners in terms of accessing works. Composers interested in an optimally appreciative public should be able to offer this helping hand through sharing what might be called their "access tools," audible musical aspects, or, alternatively, aspects of intention that could enhance the listening experience for those (new listeners) who prefer not to discover these works unaided.

It will come as no surprise that many interested in sound organization offer this helping hand already as was discovered in the original project. They are able to achieve this because of their approach to listening and their training. The more they take potential forms of the listening experience into account, the better they can create new work to enhance that experience. What is missing is the information in the middle that simply states which helping hands, that is, which things to hold on to are indeed present for those who find a new listening experience daunting. I stress the word "those" in the previous sentence, as clearly not everyone prefers such help. That said, the vast majority of listeners who participated in the Intention/Reception project (introduced later in this chapter) clearly stated that such information was of value in terms of their first experiences with electroacoustic works.

We can look at this in another way. Why do galleries and museums as well as theaters often provide viewers with relevant information concerning presented artworks? This information enhances accessibility. Why, then, are concert programs and CD liner notes normally unable to provide salient details concerning a piece's intention and how it can be accessed, whereas any good theater program does this as a matter of course? I am carefully avoiding the word "appreciated" here as this is much more individual than accessibility.

In the original "something to hold on to" project, over one hundred electroacoustic works and CD compilations were researched in which the timbral dimension outweighed that of melody or other traditional musical aspects. Each fell under one or more of the discovered categories that will now be summarized. A substantial repertoire of works, many of them belonging to the historical repertoire, was thus collected for which an access tool could easily be provided to a potentially interested public. What were those things discovered over a decade ago that people could hold on to? They are elaborated upon briefly below.

i. some parameters for a start: e.g., dynamics, space, pitch, and/or rhythm;

ii. homogeneity of sounds and the search for new sounds, e.g., pieces based on one or a few pitches, homogeneous textures, new sounds, and the voice and the special case of a live instrument plus recorded sound;

iii. textures not exceeding four sound types at once;

iv. Programs, some are real but many are imaginary, e.g., nature, recycled music and "anecdotal music,"[7] and acousmatic tales;[8] and

v. others not yet discovered.

As suggested above, part of the fourth category is dependent on the presence of a stated dramaturgy. However, nature and recycling are easily identified and fall under the listening experience part of our tale.

We can now put a bit more flesh on the bones of the items on this list.

Some parameters for a start   There are works of sound-based music that concentrate on a single parameter of sound to a large extent, whether it be loudness (the extremely quiet and the extremely loud come to mind), spatial projection of sounds or more traditional aspects including pitch (e.g., tuning, but anything that is focused on audible pitch relationships is relevant), and/or rhythm. The historical examples cited in the article were: Gottfried Michael Koenig's *Funktion* series (loudness), John Chowning's *Turenas* (space, although one does not hear the surround-sound spatialization on the stereo CD), and *Stria* (pitch relationships). Rhythmical examples are common among Latin-American sound-based composers and artists who ignore the commonly held belief that sound-based music should generally avoid using a beat.

Homogeneity of sounds and the search for new sounds   Where offering one or more parameters as an access tool is clearly related to aspects of traditional forms of music, offering homogeneity of timbre or texture is the timbral equivalent. (a) Phill Niblock best exemplifies an artist who has made pieces based on one or a few, often adjacent pitches to create a timbre of these pitches woven together. Their interplay is what the listener is able to hold on to (not to mention the visualization he often employs). (b) Similarly, a large number of composers focus on just one or a few homogeneous textures as the binding force in some of their works. In this research, homogeneity was reached in one of two manners. Either, as suggested above, a few textures are prominent throughout a piece, making their development the center of focus for the listener; or, as is the case in Bernard Parmegiani's well-known *De natura sonorum*, each movement is based on the homogeneity of sound, but there are extreme contrasts between the separate movements. (c) Some composers have focused on (if not been obsessed with) the discovery and application of new sounds. Iannis Xenakis was fascinated not only by the musical application of various branches of mathematics and architecture for which he is perhaps best known, he was also fascinated by the quest for new sounds. Several of his works in which sounds were synthesized present rather noise-like textures, often indescribable or, at best, distantly related to any known sounds from the real world. The listener will typically focus on these new timbres and how they evolve and interact in such works. (d) It is a well-known fact that, in virtually any musical context, if a voice is present it will most likely capture the attention of the listener. Sound-based works that employ vocal textures, whether recorded and then manipulated or synthesized, are no different. How the voice or voices are treated and what they are articulating is doubtlessly something for the listener to hold on to. This holds true for works such as Luciano Berio's *Thema: Omaggio a Joyce*, as well as those in which vocal sounds form only part of a whole. Similarly, there are several works in which live instruments are involved and yet timbre is the focus of a composition; Horaccio Vaggione has realized several mixed works for live performance and recording where the instruments' sounds often form a significant part of the recording's sound material. Here, the identifiable timbres related to the instrument(s) in question offer a means in which to enter a work.[9]

Textures not exceeding four sound types at once   Those who have had a reasonable amount of experience in terms of listening to sound-based music will have noticed that many works seem to evolve through the use of layering different (classes of) textures. This horizontal approach to structuring might be seen as a modern equivalent of counterpoint. What is relevant here is that transparency can be achieved through the consistent use of a relatively modest number of levels of texture at one time combined with the reappearance of sonic material. Lars-Gunnar Bodin has coined the term *polysonic* for this type of layering in sound-based music (Bodin 1997, 223). For example, much of Denis Smalley's oeuvre seems to focus on this principle. As listeners become increasingly acquainted with the various textures, familiarity aids them in becoming more comfortable with a work.[10] In contrast, works in which new material is introduced fairly regularly, normally need to be listened to several times before such familiarity can be developed. Yet how many people will be offered or choose to take the chance to hear such works more than once, given the current state of the art?

Audible programs   Sound-based music's first major developments took place at the French radio studios and were born of the history of radio plays. Early musique concrète can be seen to belong to the world of radiophonic art, here without a sense of clear narrative normally associated with most radio plays. Many early works did, indeed, have a clear program already implied in their titles. This genre moved program music from the world of notes to the world of real-world sounds. Musique concrète was in fact the first form of music in which both surrealism and abstract narrative seemed to be obvious aspects to pursue. Needless to say, those real-world sounds (whether recorded or perceived as such) offer something to hold on to as well. As I wrote in the original article: "[T]he listener is often (un)consciously trying to place sounds within personal experience. When we try a new cuisine, we tend to say that something tastes like something we have already eaten; when we listen, we react analogously" (1994a, 55).

Many works that fall under this category also fall under the previous one, homogeneity. (a) From François-Bernard Mâche's analog work, *Terre de Feu*, to more recent soundscape compositions, nature has often been brought back as a form of musical inspiration, evocatively in the former case, quite literally in the latter. (b) Citing or playing with reminiscences of existent music is a recycling tool often used in sound-based music. Similar to the case of the voice, above, the moment a familiar piece of music appears in any form within the context of sound organization, it forms something to hold on to. The range of examples in which longer segments are treated is quite broad. John Oswald and his plunderphonic[11] works come to mind when discussing more microlevel collages of existent musical materials. "Anecdotal music," a term coined by Luc Ferrari, falls under the same category as soundscape composition, where lengthy real-world recordings serve as the basis of a sound-based work, whether further treated sonically or not. In its most basic form, the presentation of audio recordings of a given environment, one speaks of "phonography" (a term taken from Mâche), not to be confused with the use of this term relating to the phonograph. Ferrari's very lightly edited beach recording, *Presque rien no. 1, Lever du jour au bord de la mer*, exemplifies the presentation of a work of phonography as a musical composition.

Recycled sounds, including audio samples, do not form the majority of sound perceived in a work, yet they can still form a key focus in the listening experience. There are pieces that play with what Germans call *Schein und Sein*, semblance and reality. John Chowning's *Phoné* exemplifies this tendency in a work where the listener is left guessing which sounds are vocal and which synthesized. He seems to be able to act as a magician manipulating the listener's perception. There is a risk in such cases, as in works where real-world sounds are prominent, but not necessarily placed in a known context, that the listener zooms into the sounds or the semblance–reality confrontation and therefore, at least for a short time, zooms out of the piece. This will be returned to below when the *5ième écoute* (fifth mode of listening: listening to technology) is introduced.

(c) The rubric of timbral acousmatic tales, that is, works born out of the radiophonic tradition, is a copious and a complex one. As program is relevant here in its widest (e.g., nonnarrative) sense—the term *cinéma pour l'oreille* again comes to mind—only those works whose program is decipherable at the first listening qualify as belonging to this type, in terms of the listening experience only. In other cases, as will be presented in the next section, the addition of the work's dramaturgy, where relevant, aid accessibility to a work as people are offered an opportunity to see whether they experience the intention related to a work.[12]

And there is more   A few obvious categories have not yet been covered, as in these cases the work's sound may not be playing the leading role. In live electroacoustic performance, for example, where no traditional instrument is present (such as in several works by Michel Waisvisz), it is the visual performance which triggers the sounds—as long as there is a largely isomorphic audiovisual relationship between movement and sonic result—that offers something to hold on to. I am particularly fascinated by new work in which performers such as dancers conduct sound performances through their movement. Experiencing the result can be like an exciting adventure when the relationship between movement and sound is neither overly predictable nor totally puzzling.

One example will be introduced even though its appreciation is probably limited to specialists. This example is a product of our technology-driven field and involves listeners' sometimes paying attention to how sounds have been made more than how they have been placed in a musical context. In other words, listeners may focus on trying to puzzle out how an artist made something sound a certain way or, alternatively, may recognize the sound of a particular type of synthesis or preset from a synthesizer and lose his or her place in a piece. Denis Smalley has called this specialist attitude "listening to technology" (Smalley 1992, 551); I have often called it *recipe listening*. Here specialized listeners pay attention to sound production, manipulation, and structuring techniques more than the sonic artwork itself, at least during periods of the work. This mode of listening is one that Schaeffer does not include in his *quatre écoutes* (four listening modes, to be introduced in chapter 2, section A1). I have therefore suggested that this be called the *5ième écoute*. It is a useful approach, of course, when a listener is attempting to figure out how a composer produced a work, but that is not what this chapter is about.[13]

The above list is still incomplete[14] but gives an indication of various types of approaches that offer listeners a means of crossing a threshold into a new work of sound-based music. As one becomes more familiar with the artistic approaches, more complex works may become accessible to them, but what is certain is that, when something is offered, taking the first step into the unknown is made much easier. Many of the roughly 100 works investigated were by no means simple or sparse. Their ability to be accessible to (new) listeners came through their composers' knowledge of human response to familiarity of sonic material and/or of structure.

The research I report on here was influenced by earlier work published by Simon Emmerson. This will be introduced at this early point as it provides complementary information to the list presented above. Emmerson introduced an important tool, his "language grid" (Emmerson 1986, 24, originally formulated in Emmerson 1982), which is useful in terms of finding a framework for the placement of works or their individual sections. It can also be useful in terms of finding something to hold on to in any given work in terms of materials used and, where relevant, in terms of musical discourse. It is here where we see evidence of the fact that many composers make *bottom-up* works, that is, works based on materials they have assembled which they subsequently manipulate and place in sequences to form structures. I would suggest that fewer works relevant to this book are made from the *top down*, that is, from a given structure that in turn is filled with sound,[15] in contrast to most traditional music that is made in this manner. In chapter 2, section A, we will discover that in fewer cases still, ordering principles are applied simultaneously at the micro- and macrolevel. Using Emmerson's grid one can conclude that a work's general sound may turn out to be a better identifier than any existent category name.

In 1986, Simon Emmerson published a chapter entitled "The Relationship of Language to Materials" that presents a 3 × 3 matrix, a language grid for the potential placement of sound-based works. Each axis has two endpoints and a midpoint where combinations take place. One axis concerns syntax, and the other, discourse. Emmerson exemplifies each of the nine boxes with at least one well-known composition of the day in his article.

His syntax axis runs from what he calls "abstract syntax" to "abstracted syntax." The former implies a formalist approach to structuring a work. Abstracted syntax implies that the source material is the building block of a work, as it were, what I have called bottom-up composition. Emmerson's discourse axis runs between what he calls the dominance of "aural discourse" to that of "mimetic discourse." In this case the more abstract the sound quality, the more likely a work is to lean toward the aural discourse side. The more identifiable a sound, the greater the chance mimetic discourse will be present in a given work. We will, however, associate aural discourse of real-world sound objects with the Schaefferian notion of reduced listening in which source recognition is not of primary concern in the discussion of Schaefferian theory in section A1 in the following chapter. Abstract electronic sound material will also normally be associated with aural discourse. Soundscape composition and electronic composition where the timbres resemble, say, traditional instruments form two straightforward examples of mimetic discourse.

Clearly not all works are able to be pigeonholed into a single grid category throughout their entire duration; they may move around Emmerson's grid as they evolve. In between the grid's extremes, the "gray area" is quite wide, too. His 3 × 3 construction is offered for ease of comprehension. This language grid takes the distinction of bottom-up (mainly abstracted) versus top-down composition (mainly abstract) and that of abstract (unidentifiable) versus perceived identifiable sound sources into account as a means of classification and is the first example of an attempt to create some cohesion in sound-based repertoire that goes beyond the historical ones found in most textbooks. Emmerson's language grid was cleverly devised on the basis of both how compositions have been generated and how they have been received. It was highly influential on the "something to hold on to" factor that was first published almost a decade later, which focused solely on reception.

Works that fit neatly into each of his grid's boxes may share a number of things in common from the listener's point of view; therefore the language grid represents one very useful way of creating coherence among sound-based works. Emmerson has devised a different approach to things to hold on to from mine that is useful for the general listener as well as for specialists studying this repertoire.

(B)   Communication from the Maker's and the Listener's Points of View

This section of the chapter follows up the suggestion that artists working with sound consider the use of relevant means to support access and accessibility. First, the extension of the original concept behind the "something to hold on to" factor to issues of dramaturgy will be proposed. This is followed by the introduction of a methodology investigating to what extent a composer's intention is received by the listener. It is here where we will discover that a much wider audience for much sound-based music is quite feasible.

It must be admitted that at the time of writing the 1994 paper, I was wary of combining information gained by the listening experience with that offered by others, in particular the artists making the works. Today, I have another view, namely, that the access experience is ideally holistic. Not only should works be accessible by way of their content, but equally, where appropriate, by means of information concerning the work's communicative intention. The reception of communicative intention forms an important part of our experience of meaning in terms of a given artwork in my view. The sharing of meaning brings us directly to the subject of dramaturgy.

The Dramaturgy of Sound Organization

The worlds of music have unfortunately never found a word similar to dramaturgy to be used in its own context. Having worked regularly with other art forms including the performing arts, I have found that the entire concept of dramaturgy has become an essential element of my own artistic work. Yet no one ever taught this to me as part of my study of music or even introduced the notion.

People tend to have a strong view about the presentation of dramaturgic information to potential listeners. At one extreme, Kodwo Eshun writes: "Good music speaks for itself. No Sleevenotes required. Just enjoy it" (Eshun 1998, –7; yes, his page numbering and his writing style are unusual). This opinion is not that uncommon. It is similar, for example, to many choreographers' remarks that if you want to know more about their work, come and see it, all a product of the "art for art's sake" credo. Commercial popular music can accept this credo owing to listeners' repeated exposure to it, popular press portraits of its artists, and the fact that it is often instantly accessible. Some more esoteric forms of popular music, on the other hand, can be compared with some types of contemporary art music discussed above. It is here where Eshun's remark might come across as a bit arrogant.

When there is a program, it is not always useful. Christian Clozier has suggested: "The information given in programme notes deals with 'how' (technical), and sometimes with 'for whom' (place, year, commission), but only rarely with 'what' and 'why,' that is, with the conditions of the 'message' rather than its nature" (Clozier 1996, 31). Readers' views may differ about the quality of program and sleeve notes. As Clozier suggests, the information provided tends to be either technical or something concerning an inaudible aspect of a piece's inspiration. Both may be relevant, to an extent, but neither offers proper information that confers accessibility on the piece (or *access information*, for short) unless the technical information or the source of inspiration is a key goal of audition.

Working in collaborative theater contexts as a composer/sound designer, there would have been a certain level of potential conflict if I were simply to arrive with material and try it out. This manner of working would have been in sharp contrast with the dramaturgic preparation by the entire team involved in a theater production before actors start rehearsing. In short, when an ensemble is attempting to achieve a certain dramaturgical concept, every aspect of performance should support that goal. I, therefore, have to create a dramaturgy of sound to fit the dramaturgy of the entire performance, no matter how radical the sound design might be. If the other members of the team or outsiders brought in to provide feedback cannot experience this dramaturgy, this is cause for alteration. Does this imply a loss of integrity? This has not been the case in my experience. The least one can do as an artist is make work that achieves what one sets out to achieve while meeting the challenge posed by the collective dramaturgical views supporting a given collaborative performance.

It was through such experiences that the power of dramaturgy became evident to me. It led me to learn about notions of triangulation associated with the action research model where feedback is integral to the development of the given research project. In an ideal world, artists should consider triangulation. It is not synonymous with loss of integrity, but instead forms a feedback mechanism in terms of whether communicative goals are being achieved within the community being addressed.

Although the research on the "something to hold on to" factor is by no means at its end and other items still need to be discovered and clearly described, what has been missing in that research is the holism that can be gained by not only offering things to hold on to aurally, but also offering information of intention as a potential access tool. One is by no means obligated to inquire about or follow this information. However, when intention meets reception in the listening experience, accessibility is made more likely. Thus, dramaturgy must be added to the list of things to hold on to presented above. This combination has served as the basis of the Intention/Reception project that will now be introduced.

To What Extent Does the Composer's Intention Find Resonance in the Listener's Reception?

I could perhaps be accused of being "an armchair scholar" in this chapter, making demands of artists and scholars while testing the "something to hold on to" factor through personal experience. But the project and its ideas must be brought to listeners with varying levels of experience. The natural next step after the research into the "something to hold on to" factor was a project which now carries the name the *Intention/Reception (I/R) project.*

> To summarize the situation of composer, listener and mechanisms of perception in a metaphor, I would say that the listener has his eye trained on the viewfinder of the camera, the composer chooses the landscape, the perception works the zoom, sometimes focusing, sometimes not. It is clear that in this metaphor, perception is not an independent third party. (Manoury 1984a, 132)

> [P]erception: what is received as a phenomenon; what is transformed by outside interference (by interpretation, by the psychological state of the receiver . . .); what was not foreseen by the conceiver; what in the course of time ends up disappearing or, on the contrary, revealing itself. The path which joins these two tortuous and undependable territories is the most complex there is. We can see that at the very outset of the problem we encounter a paradox, because for the conceiver the stakes are doubled. (Manoury 1984b, 147)

The Intention/Reception project   I have described the I/R project as follows:

> The "Intention/Reception Project" involves introducing sound-based works that are unknown to the listening subjects, and then evaluating their listening experience. Through repeated listening and the introduction of the composers' articulation of intent (through a work's title, inspiration, elements that the composer intends to be communicated, eventually elements of the compositional process itself) listening responses are monitored. The purpose of the project is to investigate to what extent familiarity contributes to *accessibility* and *appreciation* and to what extent *intention and reception meet* in the very particular corpus of electroacoustic music. (Landy 2006a, 29)

As Simon Waters once put it: "[T]he listener is an interpreter, not a receiver" (Waters 1994a, 134). He uses the postmodernist term "emergence" to describe "a conscious utilisation of the changing boundaries between the subject (listener, interpreter) and the maker (artist, composer), in which the former *interacts* with what the latter has made, such that the work can be said to emerge in its 'use,' rather than having been designed in its entirety by the artist and then 'presented'" (Waters 2000a). With this in mind the project's goals are twofold: to demonstrate the need for better means of access than the ones currently on offer; and, consequently, to illustrate that a significant amount of sound-based music is (much) more accessible than one might think. This is achieved through gaining reactions from listeners with very different levels of experience with this music.

Listener-based research is not totally new within this field. It is, however, the exception rather than the rule. A few examples will be introduced of work undertaken in a somewhat similar fashion to the I/R project thus far to contextualize this project. A related though slightly dissimilar example undertaken by François Delalande will also be presented in the following chapter, section A1.

(1) Michael Bridger published his first findings concerning listener-based research in 1989 (Bridger 1989). In 2002 (Bridger 2002), he revisited his work having expanded his project. This latter text commences as follows:

In some ways, electronic and computer music often seem to be more directly suggestive of pictorial imagery than other music, but there is ample evidence that many listeners find it disturbing and alienating. This paper explores this paradox in the light of the author's research into listeners' response, which has suggested that processes of musical communication and the engagement of listeners' pleasurable interest are in several respects similar to processes of narrative as exemplified in literary and film genres, even to the extent that the surface structures of these different narrative manifestations may both relate equally to a deep narrative grammar, perhaps akin in some respects to Chomsky's notion of deep structures in linguistic grammar. (Bridger 2002, abstract)

What one ascertains from these remarks is that the author is interested in both information related to appreciation as well as what he will later call "quasi-narrative" in sound-based music.

His earlier project, highly influenced by the work of Roland Barthes' *S/Z*, and employing some key, if difficult, works in sound-based music history (Luciano Berio's *Visage*, John Cage's *Fontana Mix*, György Ligeti's *Artikulation*, Karlheinz Stockhausen's *Gesang der Jünglinge* and

Telemusik, and Edgard Varèse's *Poème électronique*), listeners were offered the opportunity to discover salient features in the chosen works. His methodology is unfortunately not fully detailed, and one must assume the participants possess a rather considerable basic knowledge when regarding the author's main conclusions. Here follows a summary (Bridger 2002, main text):

• A number of shared concerns were evident in the pieces, despite their apparent heterogeneity—with spatial and timbral modulation, broadening of dynamic fields, and a radical rejection of other musical languages and grammars.

• Links were apparent with concerns in other arts—a shared zeitgeist with respect to material, arenas of performance, challenge to the audience, redefining of form and process—all those characteristics of confusion and radical iconoclasm that were in the air as modernism shaded into postmodernism.

• There was a positive response to spatial modulation.

• The predominant mode of expression nevertheless appeared to be metonymic rather than metaphoric.

• Listener alienation was clearly a problematic issue.

Bridger adds that listeners seem to want to find causal relationships in such works, a pertinent conclusion when dealing with accessibility. These points provide useful information in the sense that they indicate to an extent what listeners may be looking for. But to be certain, we would need to have spelled out what their musical experience was and also be told by the author why he chose these particular works, many of which do not easily fall into the class of accessible sound-based compositions.

Bridger's more recent project involved over 400 test subjects, including children and adults (not further specified) and "a range of pieces in a variety of idioms, including electro-acoustic music" (ibid.). Not surprisingly, Bridger has discovered that children generally respond more favorably to the new than adults. More importantly, he investigated both the areas of associative imagery as well as what he calls 'liking preferences' through repeated listening. His main conclusion is that there is a "need for electro-acoustic . . . music to develop a non-semantic quasi-grammar equivalent to that of the tonal system" (ibid.). This is based on his as yet unpublished appreciation statistics that are said to be clearly disappointing, a result that is in stark contrast to I/R data acquired thus far.

(2) Andra McCartney's work is linked to the I/R project in more ways than Bridger's and has provided its greatest inspiration. Still, there are also crucial differences between the two projects, as we shall discover. Her great advantage is that she is a musician, musicologist, and communications scientist; she specializes in a combination of fields that seems to occur in Canada more frequently than elsewhere. She has, therefore, research tools at her disposal that others spanning fewer fields might not readily possess.

McCartney has shown an interest in finding relationships between intention and reception for years. Her choice of participant-based research projects was therefore quite a natural one for her. McCartney is specifically interested in relating the listener experience to the communicative desires of the composer of soundscape compositions. In contrast, the I/R project uses this "conversation"—over a broader repertoire than McCartney—as a means to discover how accessible works are, as well as on what bases appreciation is founded. Her doctoral dissertation, *Sounding Places: Situated Conversations through the Soundscape Compositions of Hildegard Westerkamp* (published in 1999) focuses on Westerkamp's work. Using an approach reminiscent of Margaret Mead's fieldwork in anthropology, McCartney gets to know her subject well, forming a friendship as a means to gain insight into Wasterkamp's motivations and the vision behind her works. In this way, she becomes a well-informed spokesperson of Westerkamp's intentions when she introduces her subjects to the researched works. In contrast to Bridger's project, all works are user-friendly involving readily identifiable sounds, sources, and contexts.

Canada is the country in which the soundscape notion was born. Soundscape composition tends to involve material offering a connection with a listener's life. McCartney has written:

[W]hen we listen to a processed real-world sound, and recognize it as such, we regard the composer as "doing" something to familiar material. Processing becomes an activity that guides, and changes, our previous understanding of the source; it offers an interpretation. . . . [I]n offering a new interpretation of something that, nevertheless, remains "known" from reality, real-world music invites us to deploy, and develop, "ordinary" listening skills; it encourages us to feel that we are involved, and participating, in the creation of a story about real life. (1999, chapter 5)

There are no direct references in McCartney's dissertation to triangulation. However, one assumes that the informants' responses were relayed to the composer; all McCartney would then need to investigate is whether Westerkamp found this information of relevance to her future composition work.

An interesting factor in her project is the choice of listening subjects. Her groups ranged from university music classes, to university gender studies classes, to secondary school music classes, to a small group volunteering after a performance of a work at a public venue. Some were not necessarily trained or being trained in music; some were older children. The author admits that the majority were interested in the work in the first place.

McCartney discovered that the groups in which her tests took place offered a particular slant on the way the responses were gathered; the gender studies group members were more interested in the challenges involved in becoming a successful female composer, the composers with more technical issues. Predictable, perhaps; nevertheless, the quality of information gained from the composer, herself, as well as this particular selection of informants was unsurpassed at the time of her research.

She did not choose to perform her experiments primarily on people who had had no previous experience of listening to soundscape composition, in contrast to the I/R project. That aside, McCartney took the first steps toward the understanding of music involving the combination of information on a composer's intention and listener response; she deserves great credit for these initiatives. The method McCartney pursued has provided a great stimulus to undertake the I/R project.[16]

Related to McCartney's work are two participant-based projects of note. These have both appeared as part of the Groupe de Recherches Musicales' *Portraits Polychromes*, a series consisting of several sound-based composer portraits. The portraits can be found at http://www.ina.fr/grm/acousmaline/polychromes/index.fr.html/. The site includes multimedia information as well as associated published booklets. In one case

François Delalande and Dominque Besson asked eight participants (of whom six were professional sound-based composers and two amateurs) to listen to Bernard Parmegiani's "Aquatisme," a movement from his work *La création du monde*, in the presence of the author and, more importantly, the composer who provided commentary while starting and stopping the recording during the first set of two listening sessions. Afterward, the participants were asked to listen to the work three more times, first in a concentrated manner, followed by ten to fifteen minutes of discussion involving the use of a questionnaire; the pattern was repeated for the second listening, and finally the participant was allowed to start and stop the tape individually for the final listening, commenting on what was heard. The resulting interview material was used to create evocative transcriptions of the work that form part of Delalande and Besson's analytical presentation.

Their search was for the identification of perceived semiotic units, and the researchers' view was that this could best be achieved in an empirical manner using knowledgeable participants. The authors and their colleagues made transcriptions based on the compiled data. Two questions deserve to be raised here. To what extent were the participants influenced by the views of the composer and the researchers? Working with a group that did not receive such information might have added value to their findings. And, how would the results be affected by using less-learned participants? This question would have been relevant if the researchers had been interested in combining the discovery of semiotic units with accessibility issues. Delalande has applied this approach in other contexts: to a work of the earlier sound-based composer, Pierre Henry (Delalande 1998a) as well as to a work of Debussy (Delalande 1989a).

The second portrait concerns Jean-Claude Risset's well-known work, *Sud*. Jean-François Lagrost invited thirteen participants aged 15 to 60, all involved in some way with music, to listen to the first of the three movements of *Sud* twice, once just listening and the second time writing, making annotations. After each listening, the individuals discussed their experiences with the author. These interviews were recorded. The participants were asked to pay particular attention to the following four categories: materials, space, light, and evolution. On the basis of what they wrote down during the second listening experience and their interviews, the author was able to summarize collective and individual experiences that proved useful in terms of judging the listening experience of participants and how they varied in terms of age and experience. (The website includes an evocative transcription accompanying the recording of this movement, although it is unclear how this influenced or was influenced by the research itself.)

The examples discussed above have all focused logically on analytical issues. This follows the current pattern of interests one can discover in publications. The I/R project has no pretense of offering significant analytical insights at this point. Instead it investigates the relationship between composers' intention and the listening experience as a means to gauge accessibility and appreciation information.

The project uses three questionnaires that solicit qualitative information in order to acquire data. Informal conversations between project leaders and listener groups take place to "top off" information that is acquired consistently by way of these questionnaires. The questionnaires are printed in full in this chapter's addendum below.

The choice of works thus far has involved two restrictions. First, all works included in the study must contain real-world sounds that are identifiable, either because the sounds are recorded and thus "re-present" real-world sounds (ten Hoopen 1994), or because they have been created so as to represent real-world sounds clearly. This restriction, which will most likely be dropped now that the project has achieved its first batches of significant results, was chosen because the underlying hypothesis in the I/R project was that these types sound-based artworks are much more accessible than one might imagine. Allied to this hypothesis was the thought that using sounds from our daily lives created common ground between the creator(s) of these works and their public. Although the sounds themselves do not necessarily act as an access tool, they may serve as providing a way into a given work.

The second restriction, which again will most likely be dropped at some future date, is that up until now only "tape works," that is, works that exist on recorded media, have been investigated. This was another practical choice. As listener testing takes place in a wide variety of venues, the only equipment needed for such works is playback. It should be stated, however, that playback has thus far been restricted to stereo. Composers have been asked what their view is concerning stereo versions of their works (if the word "version" is appropriate). Only those who acknowledge a stereo version have been chosen thus far.[17] There is no reason why one could not include, for example, a sound installation in the future—as long as listening participants could have the installation present during testing, or a performance of the sound-based work with the performers present.

A third factor that might be considered a restriction is that only works have been accepted to the study where the composer(s) was willing to provide us with intention data. There are many artists who either do not want to discuss or, alternatively, do not believe in sharing intention information. Some claim not to have any particular intention at all. Intention-less works have been excluded from the study for obvious reasons.

Let's now look at this project in greater detail. After a work has been chosen, the composer in question is approached and the composer intention questionnaire is filled in. Program notes and the like are also collected. At this point groups are approached for testing. The two broadest categories of groups are those of "inexperienced listeners" and "experienced listeners." The former category is more or less synonymous with the general public; its listeners have no previous knowledge of sound-based music. In most experiments held thus far, this group has been split in two: those with no formal musical training, and those studying music at a further education level (ages 16–19 in general) who have had no introduction to this musical corpus. Experienced listeners range from those who have introductory knowledge of sonic artworks to specialists, and are subdivided in two subcategories, experienced and highly experienced listeners, the latter (usually smaller) group providing control data.

Listeners fill in two types of questionnaires. The "real-time questionnaire" is used during all three rounds of listening during a single test session and captures listeners' immediate responses to the work. The more focused "directed questionnaire" is filled in after the first listening only. This latter questionnaire is of central importance in terms of being provided with accessibility information. The real-time questionnaire follows the listeners' progress as more dramaturgic data is fed in. It is here where intention and reception comparisons can be made.

During the first listening, test participants hear a work with no contextual information provided at all. After filling in both forms, the second listening takes place, before which only the title or—if this is not useful—a single pertinent aspect of the composer's intention is shared. Before the third and final listening the composer's intention data are shared in full. This is a summary of responses taken from the questionnaire, program notes, and the like.

As mentioned above, after the third listening, an informal group discussion takes place where experiences are shared. Notes are taken of these discussions and supplementary data are acquired beyond those filled in on the three real-time and one directed questionnaire for each work.

In the discussion below, results from tests run by Rob Weale will be included. For his Ph.D. dissertation (Weale 2005), three works were chosen: *ABZ/A* by Pete Stollery, *Deep Pockets* by Larisa Montanaro, and *Nocturne* by Simon Atkinson. These three pieces ranged from one in which untreated real-world sounds are fairly prominent to one in which the sounds are much less easily identifiable and one that fell in between, as it were. The works were chosen from dozens of international submissions that were not terribly well known; therefore Weale was not running the risk that many of his experienced informants would have heard the works already. A second test that I ran (see Landy 2006a), although Weale held the trials, involved just two pieces that I chose myself, *Prochaine Station* by Christian Calon and Claude Schryer and *Valley Flow* by Denis Smalley. Here the works are readily available to those in the know. The Calon/Schryer "électro clip" is a pure urban soundscape three-minute composition focusing on underground train (métro) travel in Montreal; the longer Smalley work is comparable with the Atkinson composition at the other end of our current testing spectrum: its source material is rarely overtly exposed, its narrative more evocative. We will now look into this second test in some detail.

Test participants were divided as follows. There were twelve nonmusicians participating. All inexperienced musician participants came from

Leicester College (U.K.), a Further Education College (similar to a community college in the United States). Ten students took both tests. Furthermore, five additional students took only the Calon/Schryer test and three additional students took only the Smalley test. Students participating in only one test are listed separately in table 1.1 below. The experienced group consisted of thirteen final-year undergraduates at De Montfort University, Leicester (U.K.). The highly experienced benchmark group consisted of four postgraduate students of electroacoustic music at Birmingham University. There was no particular age or gender-based pattern of behavior observed in terms of the assembled data, with the exception that the older listeners of the inexperienced nonmusician group demonstrated less open-mindedness than other groups; however, one must take the modest sample sizes into account.

As stated, *Prochaine Station* is a short work in which brief scenes are woven together turning soundscape recordings into an urban soundscape composition. *Valley Flow*, on the other hand, is a 17' work that is more open to interpretation.[18] Smalley offers the following words to accompany the CD recording[19] of the work: "The formal shaping and sound content of *Valley Flow* were influenced by the dramatic vistas of the Bow Valley in the Canadian Rockies. The motion is stretched to create airy, floating and flying contours or broad panoramic sweeps, and contracted to create stronger physical motions, for example the flinging out of textural materials." He adds that the listener is expected to "adopt changing vantage points" in which "[l]andscape qualities are pervasive" (ibid.).

Predictably, the composers approached their intention questionnaires rather differently. Calon and Schryer focused on the specifics of the background to and detail of the work; Smalley related his vision in a slightly more poetic manner as demonstrated by his remark concerning motion in his program note. His goal was to have his new listeners introduced to and his existent listeners experience a new form of his personal approach to spectromorphological composition.[20] The Québecois composers spoke of "impressions of the city . . . on a normal day punctuated by unremarkable events." All three composers preferred the listener to be offered dramaturgic information after listening to the work although none obviously had any problem concerning the works' titles being known. When it came to things to hold on to, again the sound-scape composers were very specific about the chosen sounds and the city of Montreal whereas Smalley restricted himself to the work's title, the layering of sonic material and the work's language. All three composers agreed that their works were intended for as wide an audience as possible. Calon and Schreyer had no preference about the circumstances of performance, although they thought the traditional concert ambience was not ideal; Smalley claimed to offer the listener the opportunity to hear his works in what he calls ambient (multichannel diffusion in a larger space) and intimate (stereo) listening environments. None of the composers was at all interested in listeners following the technological elements in their works.

Let's now follow some of the reactions of the test participants to these two very different compositions before discovering how they replied to the accessibility directed questionnaire. Remarks will be restricted to the inexperienced groups as, predictably, the more experienced groups felt more at ease with both works in general.

Prochaine Station   This piece has a built-in access tool, namely the presence of untreated sounds from daily life. However, the use of unedited field recordings did lead to some negative responses. One inexperienced listener found the work "not musical at all," similarly to a highly experienced listener who claimed that "collage isn't enough." On the other hand, positive responses included a participant's claim that "hearing life from someone else's perspective" was enjoyable and others' discovery that a work of "organized sound" could be so interesting while allowing "a person can relate to everyday sounds." In fact, responses fell into two categories: those who "observed" the voyage the composers constructed for them and those who personalized their own voyages (or other narrative for that matter, for those who did not recognize the form of transport or the urban location). In the latter group one participant made the following insightful remark: the work was "quite gripping through individual association," which allows the listener to focus on "emotions based on memories."

All but one participant found the work engaging, one claiming that the piece offered the opportunity to "pay attention to daily life [via] sounds which are beautiful." Despite the fact that the word "Montreal" can be heard on an English language radio broadcast, many had difficulty placing where the piece takes place owing to their not recognizing the vocal accents in the piece or understanding the language used throughout most of the work. This meant that very few caught that the *prochaine station* (next station) called throughout the piece is always the same one, the one surreal twist in the work. During the informal postlistening session with the largest group, once the work's anecdote was related, the participants took a liking to the idea of movement without movement, as it were. Even though this soundscape composition is rather straightforward, it was discovered that the provision of increased dramaturgic information added to the participants' engagement.

Valley Flow   Predictably, this work received a wide variety of reactions leading to a broader response in general and a broader range of engagement. Understandably, some found the work more difficult; one claimed its sounds were "unmusical," while in contrast two others independently wrote of being "on the edge of my seat." Similarly, source identification ranged from some listeners making accurate or approximate choices, to many who misidentified perceived sounds that were not actually used, to some who felt that all sounds used were synthetic. In one case a listener identified "sounds not normally heard, like using a microscope." As identification was not something to hold on to in the work, people came up with more descriptive terms such as "eerie" or "cold." A number of participants felt that the work was related to science fiction; many felt that the work would fit well or even improve with visuals (e.g., a film or video). Several were aware of the fact that the composer was focused on layering evolving sounds throughout the piece.

The title was found useful by just over one half of the inexperienced listeners. Many wanted to create their own personal scenarios; however, one participant suggested that the title was beneficial, as it was not too prescriptive and thus did not stand of the way of listeners' being able to read the piece individually. The vast majority found repeated listening valuable and approximately two-thirds found the intention information useful, although some complained about what was considered to be academic language used by the composer. Exceptions, in particular within the small group of highly experienced listeners, were participants who preferred to be responsible for their own interpretations. A member of the inexperienced group noted that Smalley's intention information "closed off other options" of interpretation, but this type of response came from a minority especially in that group. The informal group discussion at Leicester College again demonstrated the value of people's sharing their listening experiences, and led to the work being played for a fourth time in a darkened space.

So how did the project participants react to the two works? Was there a great difference in terms of appreciation? As can be seen in table 1.1 the reactions were not hugely dissimilar. Before interpreting this data, it should be mentioned that one quirk was discovered in the methodology while running these tests, namely that the directed questionnaire devised by Weale (see the addendum below) had included a few questions that were not ideally formulated. This concerns two of the four accessibility questions in the directed questionnaire, questions 11 and 12, that concern potential concert attendance or purchase of recordings. Many casual listeners rarely or never attend performances with the possible exception of events involving DJs. (But who is watching them?) Some purchase many recordings, others few. Regardless of the total, many purchase only their favorite type(s) of music. In short a response concerning concert attendance or acquisition of other recordings had more to do with the responder's habits than with the test itself. Nevertheless, a positive response to either question usually was reflected in the other answers. It was decided, therefore, that accessibility statistics would need to be determined in a particular manner that can be found in the key to table 1.1. Consistent "no" answers led to a "no" result. One positive answer between questions 9 and 10 plus "possibly" answers elsewhere, of which there were several, led to the originally unplanned "±" category. Finally, at least two positive answers led to a "yes" result. Future investigations will involve relevant revisions. Table 1.1 contains the final statistics for both Weale's original project and the one presented above. Please note that the accessibility statistics were collected after the first listening, that is, before any dramaturgic information had been offered and without repeated listening.

Table 1.1
Access Statistics

	Yes	±	No	Yes %	± %	No %
ABZ/A (many recognizable sources)						
Inexp/1 (both tests)	15	4	1	75	20	5
Inexp/2 (only one test)	9	3	1	69	23	8
Inexp-all	24	7	2	73	21	6
Exp	16	2	2	80	10	10
H-Exp	7	0	0	100	0	0
Deep Pockets ("in between" work)						
Inexp/1	14	2	4	70	10	20
Inexp/2	8	3	2	62	15	23
Inexp-all	22	5	6	67	18	15
Exp	12	4	4	60	20	20
H-Exp	5	2	1	63	25	12
Nocturne (little to no source recognition)						
Inexp/1	12	4	4	60	20	20
Inexp/2	9	5	3	53	29	18
Inexp-all	21	9	7	57	24	19
Exp	14	3	3	70	15	15
H-Exp	4	1	1	66	17	17
Totals—all three works						
Inexp	67	19	17	65	18	17
Exp	42	9	9	70	15	15
H-Exp	16	3	2	76	14	10
Prochaine Station (soundscape work)						
Inexp/1 (non-musicians)	9	1	2	75	8	17
Inexp/2 (students-both tests)	5	1	4	50	10	40
Inexp/3 (students-one test)	4	0	1	80	0	20
Inexp-all	18	3	7	67	7	26
Exp	11	1	1	84	8	8
H-Exp	4	0	0	100	0	0
Valley Flow (little to no source recognition)						
Inexp/1	7	1	4	58	8	34
Inexp/2	7	2	1	70	20	10
Inexp/3	3	0	0	100	0	0
Inexp-all	17	3	5	68	12	50
Exp	10	2	1	77	15	8
H-Exp	4	0	0	100	0	0

Table 1.1
(continued)

	Yes	±	No	Yes %	± %	No %
Total—both works						
Inexp	35	5	12	67	10	23
Exp	21	3	2	81	11	8
H-Exp	8	0	0	100	0	0
Totals—both tests (all five works)						
Inexp	102	24	29	66	15	19
Exp	63	12	11	73	14	13
H-Exp	24	3	2	83	10	7

Key: A "yes" answer signifies that the listener answered positively to at least two of the access questions (9–12) listed in the directed questionnaire in the addendum; a "±" answer signifies that the listener answered "yes" to only one of these questions or "possibly" to a combination of them; a "no" answer means that no question was answered in the affirmative.

When presenting our work at conferences and the like, one question raised has been whether through repeated listening one's interest is increased. The answer is obviously an affirmative one. The vast majority of participants, particularly those in the inexperienced group, claimed that their understanding and, most often, their appreciation of the works increased with the addition of dramaturgical information. This is important as it challenges our current culture in which we typically hear less-known works only once. It also challenges that often-heard opinion that works should speak for themselves, that is, that no dramaturgic information is needed in order to appreciate a piece.

Even if two-thirds of the results above were discounted because of the unusually controlled or "safe" situation of these tests, the outcome would still be startling. All one has to do is compare these statistics with the current demography of noncommercial sound-based music appreciation which in fact makes up far less than one percent of the population. If nothing else, the Intention/Reception project serves as a lobbying tool to demonstrate the potential interest in this music by allowing people to discover it.

The key conclusions of the I/R project thus far are fairly predictable. First of all, dramaturgy must be added to the "something to hold on to" list introduced earlier in this chapter. It is equally clear that the more research similar to the I/R project takes place, the more that list will be refined and will expand in the future to include other things to hold on to not directly related to the listening experience per se. The project has demonstrated the usefulness of linking composers' intention information to the listening experience. Such an approach may be of service to those involved with analysis, as McCartney has so successfully demonstrated. It can also provide feedback to composers who are already allowing triangulation to take place, that is, taking listener feedback into account in their future works or in a work's revision. The combination of the intentional aspect of poiesis and aesthesis has led to a powerful research tool in our case. Most importantly, this project is demonstrating that its hypothesis is indeed correct: the potential public for certain works of sound organization is much greater than is currently the case and than is currently assumed. The project needs to be extended and tested on more sonic artworks, in other communities and eventually with other relevant types of contemporary music.[21] To support access and accessibility further, this project should take place with inexperienced groups in conjunction with workshops using appropriate audio software to facilitate creativity for those interested in learning more about the composition of sound-based music regardless of previous experience. We intend to affiliate the project with Unesco's DigiArts initiative, in which exciting audio software is being developed for users in developing countries. Another future question the I/R project will tackle is one that will be a focus of the next chapter, especially section B, namely, how do we best categorize this sort of work?

The I/R project is an example of a foundation-level project in the studies of sound-based music; it is an exception, not the rule in terms of current scholarship. It has succeeded in achieving its goal by way of the unexpectedly positive data that have been gained. The statistics gained thus far provide the right kind of data to sound-based music's future lobbyists, data that will offer them much more punch when they try to create a greater opening to the art form in today's society in terms of education and the media. This project has also helped me to reassess and increase my estimate of the potential value of the areas of sound-based music studies, the subject matter of chapters 2 and 3.

(C)   Further Issues Concerning Access and Sound-based Music

Section B's sequence, starting with the "something to hold on to" factor regarding sound-based artwork and then moving on to the addition of dramaturgy and arriving at the I/R project, forms a demonstration of the potential of greater access to much of the body of sound-based music. There are obviously other related issues that are also worthy of mention here. Although they will not be given the same amount of attention, this does not underestimate their importance. A few problem areas will now be introduced separately, all crucial to supporting access: education and the communications media, communities and participation, the retention of local values, and the social function of sound-based music.

Education and the Communications Media

In an ideal world the voyage of access to an artwork or art form starts when people are quite young. In today's education system, however, this is not on offer for most children. That there is a fairly general embargo in terms of the contemporary arts can be found in most nations' arts curricula. In many countries, the pressures to have children do well at the "three r's," reading, 'riting, and 'rithmetic, has led to the arts being given less (or no) time in the curriculum. This is an odd development for two important reasons: the skills the arts offer any individual and the size of the cultural industries. Then there is the relative embargo by the major communications media as far as much sound-based music is concerned. If a peer or teacher or family member does not introduce these opportunities, no one will. Given the I/R results shared above, neither of these situations seems to make much sense.

Anyone who has encountered public sound installations, particularly those in which interaction is possible and relatively transparent—that is, where one is aware of how sounds are triggered and eventually manipulated—knows how young people can be fascinated by such works and can even enjoy them for several minutes at a time. Both haptic and movement tracking-based installations are popular with the young. So why, then, does the road that starts at primary school with ensemble singing normally lead toward an education within a fairly narrow scope of music?

R. Murray Schafer and John Paynter are but two pioneers who spent years fighting for a more representative form of music education.[22] Schafer made people of all ages more aware of their sonic environment and of how sounds from the environment could be incorporated into music. Paynter, following major developments in contemporary music, focused in his research on aspects such as silence, new forms of structure, and new types of sound material. Yet how much impact did these pioneers have in terms of music curriculum developments around the globe? We have seen that the artwork we are discussing is not necessarily particularly esoteric and difficult for young people. The road to the discovery of sound organization can easily be opened up to children at preschool age and onward.

Fortunately some countries are striking back, adding aspects of music technology particularly at secondary school levels, albeit on a voluntary basis. The A-level in Music Technology in Britain concentrates much less on sound-based music than it might, but it is at least a step in the right direction. Interest in music technology courses at the tertiary level in Britain has increased significantly in recent years, partially reflecting a number of initiatives in the field of popular music, but also indicating increased interest in sound-based musical opportunities. As student numbers in such courses continue to rise rapidly, perhaps those responsible for primary and secondary education may consider updating their music curricula.

Other countries are more forthright as far as music technology is concerned. France's education ministry has actively supported several types of research for application in schools, focusing on aspects relevant to sound-based music. It also publicizes its interest in the field. For example, in 2003, *Les Dossiers de l'Ingénierie Éducative* published its second themed issue on music technology. In one of this issue's articles the sociologist Serge Pouts-Lajus reports that at that time approximately one million "amateurs" were composing music in France using a computer, and that a very large percentage of these people were *sampleurs*, that is, were using and manipulating sound samples (Pouts-Lajus 2003, 16). Although not all of these people will be making sound-based music, the fact that the French school system is supporting an increasingly significant percentage of people in the use of technology to make music with sounds is a major step in the right direction. This issue of *Les Dossiers* makes it absolutely clear that where there is a will, there is a way in terms of introducing music, technology, and organized sound into the curriculum.[23]

The *communications media*, radio, television, and the written media have also done far too little to combat these marginalization issues. Newspapers tend to write up concerts after the fact, if at all, as opposed to discussing certain works well before they are performed, taking into account dramaturgic issues and indicating aspects that listeners will be able to hold on to as an incentive to support appreciation and eventual attendance.

Television seems uninterested in the subject, regardless of the fact that many organized sound works exist in viewable audiovisual versions. Of course there are quite a few sound designs for films, television programs, and advertisements on the air, but to a large extent this happens by stealth. Most viewers may perceive these sound designs, but they are not able to place the work in a broader context.

Radio has more or less given up on contemporary art music. Less than 5 percent of airtime is offered to living composers by many countries' hardly listened to classical music stations. I doubt that sonic works earn any more than 1 percent of airtime on art music broadcasts excluding those advertisements and the sound designs for radio documentaries and radio plays, which rarely are acknowledged. As will be investigated later on, the Internet looks like it may become the place where communities will find the types of works that they are interested in hearing. Please note that the fact that much information is becoming available on the Internet does not, in itself, mean that people know that it exists and may be of interest to them. More must be done to bring sound-based music to new listeners of all ages.

An Example
Let's look at an example demonstrating how access is restricted as a result of inadequate media support and also a lack of infrastructure linking education to culture, as it occurs in the Bourges Festival of Electroacoustic Music (regardless of the fact that the festival in question is

in France).[24] At the time of writing this chapter (2005), the festival celebrated its thirty-fifth year of existence. Much credit can be given to those
who have hosted and supported this event throughout the decades. It has
always been an international crossroads for composers who are offered
an opportunity to share much music and meet informally in relaxed surroundings. Although never subscribing to a single aesthetic, Bourges did
develop a particular francophone "sound" or "sonic signature"[25] by the
1980s, one that will be discussed further under the header of acousmatic
music in chapter 2, section A1. Ironically, the part of Bourges that I was
often most enthusiastic about was their insistence on including installation works before such works were widely celebrated. Not only this, the
placement of most installations was in a municipal building where their
administration and studios used to reside as well, into which walked
people of all ages and backgrounds. A large number of people passing
by came to visit and, where relevant, play with the installations; there
was often a clearly positive emotional response shared during these visits.
First-time visitors rarely demonstrated timidity in these particular surroundings. So, given this and Bourges's and France's initiatives in music
education and their relatively high support for sound-based music broadcasts on the radio, this story should have a happy ending.

Yet year after year most Bourges festival concerts are filled with the
participants and hardly anyone else. One would think that after thirty-
five years of those installations, education initiatives, and better media
contacts than many other festivals, some combination of continuity and
curiosity based on the presence of the installations and publicity in
general would lead to substantial audience development. This is sadly
not the case.

This issue is exactly what I alluded to when presenting the first two
of the four examples (the installation and the electroacoustic work) in
the introduction in the discussion of whether sound art is music. Appar-
ently at Bourges the two barely meet in terms of appreciation. The questions that emerge from this example are hugely important. For example,
must one deduce from this history that acousmatic music is therefore
inaccessible and thus doomed to permanent marginalization? Do we
need, therefore, to separate such installations from concerts, effectively
making them two separate art forms? Granted, one can walk out of an

installation without anyone turning a head. Still, one would think these two types of work need not be seen as separate.

The Bourges festival with its fairly recently added Académie where themes are discussed relevant to sound-based music could be to this art form what Cannes is to cinema. However, three and a half decades have led to performances of many extraordinary works—the winner's list of their competition demonstrates how many talented artists support their initiative—and, sadly, to a largely *entre nous* group of participants.

So what is missing? What has not taken place is, for example, an outreach program of any significance. Why aren't there loads of school children attending? (The festival does take place in June, perhaps an awkward time of year.) In fact, why aren't concerts put on especially for children, as happens as a natural part of the outreach program of many festivals in the U.K. and other countries?

Ironically, given the terms of Bourges' funding, it does receive international broadcast time, albeit usually after the fact and hidden in the late hours of the evening during slots that only the participants and their immediate colleagues know about. It would be much more useful for pieces on the works and interviews of the artists to be offered regularly on radio stations in and nearby Bourges, making the pieces more accessible to a wider audience and turning these concerts into a welcoming environment for newcomers. In fact, the notion of "welcoming environment" may be a significant clue here: Bourges' apparent lack of one is its fatal flaw, in my view.

The festival provides an example of the clear need for greater synergy between education, the media, artists, and arts organizations. One of the morals of the Bourges story is that people like to feel they acquire a sense of ownership of sonic artworks as is clear from the response to the installations they have offered. Fortunately, a number of programs similar to Bourges, at least in Europe and to a lesser extent elsewhere as well (see the Copeland example discussed below), are now being asked to implement an outreach program to accompany the event. This might involve schools' participation in putting together a performance tackling one of the festival's chosen themes or working with one of the festival's artists. This would make a difference in terms of people's crossing the threshold and attending festival events. It also crosses the boundary between art appreciation and art participation, thus offering people the opportunity to feel they are truly participating in the festival. The desire to feel part of art making is at the heart of the issues of participation and interactivity. I have suggested that in such cases a little care in choosing prepositions can make all the difference (Landy 1998b, 321–323): the difference between making artwork *for* people and making artwork *with* people, the basis of what is known today as community art.

There have been, of course, some individuals who have attempted to take works of sound-based music to new audiences.[26] For example, Darren Copeland (2003) has written about his experiences as artistic director of the New Adventures in Sound Art Festival, which has been held in Toronto, where the event's intention included the creation of new audiences for sonic artworks. This forms an interesting counterexample to the Bourges case. One of Copeland's foci concerns social relevance and public impact: "It is my goal as a producer to increase the audience for electroacoustic music. However, in so doing I strive not to compromise the aesthetic" (2003, 59). He goes on to state that he likes to include issue-oriented electroacoustic music, a soundscape artist forum, and discussions concerning noise abatement, as well as sound installations and soundwalks[27] in tourist areas and the use of community radio for creative work and audience appreciation. He reminds us that "campus and community radio stations sometimes play a significant role in local cultural life" (ibid., 61–62). How does he go about building the audience? "Once that audience is in attendance, then it is important that extra efforts be made to support their investment in the field with access to understandable accounts of its history and aesthetics as well as by insuring their works presented in the show are relevant to the context and that production constraints are viewed as creative variables rather than obstacles" (ibid., 64). This is a most holistic way of dealing with access and accessibility and seems as good a way as any in terms of future developments in audience and participation. It also can be used in terms of what might be called community development.

The Importance of Communities and Community Development
Everything discussed in this chapter has one common denominator, that of communities possessing shared interests.[28] In the past, communities

tended to be determined geographically. Today's technology, alongside the facilitation of travel, has increased the opportunities for communities to spread out, both physically and virtually. Taking Fischman's goal to pursue an optimal public into account, one might do so by way of searching for communities that represent the combination of shared interests and experiences.

The true heroes in terms of developing new channels of access are those, like Copeland, who work in the community. For example, Bruce Cole is one of the pioneers of what is currently known as the *community arts*. He has worked with young offenders, disabled people, and a wide variety of other groups of all ages and backgrounds using music technology as a means toward facilitating creative participation while acknowledging the therapeutic aspects of such projects as well. His goal is not to offer any single exciting project, but instead to offer protocols that can be followed up once he has left (see, e.g., Cole 1996), protocols that take particular community members' strengths and interests into account. Many people he has worked with end up working in a musical field.

Broadcasters make programs for certain communities. We are already seeing the Internet used as an alternative broadcasting source, allowing for much more specific broadcasts to be offered than on our radios and televisions. It is as if our broadcasting dial is being filled with stations that really offer their own particular vision, their own color, and thus address more focused communities.

In discussing opportunities that may evolve through the Internet, Dante Tanzi looks at a broader horizon of music than sound-based work, yet his key theses are relevant to this art form in particular. "Online communicative practices have succeeded in placing relationships between individuals and communities inside a new public space. They have also attenuated the distinction between producers and consumers, especially in the creative sphere. . . . [I]t is only thanks to the widespread use of the Net that digital music can now be manipulated by so many people" (Tanzi 2003). He believes in what Sean Cubitt calls "network sound aesthetic[s]" (Cubitt 1997, 45), a basis for building communities through participation. Tanzi does offer a note of caution, "however the more the intelligibility of musical events is entrusted to online practices and the more cultural differences are approached with apparent nonchalance and without any preliminary presentation, the more the experience of immediate access may pre-empt the possibility of any cultural mediation derived from the assimilation of musical content" (Tanzi 2003). This remark relates to the difference between top-down Internet musical activities and bottom-up ones. It also focuses on the importance of local values.

Retaining the Local and Creating the "Local"

Communities go hand in hand with diversity. Of course, there is no turning back in terms of globalization. What is being suggested here is an optimal balance between massive global communities and similarly global approaches to sound-based music and local ones. The local can remain geographically sited, but other communities can be tied together through the Internet and the like, emphasizing their particular community interests. The future of sound-based music will be one that not only celebrates so-called universals, but equally one that celebrates local values in at least equal portion, an ideal manner of supporting diverse communities of interest and thus access.

The Social Function of Sound-based Music

A possible frame for our discussion on access can be found in the investigation of the social placement of works of organized sound, a subject that has not arisen here thus far. Simon Waters has complained that artists have created the genre of electroacoustic music, here used in the sense of art music, without any discussion of its social significance (Waters 1994a). There are, indeed, far too few publications that deal with this highly important subject of the cultural placement of sonic artworks and technology's impact on music making.[29] His claim is that for electroacoustic art music to move beyond its current marginal public, it must investigate its own politics, its sociocultural position, and reflect this investigation in the music's own development. The consequence of this search would be to tie (new) electroacoustic communities together.

I would take this well-founded goal one step further and suggest that people investigate whether our traditional forms of presentation are the right ones for sound-based music. The art of organized sound offers us new means of celebration, of ritual, of sharing. As technology evolves, music as celebration will take on a range of new forms. Each community will be able to define its own celebration(s). To anyone interested in achieving greater access and accessibility to sound-based music, the investigation of the appropriate forms of participation and presentation of this music, whether known or not yet discovered, cannot be ignored.

Addendum—The Three Intention/Reception Project Questionnaires

Composer Intention Questionnaire

(Please note that text in parentheses has been inserted to provide clarity to the questions.)

Please complete the following

Name:

Date of birth (dd/mm/yy):

Sex (m/f):

Ethnicity:

Country of permanent residence:

Composition Title:

Sound source(s)/source material (i.e., the place(s) or object(s) from which the sound(s) were collected/recorded, e.g., rocks, railway station, etc; and a list of each sound object that was used, e.g., the sound of rocks being scraped together, the sound of trains, etc.):

Intention Questions

1. What were your intentions concerning this particular composition? (What are you attempting to communicate to a listener? Please be as specific and detailed as possible.)

2. What methods are you using to communicate these intentions to the listener? (Are you relying on the recognizable aspects of the sounds to communicate meaning? Are you using specific sonic manipulations to communicate these meanings?)

3. Is there a narrative discourse involved? (The word "narrative" is not solely meant to imply a text-based narrative, a story, but includes

sound/structure/spatial/temporal-based narrative discourses.) If so, how would you describe this narrative?

4. How important is it that this narrative is received and why?

5. Where did the inspiration to create this particular composition come from? (What influences caused you to initially decide to create this particular composition?)

6. To what extent, and how, did your initial intention change as the compositional process progressed?

7. What influenced these changes of intention?

8. Is it important to you that your composition is listened to with your intentions in mind and why?

9. Is/are there something(s) in the composition that you want the listener to hold on to and why? (E.g., a recognizable sound, structure, narrative, etc.)

10. At what point in the compositional process did you decide on a title for the piece?

11. How much do you rely on the title as a tool with which to express your compositional intentions and why?

12. Do you rely on any other accompanying text, in the form of program notes, to outline your intentions prior to the listener's engagement with the composition and why? (Please list/attach the text that accompanies your composition here.)

13. Who is your intended audience for this composition? (E.g., all audiences, the electroacoustic community, etc.)

14. How is your compositional process influenced by the intended audience, if at all?

15. How important is it that the technical processes involved in the composition are recognized by the listener and why?

16. Do you think that detectable technical processes are an integral aspect of the composition's overall aesthetic? (Is it important in this composition that the listener is aware of the technical processes?) If yes, why? If no, why not?

17. Under what listening conditions is your composition intended to be heard and why? (In stereo, multichannel, through headphones, in a concert hall, diffused, etc.)

18. If you intended for your composition to be diffused over a multi-channel system, how did this intention affect your compositional techniques? (In what ways did you structure the composition and its contents in order for it to be best heard in a diffused performance?)

19. If you intended for your composition to be diffused over a multi-channel system, in what ways do you expect the listening experience to be changed by a stereo performance of your composition?

The Intention/Reception Project: Real-Time Listener Response Questionnaire

Please complete the following

Name:

Date of birth (dd/mm/yy):

Sex (m/f):

Ethnic origin:

Country of permanent residence:

What is (are) your general musical taste(s)?:

(You may state specific genres, e.g., metal, orchestral, indie, bhangra, rock and roll, jazz, etc.; and/or specific groups, bands, artists, e.g., Elvis, Stereophonics, Beastie Boys, Miles Davis, Aretha Franklin, etc.)

First Listening

Please list any thoughts, images and/or ideas that come to mind as you listen to the composition.

Second Listening

Now that you are aware of the *title* of the composition, please list any new or altered thoughts, images, ideas that come to mind, or try to expand on any ideas that you have as you listen.

What might this piece be about?

Did knowing the *title* help you to understand the composition? If yes, why? If no, why not?

Third Listening

Now that you are aware of the *composer's intentions*, please list any new or altered thoughts, images and/or ideas that come to mind, or try to expand on any ideas that you have as you listen:

Did knowing the *composer's intentions* help you to understand the composition? If yes, why? If no, why not?

How did repeated listening help you in understanding the piece?

The Intention/Reception Project: Directed Questionnaire
(*Candidates may refer to their initial listening notes when answering the following questions.*)

Print your name:

1. What might this piece be about?

2. What sounds did you recognize in the composition?

3. If you heard sounds that were strange and/or unnatural, please describe (if you can) one/some/any of them.

4. Did the composition conjure images/pictures in your mind? If so, please describe them.

5. Did the composition suggest a narrative, be it a story or any other time-based discourse? If so, what might this concern?

6. Did the composition seem to convey any emotion(s)? And/or did you have any emotional responses to the piece? If so, please describe them.

7. What aspects, musical or otherwise, did you find most engaging in the composition?

8. What aspects, musical or otherwise, did you find least engaging in the composition?

9. Did the composition make you want to keep listening or was it uninteresting? Why?

10. Now that you have heard the composition, would you choose to listen to a similar type of composition again in the future? If yes, why? If no, why not?

11. Now that you have heard the composition, would you choose to purchase a CD containing this type of composition? If yes, why? If no, why not?

12. Now that you have heard the composition, would you choose to attend a concert featuring these types of compositions? If yes, why? If no, why not?

2

From Concept to Production to Presentation to Theory: Creating "Co-hear-ence"

Music plus electricity equals the sound of twentieth century music.
—Joseph Schillinger (cited in Battier 2001)

[C]ommunication between composer and audience rests to some extent on a common code or at least some common expectations and assumptions. . . . [T]he discovery (not the invention) of some of these general codes is an essential task for all composers.
—Simon Emmerson (1989)

This second chapter[1] acts as a lengthy bridge between the discussion concerning access and the book's final chapter delineating the field of studies for sound-based music. It focuses on the current repertoire of sound-based works and is complemented with discussions concerning related theoretical developments. Its main agenda is to attempt to make some sense of the highly diverse body of work that has been built up over some five and a half decades. Coherence concerning the theoretical concepts relevant to the study of sound-based work will simultaneously be sought based on the chapter's featured theoretical writings.

It must be admitted straightaway that it is challenging to identify many clear or all-embracing patterns within the body of sound-based work. Histories on the topic tend to be technology driven; in some cases, one is led to believe that indeed technology and compositional procedures developed hand in hand. However, in many cases, the picture is not so clear. One need not focus only on compositional approaches—or on technology for that matter—to tie works together. One can also focus on the listener's point of view, in particular on those things that listeners can hold on to. What this chapter is designed to demonstrate is that clusters of activity can be discovered on the map of sound-based works and, furthermore, that there are more ways than one of grouping sound-based compositions together. In the following discussion the search for ways to create coherence among the works is our goal.

The chapter, following this introduction, has been subdivided into two sections. The first, lengthier section deals with the diverse sound-based repertoire and its associated theory. Supporting the view held by many working within the field of sound-based music, that of the primacy of the aural experience (or audiovisual experience where appropriate), this section will focus on sonic material, what it consists of and how it is presented, treated, and ordered. More formal architectural concerns will also be introduced, though less rigorously, as it turns out that a significant number of these concerns are inaudible to the listener; furthermore, many approaches are not especially created for sound-based composition and thus are less relevant to this discussion. This section works its way through a number of these approaches, five of which focus on material, one on formalization, and two on presentation. The position of sound-based music associated with popular culture will also be presented as a separate header, although it will be discovered that the significance of "associated with" may have more to do with musicians' roots and influences than with intention. Part of the discussion of families of works and approaches will concentrate on how formerly diverse categories have been converging in recent years, such as algorithmic works starting to use sophisticated sound morphology techniques. The notion of convergence will serve as a link to the brief second section, which investigates existent and novel options concerning the works' categorization.

An issue that will be crucial to section A is the distinction between a *genre* in the sense of a single musical or artistic grouping (e.g., soundscape composition) and a *category* in which a performance situation (e.g., installation, mixed work), an aspect of technology (e.g., microsound,[2] digital music), or an approach (e.g., algorithmic composition) holds a group of works together.[3] The problem is that the word "genre" is often used as a synonym for "category," leading to some ambiguity. For the remainder of this book, these two terms will be used as described in this paragraph.

As suggested above, a question to keep in mind is: do sound-based works that are associated with so-called popular music and those associated with art music culture need to be separated? It is heartening to see the first surveys being written from an eclectic point of view. Richard Toop's *Ocean of Sound* (1995) and Mark Prendergast's *The Ambient Century* (2000) are two useful examples. Although neither is focused solely on sound-based music or presents a detailed study of musical content, such eclectic surveys discussing music technological approaches represent a significant "hole in the market" at this point. Despite the fact that many examples below will seem to have evolved from a more *E* or *U* background, the closer we come to the present day, the less relevant those two letters will appear in many cases. This is an important aspect of sections A7 and B.

Before we embark on our journey through the realms of sound-based music, a smaller bridge must be constructed linking the previous chapter's discussion with this one. The idea is quite straightforward: the items on the "something to hold on to" list, not to mention Emmerson's language grid, can serve to support coherence as much as anything else can. Let us start with the notion of layering in a sound-based artwork as a case in point.

I have already presented the view that there is little difference between the concept of layering sounds and that of counterpoint. Both have to do with horizontal musical organization. Clearly horizontal thinking in music has occurred in many societies throughout the ages—think, for example, of the parallel second singing to be found in folk and liturgical music in southern Balkan areas. It is still important today as an often-used element of sound-based musical composition.

Those who choose layering as a tool of construction tend not to use too many sound types in a composition in order to avoid confusing the listener. The number of layers[4] of sound does not normally exceed four at any given moment. The flow or variation of textures combined with the consistent use of materials, whether these are derived from the real world, abstract, or anything in between, is what the listener holds on to.

A second example: Julio d'Escriván has suggested that in his music there are three elements with which listeners can engage. They include what he calls "refrain," the reappearance of previously introduced chunks of material; "mimesis," the use of remote extraneous elements; and "quotation," the use of borrowed material (d'Escriván 1989, 197–201). I would add to this the use of beat found in a number of his works, and one can easily see in him an example of someone who shares his "things to hold on to" with his listeners. Making such tools clear to people learning about sound-based music is a great step toward helping them over an initial threshold, by offering musical and eventually extra-musical elements that support noema.

(A)   Families of Approaches/Works of Organized Sound

Let's begin by rewinding the analog tape and recalling those history books for the moment that commence with musique concrète and *elektronische Musik* and eventually their prehistories. One can hear that works belonging to the former category used recordable sound sources and the latter synthetically generated ones. But is it not a bit too simple to say that all works based on synthesized sound form a family of works? Perhaps this is so for those who are interested in how works are constructed, but not necessarily for the listening public. Yet, interestingly, there was something that held most of the French composers together and something else that held most of the German ones together.

If we stay with this traditional point of departure for a moment, knowing well that by the time Stockhausen composed his *Gesang der Jünglinge* in the mid-1950s recorded and electronic sounds already had a history of being mixed in compositions, there is perhaps a better point of departure that helps to describe the separation between the French and the German early works. Simon Waters has introduced the terms, spectralist and formalist, as a form of separation covering a fairly substantial portion of sound-based works.[5] In the former case, the focus is the evolution of texture. In the latter, the tools of sound creation and, in particular, ordering principles and structural development are of greatest importance. Obviously there exist formalized spectralist works (Waters 2003, chapter 4). In fact, the number of such works has increased considerably in recent years. Georgina Born has described the phenomenon of this separation by making a comparison between the

GRM, the home of post-Schaefferian sound object-based composition, and IRCAM, the French bastion of formalism, as an "opposition between experimental empiricism and postserialist determinism" (Born 1995, 59).

This separation will prove useful in defining works that are built from the bottom up (most spectralist works) and those built from the top down in the sense of their structure being determined before or during the creation of sounds (most formalized works). Yet, we still have little idea of what a composition sounds like in both cases. The range of timbral and formalist composition is huge; we are only taking the first step of several in terms of creating frameworks relevant to the genres and categories of the music.

Those working on the EARS project have attempted to clarify as many terms as possible to offer a view of the range of sound-based composition. Here, again, genres or categories that restrict themselves to borrowing electroacoustic techniques have not been included in the glossary and index. A look at the current[6] genres and categories section of the EARS site offers interesting food for thought. To start, of the approximately eighty terms listed, very few represent genres, most of which have roots in popular music traditions and/or more recent electronica developments. One wonders how many of the following seven terms might be classified as genres as described above: acousmatic, *musique concrète*, ambient music, *bruitisme*[*7] (or noise music), house, soundscape composition, and *spectralisme**.

There are a few entries on the list that have to do with formalization, for example algorithmic composition*, serialism*, and stochastic music*. The list on the EARS site could be much longer if one were to include the basic processes involved in formalist approaches, yet relatively few of them are directly related to sound-based composition.

In addition, there is a fairly large list of terms involving technique (formalized music varieties belong to this list, as do collage and plunderphonics), some form(s) of technology (e.g., analog music, computer music), sound generation (electronic music), a particular choice of (virtual) venue (radiophonics, Internet music, site specific), among others. Such terms normally do not imply much about how a work might sound stylistically.

Finally, there is a fairly extensive list even more general than the above, including terms such as electroacoustic music, electronica and experimental music, multimedia, sound art, and text-sound composition. To illustrate just one, consider the term electronica. This is used within popular music, but it also covers genres such as today's noise music. It is a word, therefore, that some identify with certain related experimental forms of music in the popular tradition; to others it is also a term clearly associated with noise and laptop performance practices. I can easily imagine that to a few people it is both. Many terms associated with electronica (or other terms listed in the EARS index) turn out to be ephemeral. These are relevant, of course, but our key interest is in finding terms that are not only relevant but may prove to have a reasonably lengthy "shelf life."

All of the terms associated with the types, from formalism to venue, listed above are legitimate categories; but not one of them tells you anything about what a piece sounds (or looks) like. This is rather dissimilar to traditional musical genres, which are related directly to one or just a few forms of musical discourse. In short, most of the terms above are indeed *categories*, not genres as we have defined them here.

So, perhaps not unexpectedly, our starting point using such terms as designators is fairly weak. As the point of this book is to attempt to bring some cohesion to relevant artworks and their field of study, most of the remainder of this chapter will be focused on bringing some terminological order to this field of music. Through the introduction of related theoretical writings we can start delineating patterns of thought in the field's scholarship as well. Having reviewed many of the history and repertoire surveys, I propose the following list of subheads for this section.

- *Musique concrètement*: from acoulogy to spectromorphology
- Real-world music: from acoustic ecology to soundscape composition
- Appropriation: convergence (1)
- New sounds: from synthesis to microsound to noise
- An interim summary: all sounds are sound objects
- Formalized works: from "*Die Reihe*" to all things algorithmic
- The popular dimension

• The "split" between fixed medium and live electroacoustic performance: convergence (2)

• Sound art → sonic art: convergence (3)

Not all of the subheads relate to how the works sound; the first five focus on sound materials and how they are presented, whereas the sixth focuses more on structure-generating procedures. After discussing how sound-based musical procedures have infiltrated popular music and how in many cases the popular music–art music divide is becoming fuzzy if not invisible, in the final two subsections I focus on how and where sound-based works are presented and/or performed. Three of these subheads include the word "convergence"; this word helps to form a link to the chapter's final section concerning categorization.

In each subsection, I attempt to find relevant characteristics of works belonging to each category. I cite supporting theoretical writing that underpins each area, where it exists. One point concerning theoretical examples needs to be raised immediately. The theories that are presented relate more often to the musical experience than to practices of construction. The latter topic is more commonly available in today's literature and, as suggested elsewhere in this book, is often discussed without any mention of reception. Therefore, theory pertaining to construction and technology is introduced here mainly in those cases where it supports musical understanding and experience.

(1)   Musique Concrètement: From Acoulogy to Spectromorphology

This title has been chosen to introduce the copious œuvre that has evolved due to the introduction of musique concrète in 1948. Do we call this music by its original name, by its later version, "acousmatic[8] music" (promoted by, for example, François Bayle), or perhaps by the term coined by Michel Chion, *l'art des sons fixés* ("the art of recorded," therefore, "fixed sounds")?[9] These forms of timbral or spectral composition, originally derived from a radiophonic tradition, tend to have one thing in common: they are influenced by Pierre Schaeffer's concept of reduced listening or *écoute réduite*. Schaeffer's reduced listening theory is more concerned with the quality of sounds than their source. This is, in fact, for many listeners not an easy thing to achieve. He was interested neither in the use of electronically generated sound material nor in conscious sound recognition. His concept of *acoulogie*, translated here by its English equivalent, acoulogy, was proposed as part of an analogy between acoustics and phonetics, where phonology was chosen to investigate the function of phonetic sounds in language and acoulogy was related similarly to the art of sound organization (see below under Schaefferian theory for further discussion).

So we have two puzzle pieces. First of all, if we generalize Schaeffer's original position, there is a sense of a presence of *real-world* sounds or, at least, *recordable* sounds in the work, although the listener's identification of them is not of primary importance. Second, the sounds used in these works have typically been considered worthy of being used within a *musical* context, as Schaefferian theory calls for the use of *objets musicaux* (musical objects), that is, *objets sonores* (sound objects[10]) that have been deemed worthy of being used in a composition.

I have often found, and have heard from many others in the field, that for people who have no experience with the repertoire, works that use (perceived) natural sounds tend to be more digestible, that is, more accessible than most pieces that are based on artificially generated sounds. This supports the view introduced earlier concerning people's desire to be able to link art with experience. There are exceptions, of course, that should be mentioned for completeness, two opposites in fact: complex works that use recorded real-world sounds that have been manipulated to such an extent that no relationship with their origin can be traced tend to be difficult in terms of accessibility; and those electronic pieces that clearly offer the listener one or more things to hold on to are often found fairly accessible by inexperienced listeners. Neither of these exceptions fits into this generalization.

Pieces that belong to the musique concrète category tend to have what one might call a *narrative discourse*. "Narrative" here is by no means to be taken literally; instead, it concerns the notion of a piece's taking the listener on a sort of voyage, one in which exact repetition of longer segments is rare. This is the source of Michel Chion's description of the experience as *cinéma pour l'oreille* (cinema for the ear).

Works belonging to this category are typically realized with the composer's first collecting source material and manipulating it. The structure of such a piece evolves much more often than it is imposed, similar to a procedure common in contemporary choreography. Formalists naturally tend to experience some difficulty with this approach. H. H. Stuckenschmidt, referring to remarks by Herbert Eimert, notes in the famous pro-serial journal *Die Reihe*: "[Eimert] has disassociated himself from the 'fashionable and surrealistic' musique concrète produced at the Club d'Essai[11] in Paris, and any incidental manipulations or distortions haphazardly put together for radio, film or theatre music" (Stuckenschmidt 1958, 11). In contrast, Francis Dhomont, a well-known proponent for things acousmatic sees things differently: "Its independence in terms of systems (tonal, modal, atonal) is complete as its language obeys different criteria. There is no distant past, it is not influenced by nostalgia; its philosophy and its working methods are entirely new and its liberty is total" (quoted in Roy 2003a, 25).[12]

What separates musique concrète from most of the other categories is, as Jean-Claude Risset has noted: "In the first instance Schaeffer placed the accent on the primacy of the listening experience and on the necessity to develop a solfège of effects as opposed to causes" (cited in Thomas 1999, 37ftn.). In other words, this music is not to be appreciated primarily in terms of a deep understanding of the music's or any sound's construction, according to Schaeffer. "Cause" here is a key word, as the sounds' causality is equally not of fundamental importance as a result of the reduced listening strategy. This approach to listening can be a difficult challenge for less experienced listeners. Instead, the focus is to be on the pure sound itself.

Musique concrète was born at the home of French radio where the current Groupe de Recherches Musicales (GRM) still resides. The theories that began to develop in the late 1940s live on, whether at the GRM or elsewhere around the globe. The music associated with musique concrète has also evolved, in particular because most musicians no longer stick to the original restriction of recordable real-world sounds. Also, many of today's acousmatic musicians do not fully subscribe to the reduced listening strategy but rather introduce identifiable sounds, and their causes, wherever they please. In this sense, these more recent forms of musique concrète–influenced work can be included on the list of formerly separate categories or approaches that have been converging, particularly in recent years.

The theoretical dimension   Most of these nine subsections contain theoretical information that has been formulated especially for works of organized sound. Usually this theory will simply be integrated into the section's main discussions. However, given the relatively large amount of theory created for music belonging to or derived from this category, a separate sub-subsection is merited. Many of these discussions have a hybrid structure, containing a general introduction of concepts and, in particular, terminology of particular relevance to each musical approach, in combination with brief portraits of the work of specific writers who have been responsible for more significant contributions to these theoretical studies. Sometimes it may appear as if a valuable theory is introduced in this chapter without a particular peg (i.e., subject area within sound-based music studies) on which to hang it. By introducing significant theoretical concepts here, my hope is that a pattern of subjects of relevance to the field of sound-based music studies will emerge, which will form the basis for chapter 3, the chapter in which the key areas of sound-based music studies are introduced. To this end, some of the theorists' work will be placed in categories we will return to in the following chapter.

> Contemporary music, above all works involving electronics, has destabilised our cultural habits, our systems of reference and equally influence our choice of sonic material and formal organisation processes. . . . [With this in mind,] how do we understand music if we are not at all acquainted with its creative processes? (Jean-Baptiste Barrière 1992, 77, 79)

Michel Chion provided us with a lovely *jeu de mots* when he decided to write about musique concrète *"concrètement"*—concretely. Ironically, what has fascinated me throughout the years is how difficult it is to write about this genre in a concrete fashion. This applies not only to analyses, but to the very important body of knowledge that has been provided by Pierre Schaeffer, his colleagues at the GRM, and others throughout the years, making up a large percentage of the theory concerning sound-based music that has been formulated. What is most striking about Schaefferian theory, and what differentiates it from most music theory that developed before it, is its focus on the primacy of the ear, rather than abstract forms of musical construction. Writing about music from the point of view of reception does not have to be that difficult to concretize, but very few theoretical approaches introduced below have been applied thus far by more than small groups of specialists, suggesting that these theories are only open to restricted application. Although some of the terminology is more widely used, again, very little of it has been accepted across the board.

Pierre Schaeffer   The primary source for the following overview is Schaeffer's key treatise, *Traité des objets musicaux* (Schaeffer 1977, originally published in 1966; hereafter *TOM*), a monumental work of over 700 pages.[13] It must be said that Schaeffer can be sometimes a bit difficult to follow, particularly for people whose mother tongue is not French. Fortunately, Michel Chion published a supplementary book, *Guide des objets sonores: Pierre Schaeffer et la recherche musicale* (Chion 1995), introducing Schaeffer's terminology in *TOM* in a systematic fashion. This summary will serve as our key guide here.[14] Chion has also written another summary of Schaefferian theory in a separate book *Le son* (Chion 2002, 237–262). The only publicly available English translation that I am aware of is Schaeffer's short "Acousmatics" chapter (Schaeffer 2004) published in Cox and Warner 2004.[15]

The French critic Maurice Fleuret, never one to mince his words, has spoken of *TOM* as follows: "[a] new Bible . . . a New Testament of Music" (in Bayle 1990, 101–102) and "the first solid foundation for the future of music" (in Dutilleux 2001, 11). After introducing the state of music and musicology as he sees it, *TOM* is an introduction to what Schaeffer calls experimental music, in particular musique concrète or acousmatic music.

To begin, it is important to understand what Schaeffer meant by the word *concrete*. Schaeffer took his lead from the phenomenologist Edmund Husserl, and often introduced terms in binary pairs. In section [15][16] of his *Guide*, Chion introduces the pair of terms, *abstract* and *concrete*: "When in 1948 Pierre Schaeffer gave the name concrète to the music he invented, he wanted to emphasise that this new music came from concrete sound material,[17] sound heard in order to try and abstract musical values from it. And this is the opposite of classical music, which starts from an abstract conception and notation leading to a concrete performance. Schaeffer wanted to react against the 'excess of abstraction'[18] . . . in serial and other types of 'preconceived' musics" where "[a]ll these musics called for a 'total ascendancy of abstract intelligence . . . over sound material.'"

By 1957, Schaeffer had already retreated a bit from the denomination, musique concrète due to the ongoing misunderstanding that this might signify recognisable source material. He opted first for the more general term, experimental music, and from then on, the battle of acousmatic vs. electroacoustic vs. musique concrète vs. any other relevant term was to commence.

The term acousmatic [1]

was taken up again[19] by Pierre Schaeffer and Jérôme Peignot to describe an experience which is very common today but whose consequences are more or less unrecognised, consisting of hearing sounds with no visible cause on the radio, records, telephone, tape recorder, etc. Acousmatic listening is the opposite of direct listening, which is the 'natural' situation where sound sources are present and visible. . . . By isolating the sound from the 'audiovisual complex' to which it initially belonged, it creates favourable conditions for reduced listening which concentrates on the sound for its own sake, as sound object, independently of its causes or its meaning. . . . By repeated listening to the same recorded sound fragment, the emphasis is placed on variations of listening . . . [which arise from] 'directions which are always precise and always reveal a new aspect of the object, towards which our attention is deliberately or unconsciously drawn.' . . . Indeed, if curiosity about causes remains in acousmatic listening (and it can even be aroused by the situation), the repetition of the recorded signal can perhaps 'exhaust' this curiosity and little by little impose 'the sound object as a perception worthy of being listened to for itself,' revealing all its richness to us.

Acousmatic is an example of many terms presented here that will fall under the theoretical category, the listening experience in chapter 3.

Acousmatic's sister term, acoulogy [39], is introduced as follows. If acoustics is "the study of the physical production of sound, . . . [acoulogy is] the study of the potential in perceived sounds for producing distinctive characteristics which can be organised into music." Acoulogy is fundamental to Schaeffer's solfège, introduced below. Its object is "the study of mechanisms of listening, properties of sound objects and their musical potential in the natural perceptual field of the ear. Concentrating on the problem of the musical functions of sound characteristics, acoulogy relates to acoustics in almost the same way as phonology relates to phonetics."

As noted earlier, one of Schaeffer's greatest influences is the phenomenologist Edmund Husserl. Schaeffer gratefully borrows some phenomenological terms to help present his treatise. For example, the term *époché* [10] "describes an attitude of 'suspending' and 'putting in parentheses' the problem of the existence of the external world and its objects, as a result of which consciousness turns back upon itself and becomes aware of its perceptual activity in so far as the latter establishes its 'intentional objects.' . . . In the particular case of listening, *époché* represents a deconditioning of habitual listening patterns. . . . This disengagement of perception [is] also called phenomenological reduction." The concept of "putting between parentheses" forms a clear link with the attitude associated with Schaefferian reduced listening, suggesting that the listener "'put to one side' the consideration of what the sound refers to, in order to consider the sound event in itself [and] distinguish this perceived sound event from the physical signal to which the acoustician attributes it, and which itself is not sound." Supporting this, Schaeffer calls on the term *anamorphosis* [5], which is "[a] particular example of the correlation between physical signal and sound object characterised by 'certain irregularities' which are noticeable in the transition from physical vibration to perceived sound 'suggesting a psychological distortion of physical "reality," and which demonstrates that perception cannot be reduced to physical measurement.'" Anamorphosis applied in time leads to the concept of "time warping," where the listener's perception affords conclusions that do not concur with physical reality.

Schaeffer defines this key term as follows: "Reduced listening is the listening attitude which consists in listening to the sound for its own sake, as a sound object by removing its real or supposed source and the meaning it may convey. . . . Reduced listening and the sound object are thus correlates of each other; they define each other mutually and respectively as perceptual activity and the object of perception." We now possess an adequate background to Schaefferian reduced listening[20] [11] and can imagine why he would abhor anecdotal music and later soundscape composition (see subsection 2 below); both these approaches run totally contrary to his method. It should come as no surprise that Schaeffer was also fairly intolerant of electronic (that is, synthesis-based) music, algorithmic music, and computer music (see, e.g., Schaeffer 1971).

Our next step is to investigate exactly what Schaeffer was seeking with the concept of sound object and, consequently, his never-defined musical object. Schaeffer's discussions consist to a large extent of what the sound object is not, rather than what it is. The sound object [12] "refers to every sound phenomenon and event perceived as a whole, a coherent entity, and heard by means of reduced listening which targets it for itself, independently of its origin or its meaning. . . . It is a sound unit perceived in its material, its particular texture, its own qualities and perceptual dimensions." It can be "compared to a 'gestalt' in the psychology of form." It is not: "the sound body," "the physical signal," "a recorded fragment," "a notated symbol on a score," or "a state of mind." Furthermore, "[one] can also consider [a sound object] as a composition of small sound objects which can be studied individually." As we shall discover, the sound object and related terms are pertinent to the classification of categories: from the level of sound to that of work, and organizing sound from the micro- to the macrolevel in the following chapter.

One type of sound object is the suitable (*convenable*) object [40]: "Sound objects are called suitable when they seem to be more appropriate than others for use as a musical object." This suggests that a musical object is a sound object that has been chosen for its musical potential. Suitable objects should "be simple, original and at the same time easily 'memorable,' with a medium duration; therefore be balanced[21] typologically; lend themselves easily to reduced listening, therefore not be too anecdotal or too loaded with meaning or emotion; be capable, finally, combined with other sound objects of the same genre, of producing a salient and easily identifiable musical value." The notion of value will be returned to shortly. Suitable objects are "created and defined by a series of approximations, by to-ing and fro-ing between doing and listening." The point here is that as the primacy of the ear is a given, there are no rules, other than empirical trial and error, on which to lean to achieve suitability.

Chion includes in his *Guide* what he considers to be Schaeffer's "law of the musical," also known as PCV2, a law combining several word pairs introduced in *TOM* and providing a formula that would turn out to be fundamental to his solfège [26, end]: "amongst several (sound) OBJECTS the PERMANENCE of a CHARACTERISTIC is the CONCRETE

SONOROUS basis of a STRUCTURE of VARIATIONS of VALUE forming the ABSTRACT MUSICAL discourse." The pairs work chronologically per line: object–structure, permanence–variation, characteristic–value, concrete–abstract, and sonorous–musical. To understand this fully, one needs to study every nuance of each word pair, a task that would take up far too much space in the current work. The law is included here simply to give an impression of the wealth of ideas conceived by Schaeffer and equally the somewhat nonspecific nature of his approach.

We have now been introduced to many of Schaeffer's key building blocks. Before considering the notions behind his solfège, I will briefly discuss his concept of the *quatre écoutes* [6] or four listening modes, as this is one of his most important concepts related to the listening experience. The four modes are: *écouter*, "listening to someone, to something; and through the intermediary of sound, aiming to identify the source, the event, the cause; it means treating the sound as a sign of this source, this event"; *ouïr*, "perceiving by ear, being struck by sounds, the crudest, most elementary level of perception; so we 'hear,' passively, lots of things which we are not trying to listen to or understand"; *entendre*, "an intention to listen [*écouter*], choosing from what we hear [*ouïr*] what particularly interests us, thus 'determining' what we hear"; and *comprendre*, "grasping a meaning, values, by treating the sound as a sign, referring to this meaning through a language, a code (semantic hearing)." Schaeffer considers the first pair to be concrete and the latter to be abstract, and he considers *écouter* and *comprendre* to be objective and the other two to be subjective. It is important to note that further modes of listening have been introduced by other authors.[22] I would think that assuming the listener's ability to switch between the various modes of listening might be a very important tool for composers of music; yet this is by nature largely unpredictable. With this in mind, interdisciplinary work with specialists in areas such as perception could be very useful, not only in terms of providing relevant information for composers, but also in terms of furthering our knowledge of how electroacoustic music is experienced.

Schaeffer does not stop with these four modes of listening. He accompanies this introduction with two other pairs related to listening:

ordinary/specialized [7] and natural/cultural [8]. Ordinary listening is a lesser form of specialized: "Ordinary listening goes immediately to the causality of the sound, its origins, as well as its meaning. . . . Specialised listening concentrates on a particular manner of listening." That is, the specialized listener is more acutely aware of variations of a given type of sound. Natural listening is more involved with source identification; cultural is more involved with the comprehension of meaning. Schaeffer does not often return to the modes of listening once he embarks on his discussions relevant to his solfège, but they clearly go hand in hand with his concept of reduced listening.

Schaeffer's solfège (and his program of musical research) [38] is " 'the art of practicing better listening'; it is an 'experimental . . . and realistic' approach to the sound object, a kind of becoming aware of the new materials of music while distrusting preconceived ideas and relying first and foremost upon what is heard." However, it is "also a 'generalised solfège,' without notation, because it is intended to apply to the whole universe of sounds already available or capable of being made." Furthermore: "This solfège is situated rather in the area of hearing than making, it is descriptive rather than being operational. The criteria which it seeks to bring out are not expressed by symbols leading to (premature) notations for new scores, but as a deepening of the act of listening, seeking in sounds their musical potential, prior to any plan of notation or composition. This solfège 'is not yet music,' it is the indispensable preliminary to it. It is embodied in the five operations of the program of musical research Programme de la Recherche Musicale, [PROGREMU]: typology, morphology, characterology, analysis, synthesis." Solfège is therefore related to the listening experience as well as classification and analysis, and has primarily been created for the composer.

We will complete our introduction to Schaefferian concepts by working our way through PROGREMU. John Dack, who has been studying Schaeffer for years, has summarized it as follows (Dack 1999, 53): "PROGREMU comprises a system of five interdependent stages. . . . By means of typology and morphology sound objects are isolated from their context, classified and described. These are the most detailed, taxonomic stages of the program. Thereafter, according to characterology, sounds can be grouped in 'genres' and, by analysis, their potential for musical structures can be assessed. With this information the composer can synthesize new sound objects. Each stage has a specific function but is subservient to the ultimate aim—musical composition."

First, typology: "Typology ([41], accompanied by another term, type [42]) has two objectives: to isolate a sound object from its context[23] and to classify it. Schaeffer invented four pairs of dualisms to accomplish these aims" (Dack, 1999, 54). By way of Schaeffer's system of types (twenty-nine types + eighteen "variant" types of sound object are defined), he is seeking suitable objects. These types are summed up in his table, which shows the principal plan of the typology of sound objects (*TOM*, 442). In Schaeffer's table, the two axes represent one of his key typology pairs, mass (material) and execution (*facture*, the nature of the sound's shape in time); "balanced" sound objects are to be found near the middle, and more "original" objects are to be found toward the edges. Note that to decipher Schaeffer's tables, we require a large number of lower-level terms. Chion remarks in his *Guide* that very elementary terms were needed at the typology stage to avoid overclassifying sounds. Accompanying this table is one with even greater detail known by its abbreviation "TARTYP" (*Tableau récapitulatif de la typologie* or reca-pitulative typology table; *TOM*, 459; *Guide*, 172). Both are highly relevant for those who would like to understand Schaeffer's concepts in further detail. It is not clear, however, how to work out specifically how experimentation takes place using the PROGREMU system. There are few published statements that illustrate how these tables are to be used, unfortunately, and there are none to my knowledge that discuss their application in any great detail.

John Dack (1999) has also provided succinct summaries for the other key PROGREMU terms. On morphology: "Once sound objects have been subjected to typological classification a more detailed description is required of their characteristics.[24] Naturally, description is needed for typology but it is less specific. The more refined, precise description is the task of morphology [43]" (Dack 1999, 56). There are seven key criteria associated with morphology: mass, harmonic timbre, dynamic, grain, oscillation (*allure*), melodic profile, and profile of mass (summarized in [88], dealt with in some detail in [89–100])—these are in turn assigned to different classes [44]. Schaeffer introduces yet another pair of terms here: outer context and inner context: "The outer context of a sound object is the whole structure in which it is identified as a unit and from which it is extracted to be examined individually; its inner content is the structure of which it is itself made up and which allows it to be described and defined in accordance with the stacking principle of the object/structure rule. The identification of sound objects in their outer context . . . comes under typology. The definition of sound objects in their inner context, the description of them as structures made up of constituent objects, comes from morphology" (*Guide*, [24]). Projecting the typological onto the morphological criteria [88], Schaeffer proposes the term *typo-morphology* [58], which is where the identification, classification, and description of sounds theoretically take place.

Characterology [46] is the next stage of PROGREMU, "during which several implicit notions regarding instrumental thought are reintroduced. Characterology is in many ways the most elusive stage of PROGREMU. However, it provides important insights into the nature of instrumental thought. Characterology's purpose is the formulation of 'genres' [47]. These are sound families where sound objects' morphological criteria interact in specific ways" (Dack 1999, 57). Chion writes: "synthesis of musical objects . . . would aim at producing series of objects of the same genre capable of producing a variation of a relevant feature, or value" (*Guide*, [47]). As Schaeffer's means of classification is highly timbre-based, his use of genre here can also be associated with timbre.

The stage of analysis is next, which "complements that of characterology. Genres are examined in order to see if perceived features of sound objects have the potential for being placed in 'scales' (this term is accompanied by 'species' [49]). . . . It is the variation of values on which abstract relationships are based. If the composer decided that particular 'scale steps' were needed, new sound objects might have to be created. This is the final stage of PROGREMU—synthesis. Thus, Schaefferian synthesis aims to manufacture specific sound objects but only after stages of close, intelligent listening demanded by analysis" (Dack 1999, 57–58). Dack goes on to suggest that sound manipulation forms an important part of the synthesis stage, rightly noting (see Dack 2002) that synthesis in Schaefferian terms has nothing to do with synthesis as we normally know it today, that is, as creating sounds either *ex nihilo* or through some means of analysis/resynthesis. Analysis and synthesis are accompanied by their own special terms. This pair appears to be the least worked out of the five PROGREMU levels. This is rather unfortunate, as these terms seem to take the user close to the level where compositional experiments could start. So again Schaeffer's tables in *TOM* introduce many useful terms, but offer few protocols regarding their operation. We will discover why in due course.

All five levels are summed up in Schaeffer's most complex table in *TOM* (584–587; *Guide*, 173–177) known again by its acronym, "TARSOM" (*Tableau récapitulatif du solfège des objets musicaux* or Recapitulative table on the solfège of musical objects). This massive table takes terms from all five levels and places them in a two-dimensional field interrelating criteria with relevant terms and examples of sound types where relevant. This is as close to a description of potential musical objects as Schaeffer gets. Again, TARSOM seems not to have led to musicians' sharing reports on how they specifically applied it.

Schaeffer's terminology is generally used by people who make or study music (music analysis, music philosophy) with real-world sounds, Francis Dhomont and Annette Vande Gorne being not the least important; however, there are interesting exceptions which do demonstrate that what he created is not solely applicable to the corpus and approach that he represents. For example, John Bowers has called on Schaefferian terminology in discussing improvised real-time electroacoustic music work (Bowers 2003); John Dack has used Schaefferian terminology in a discussion of Stockhausen's *Kontakte* (Dack 1998); François Delalande often uses relevant terms in his pedagogical discussions including discussions of sound awareness from pre-birth to early childhood (see, e.g., Delalande 2001a). Most authors I discovered while preparing this publication and as part of ongoing EARS research tend to use the Schaefferian approach primarily for analytical purposes as opposed to compositional ones. This may be partially a result of the fact that very few composers have offered details on their specific usage of Schaeffer's system. Although Schaeffer composed an important series of works in his lifetime, his theory seems to have remained incomplete if not a bit too open to interpretation. Given this nonspecificity and without cases in point (the published CD set *Solfège de l'objet sonore* which focuses on illustrations of sonic objects [Schaeffer and Reibel 1998] being a rare and important exception), applying his theory seems to require the user to make several decisions unrelated to the theory. Of those who have followed in Schaeffer's footsteps, Denis Smalley (see below) comes closest to someone whose approach to theory is suitable for others' analytical application. Finally, Schaeffer worked at the level of the sound object, but he hardly discusses musical structure throughout his large series of writings. This seems awkward in terms of application and is perhaps the theory's most significant omission.

François Bayle is another former director of the GRM. In a sense, his work picks up where Schaeffer left off; his views focus completely on the acousmatic[25] and are possibly more difficult to grasp, though they are not as voluminous as Schaeffer's. Bayle has been known to suggest that his thoughts on music are a bit like poetry. Poetry is, of course, open to interpretation, as is music. This brief summary will limit itself to an introduction of Bayle's key concepts which all appear in his compendium *musique acousmatique: propositions . . . . . . positions* (Bayle 1993), but which seem to be better clarified in the bilingual (French/German) *François Bayle L'image de son/Klangbilder: Technique de mon écoute/Technik meines Hörens* (Misch and von Blumröder 2003). Some of his key concepts can also be found in English in "Image-of sound, or I-sound: Metaphor/metaform" (Bayle 1989). An article that accompanies this 1989 English translation is by a colleague who clearly influenced him, Jean Petitot, and is entitled "Perception, Cognition, and Morphological Objectivity" (Petitot 1989).

Petitot introduces the context of Bayle's theories as follows:

The study of "form-bearing elements" presupposes the possibility of developing a specifically morphological analysis of sound forms. . . . One of the most striking things about acousmatic music such as that of F. Bayle—apart from its specifically aesthetic and artistic qualities—is its wealth of morphological components. The morphological, indeed morphodynamic, lexicon used by the composer in the phenomenological description of sound images, sound structures and sound organisations is very diverse; it includes figurative salience, clear and fuzzy contours, attacks and fronts, not to mention deformation, stretching, mixing, stability and instability, rupture, discontinuity, harmonic clouds, crumbling and deviation of figures and so on. (Petitot 1989, 171–172)

Bayle, himself, summarizes his writings as follows: "The central question . . . is that of conditions or criteria of the listenability [*écoutabilité*][26] of organised sounds projected into a listening space by electroacoustic means. Based on their morphological 'appearance,' . . . effects of salience and pregnance,[27] as well as distinguishing features of reference and coherence, [are] assessed" (Bayle 1989, 165). Thus he claims to be interested in cause, in contrast to Schaeffer, but he also states that causality in acousmatic music works best when imaginary, when space is fictional (Misch and Blumröder 2003, 28). For those already acquainted with the subject, these remarks can be clearly seen as a midpoint between the work of Schaeffer and the work by Denis Smalley, which will be introduced shortly. What Bayle desires to achieve is a reconciliation of the physical aspects of sound with its morphological aspects. Given the reduced listening environment in which he works, the morphological becomes a space for metaphoric thinking. (Bayle is known to have said that the first technology in semiotics was clearly that of the acousmatic curtain, Misch and von Blumröder 2003, 16.)[28]

More specifically, Bayle is interested in what he calls the "trichotomy of the audible": "i) hearing and 'presentification' (activating audition), ii) listening and identification (activating cognition), and iii) comprehending and interpretation (which activate 'musicalisation')" (Bayle 1989, 167).[29] The Schaefferian inheritance is clear if for no other reason than the use of three of the four modes of listening. Bayle relates this Schaefferian triad to his own terms, which fall under the umbrella of *i-sons*, images-of-sounds, the building blocks of acousmatic music. These *i-sons* are based on the double disjunction, physical and psychological, of a perceived "projected sound," that is, one heard by way of loudspeaker diffusion,[30] and comprise "i) the isomorphic image (iconic, referential) or *im-son*,[31] ii) the diagram, a selection of simplified contours (indexical), or *di-son*, and iii) the metaphor/metaform, associated with a general concept (sign of) or *me-son*" (ibid., 168). Bayle openly admits that this part of his terminology is highly influenced by the work of Charles Sanders Peirce (Misch and von Blumröder 2003, 54).

Bayle's terminology may appear to be a bit piecemeal, perhaps owing to the difficulty of coming to grips with his ideas. It may also have to do with the fact that Bayle does not seem to deliver as complete or enclosed a theory as Schaeffer, leaving the application of his terms even more open to interpretation. They are working in the same areas of theory, however, as Bayle is particularly interested in the listening experience and, to a lesser extent, in classification and discourse. He also poses some worthy straightforward questions in his book that boil down to: What is the significance of the "quantum leap" acousmatic music represents? What significance does the technological studio have in terms of this experimentation? And, to whom might this music be addressed—how does one value it, communicate it (Bayle 1993, 29)? It seems curious, though, that after raising such important issues, he hardly goes on to address them in general terms.

It is also interesting to note that Bayle is concerned with the "literature" of electroacoustic music and proposes that "[w]e need graphic representations to create a literature that one can quickly scan, like one leafs through a book to find a key phrase" (Desantos 1997, 17), a suggestion relevant to the following chapter's discussions of representation. This proposal seems slightly at odds with his often-cited alternative means of description. But, as with Schaeffer, what is most important here are the questions: how many people use Bayle's terminology for compositional and analytical purposes, and how many have incorporated Bayle's terminology alongside that of others?[32] Even in analyses of his works, not many people have mastered the terminology sufficiently to apply it, or else they have chosen not to. For example, Pierre Couprie openly uses Schaefferian terminology in his discussion of one section of Bayle's *Trois rêves d'oiseau* without calling on the *i-son* concept (Couprie 1999). That said, this same author successfully combines Schaefferian, Bayleian, and Schaferian (that is, R. Murray Schafer, introduced below in subsection 2) terminology in an overview entitled "Le vocabulaire de l'objet sonore" (Couprie 2001). The dearth of usage of Bayle's ideas is a bit unexpected, as many of his ideas seem potentially powerful. Perhaps as less poetic treatises on his theory appear, such as the 2003 bilingual publication, his concepts will be better understood and, ideally, assimilated with the concepts of others, as Couprie has done in his terminology article.

Michel Chion is not only a specialist in deciphering the concepts of Schaeffer; like most theorists in the subject area, he is also a composer.

Like Schaeffer, he writes with ease. But Chion also has another vocation, namely that of a writer about cinema. On occasion his two "halves" coincide. This has led to key works, including his well-known title, *Audio-vision: Sound on Screen* (Chion 1990) and his books *Le son au cinéma* (Chion 1985) and *Musiques, medias, technologie* (Chion 1994). His book *Le Son* (Chion 2002), however, focuses more on audio than audiovisual work. He has also presented his ideas behind musique concrète in *La musique électroacoustique* (Chion 1982) and *L'art des sons fixés ou la musique concrètement* (Chion 1991). Chion has often noted that there is not enough musical analysis of sound-based music, but then he chooses to avoid the practice himself. What he does achieve, similar to these other French specialists, is the addition of terms relevant to the study of sound-based music with and without visual images. Many of his publications also include helpful glossaries which contain newly proposed and borrowed terms.

True to his colleagues' practice, Chion is not terribly interested in discussing or documenting any real-time music making, whether purely electroacoustic or mixed. His sound world is that of *sons fixés* (fixed, that is, recorded sound), and his genre remains that of musique concrète. He rejects both of the terms electroacoustic and acousmatic as inappropriate to the music of sounds that have been captured by microphone and further treated in the studio. It was indeed Chion who proposed the term "cinema for the ear" (e.g., Chion 1991, 62), a term that seems appropriate as many of his books concern aural experience in the cinema. In both audio-only and audiovisual contexts he celebrates the art of montage and its presentations of what is perceived to be natural or unnatural sequences of sonorous events. Chion's preferred *modus operandi* as a composer is, of course, the latter.

A true disciple of Schaeffer as far as reduced listening goes,[33] he offers "10 commandments for the art of fixed sounds" (Chion 1991, 22–25). These make clear that source identification is off limits, as is any sense of physical causality. That said, he is the first of these three authors to spend time writing about the recording experience, introducing the term *tournage sonore* ("audio shoot"),[34] a term clearly borrowed from film. His goal here is to emphasize that sound recording is an intentional act and, whether done for professional or creative reasons, the act of sound recording forms an essential part of the art of fixed sounds. Terms such as this one are associated with the category of "new virtuosity," discussed in the following chapter. Once a work is completed, he describes the work's space as being internal to the recording itself and also external, in that it depends partly on the listening conditions present at any given moment the work is heard (ibid., 50).

Below, I list other useful terms, separated by whether they have audio-only or audiovisual applications. It is regrettable that Chion does not consider audiovisual terms that might be useful in nonfilm (or theater) contexts, such as audiovisual works of sound art, or video/new media works.

Audio

Auditum—something heard (Chion 2002, 271–272).

Cause figurée, cause réelle, cause attribuée (figurative, real, attributed cause)—three terms dealing with the perception of cause. The first is often accompanied by the term *flou causal* (blurred causation), which leaves cause to the imagination; the second focuses on the object itself, which is recognizable, but its cause needs to be worked out in a sense; and the third allows the cause to be determined within the context of the work's perceived sounds (ibid., 118–122).

Indices sonores matérialisants (materializing sound indices)—an aspect of a sound, in whatever form, which aids in the listener's perceiving the material nature of the source and the concrete history of its becoming sonorous (ibid., 102).

Modelage (shaping)—designates certain "manipulations" of fixed sounds that imprint them with such a particular form that this resultant form becomes the essential essence of the sound (Chion 1991, 98).

Phoniurge—one who is the creator of a sound in every sense (ibid.). Perhaps a synonym for *sound designer*.

Audiovisual

Acousmêtre (from acousmatic and *être*, to be)—a kind of voice-character specific to cinema that in most instances of cinematic narratives derives mysterious powers from being heard and not seen (Chion 1990, 221).

Added value—the expressive and/or informative value with which a sound enriches a given image, so as to create the definite impression (either immediate or remembered) that this meaning emanates "naturally" from the image itself (ibid.). Related terms are: *anempathetic sound*—sound that exhibits conspicuous indifference to what is going on in the film's plot (ibid.); and *empathetic sound*—music whose mood or rhythm matches the mood or rhythm of the action on screen (ibid., 222).

Audio-vision—designates the type of perception relevant to cinema and television (or in daily life) in which the image is the focus of attention, but where the sound contributes a series of effects, sensations, and meanings at any moment which, by means of the phenomena of illusion and projection, are taken into account and seem to be released naturally from the visual content (ibid., 96). Its converse, visu-audition, concerns audio-driven events (e.g., concerts) at which visual aspects can influence certain aural perceptions.

Synchresis—the forging of an immediate and necessary relationship between something one sees and something one hears at the same time (from *synchronism* and *synthesis*). The psychological phenomenon of synchresis is what makes dubbing and much other postproduction sound mixing possible (ibid., 224).

François Delalande has been working at the GRM for years as a musicologist and music education specialist in residence, alongside the musicologist Jean-Christophe Thomas. Delalande is another active writer, specializing in GRM-like work, although in recent years, his output has diversified to an extent.[35] A great deal of his writing concerns potential means of analysis; a somewhat smaller percentage is involved with pedagogical tools related to musique concrète. He has been involved with widely distributed publications created by the French Ministry of Education. France is, after all, one of very few countries that celebrates its contemporary music, for example by choosing electroacoustic compositions as national examination material at secondary school level. Nevertheless, Delalande's work tends to be more theoretical than empirical.

His works on analysis, description, and comprehension of electroacoustic music form the bulk of his publications. The earlier works are

useful in that they carry on the Schaefferian theoretical tradition, sometimes in greater depth than had previously been published. To discuss
this, however, would only continue the thread of what has already been
introduced. Instead, I will focus on two highly empirical and thus exceptional articles, as they are directly pertinent to my aim of creating a
framework for understanding sound-based music; I will return to a major
concept of his, the electroacoustic paradigm (Delalande 2001b), in the
final section of this chapter. Traditionally and predictably, Delalande has
been a propagandist for aesthesic analysis. Given Schaeffer's credo concerning the primacy of the ear, Delalande believes that analysis should
take place logically from the listener's point of view in the first instance,
and consider composer feedback only for the purposes of verification of
aural analytical findings or ambiguities.[36] Later in his career, Delalande
became part of the team that would create the acousmographe, a representation software for the evocative—that is, not solely physics-based—
transcription of electroacoustic works. His ideal, announced in the article
"Écoute interactive, imagerie musicale" (Delalande 1998b), is analysis
through interactive listening.

The two chosen articles are opposites, in a way. One is analytical and
based on aesthesis, but does not primarily focus on Schaefferian notions
(Delalande 1998a). The other, a real exception for Delalande, is clearly
based on poiesis (construction), as it involves composition (Delalande
1989b). The former, English-language analysis (his only publication in
English) involves eight experienced listeners who study a single movement of Pierre Henry's early work, "Sommeil" of *Variations pour une
porte et un soupir*. Delalande begins this article with a large and very
informative contextual introduction. Here he admits to having spent a
great deal of time, particularly in the 1970s, performing what he calls
morphological analyses, something he now finds problematic and unsatisfactory: "The morphological analysis of electroacoustic music (based
on a resolution into sound objects) is a 'syllabic' analysis, which does
not provide the means of highlighting pertinent configurations either poi-
etically (a 'trace' of compositional strategies) or aesthesically (contributing to explaining the behaviours and representations of listeners)"
(Delalande 1998a, 20). He suggests that Schaeffer's work needs to be
"revised, completed and adapted to the types of sounds now more com-

monly used in music" (ibid., 18), and refers to Denis Smalley's work in spectromorphology (which he considers to be more "semiotically inspired" [ibid., 22] than morphological), introduced below, as an important advance in this direction. His key goal, therefore, is the discovery of what he calls *pertinences*. He believes that there are various paths which, when combined, help in achieving this: analysis of the physical signal (e.g., using the acousmographe or a sonogram); discovering morphological characteristics of a work, which he claims is more complex than the Schaefferian discovery of morphological units; various other ways, particularly through the listening experience, which is not primarily taxonomic in character; and triangulating this information with feedback from the composer wherever possible. "The objective of music analysis is to bring to light configurations which either reflect the choices (implicit or explicit) and actions of the composer, or which are needed to explain the reception behaviours of listeners, . . . or both at once" (ibid., 18).[37] Delalande admits that our listening behavior is inconsistent—that one never hears a piece the same way twice in a row and that no two people hear a piece in the same manner either—but claims that this need not detract from the specific goal of finding pertinences.

His research leads him to coin the term "listening behaviors" instead of modes of listening as, in five of his six cases (see the next paragraph), they all involve Schaeffer's *comprendre* (understanding) to a large extent. Listeners may be able to engage in more than one of these behaviors, according to Delalande, but not simultaneously. In collaboration with his GRM colleague, Thomas, trials were held with eight experienced electroacoustic music specialists who listened to "Sommeil"; three listened to the movement once, two twice, and three listened three times. (Delalande does not focus much on the differences between repeated listenings and a single listening, perhaps because of his small specialist sample.) It is this project that I referred to in chapter 1 when introducing participant-based research projects as part of the I/R project discussion. Before elaborating on his listening behavior typology, he claims that this experiment demonstrated that: (a) there is a coherence in listening behavior where "expectations and specific interests determine a strategy, and therefore . . . [evoke] significations and aesthetic appreciation" (ibid., 25); (b) analogies between certain testimonies emerge clearly; and

(c) it is not difficult to take each of these behaviors as an analytical point of view (ibid., 25). Delalande admits that once testimonies are collected, the analyst is not always entirely impartial in terms of potential interpretation.

Delalande identified three main listening behaviors and three peripheral ones: (1) In *taxonomic listening*, "the most artificial, indeed artifactual" (ibid., 26) approach, the experience is more laborious than pleasurable. Listeners distinguish sufficiently large morphological units, qualify them, and notice how they are arranged in relation to one another. Descriptive metaphors are used and sometimes pictures are created to organize these thoughts. (2) *Empathetic listening* focuses on feeling, the immediate reactions to sensations that the listener has no interest in scoring. As in taxonomic listening, metaphors are created and general images of the piece constructed, leading more easily to aesthetic reactions. In this case morphology and impact may coincide, whereas in the first case, selection and description are more important. (3) In *figurativization*, the listener searches for narrative discourse within a work, for movement, for traces of life, for contextual function, according to Delalande. Here "form becomes narrative" (ibid., 49), responses are perhaps more "childlike . . . as opposed to 'scholarly' " (ibid., 51). In this project appreciation is thus as relevant as, for musique concrète specialists at least, the ambiguity between realism and abstraction (ibid., 58). (4) Listeners may *search for a law of organization*: in an epoch where formalization (see under subsection 6 below) plays a significant role in composition, one form of listening behavior is that of the search for structure(s) and models. (5) In *immersed listening*, the listener feels part of a context, partaking in the flow of a sequence (which was impossible in the trial, given the work in question). (6) Finally, there is *nonlistening*: the participant loses concentration or interest in the work.

This article stands out in the long list of Delalande's publications and is a tribute to the GRM team of musicologists. It combines contextual issues with empirical data. It is a wonderful case of the listening experience as a category being integrated with analytical investigations into musical discourse and salient sound qualities. This can subsequently be linked to the classification of sound and musical gestures. What is perhaps frustrating is the isolated nature of this type of project. Now that these ideas have come to the fore, they should, it seems, be tried out on listeners with various levels of experience, taste, and so on, and with other works.[38] That said, this article offers a framework for building a greater awareness of works of organized sound. Complementing this article are three volumes at the GRM where the raw data can be accessed.

In a sense, the second article uses the methodology of the first article taken through the looking glass. Here, based on an project of Bénédict Maillard, Delalande and Thomas worked together with fourteen composers (twelve of whom were interviewed at the end of the project), all of whom were given very short "germ cells" of sound of a few seconds' duration each (no two composers were given the same one) and were subsequently requested to create their work in the same studio at the GRM, that is, using the same equipment. Only the final mix-down took place in a separate studio. The article chronicles some of the patterns of behavior that were discovered. No one in particular worked in an unorthodox manner, so the goal was to see how the composers phased their work. (There is oddly no analysis of how the pieces represented either the GRM spirit or the particular studio that was chosen.) What is fascinating, given this group's known conscious avoidance of formalization, is the interplay between discovery (*trouvaille*), the search for suitable (*convenable*) material, musical ideas, and stylistic rules. The article claims the purpose (*propos*) of the experiment is the only part of the project that could be formulated; yet through repetition in behavior, particular stylistic "rules" are discovered.

What makes this project special is that the composers are the ones who are directly involved in this poietic investigation, albeit through a structured interview approach. The paper is unusual in that the composers are dealing not with models of synthesis and manipulation, but instead with process, an aspect of sound-based music that is relatively underdocumented. This paper is useful in identifying a wide variety of aspects relevant to the analysis of works of sound organization. By participating in a totally different type of investigation than those with which he is typically associated, Delalande helped to define the boundaries of the potential investigation of the music of sounds. This article belongs to the categories of new virtuosity, organizing sound, and modes of discourse and analysis within sound-based music studies.

There are, of course, others who are well known for their analytical work founded on Schaefferian concepts, Stéphane Roy being one of the better-known specialists. People who have forwarded these concepts in analysis will be introduced in the following chapter in the discussion concerning discourse analysis, and representation (section B3). Before closing this first subsection, I will introduce Smalley's concept of spectromorphology.

Denis Smalley is the only person to have taken a significant step beyond *TOM* while acknowledging its influence on the development of his concepts of spectromorphology and spatiomorphology.[39] These concepts are related to the following theoretical categories: organizing sound from micro- to macrolevel, modes of discourse, analysis and representation, new means of presentation (as far as spatialization is concerned), the listening experience, and classification.

The following remark demonstrates that Smalley is a product of the Schaefferian tradition. He, too, believes in the primacy of the ear and, to a large extent, in reduced listening:[40]

My musical ideas come out of the sounds themselves. I explore their characteristics. I discover. With digital techniques, for example, I can isolate fragments that the ear can't otherwise hear. (Smalley, cited in Chadabe 1997, 130–131)

Smalley's approach is one in which structures evolve from sounds that are organized in time. This discussion will focus on his three key texts: "Spectro-morphology and Structuring Processes" (Smalley 1986), "Listening Imagination: Listening in the Electroacoustic Era" (Smalley 1992a), and "Spectromorphology: Explaining Sound Shapes" (Smalley 1997).[41] Smalley defines spectromorphology as follows: "Spectromorphology is an approach to sound materials and music structures which concentrates on the spectrum of available pitches and their shaping in time" (Smalley 1986, 61). In this definition he acknowledges the premise of "the inherent musicality in all sounds" (ibid.), a slightly different standpoint from that of Schaeffer. He also acknowledges "the abstract and concrete aspects of sound" (ibid., 64) in the Schaefferian sense. This leads him to the view that analyses of the type in which he is interested must involve an awareness of the listening experience, in particular if a reduced listening approach[42] is called for. With this in mind, Smalley reexamines Schaeffer's *quatre écoutes*, choosing three of his own (in Smalley 1992a—he translates the term as "ways of listening") plus a separate mode launched elsewhere (in Smalley 1997). In interpreting Schaeffer he calls on Ernest Schachtel's terms *autocentric* ("subject-centred senses [which] focus on basic responses and feelings of pleasure and displeasure") and *allocentric* ("[which] is object-centred in that it involves perceiving something independent of the perceiver's needs," Smalley 1992a, 518). Linking these two concepts to Schaeffer's four, Smalley introduces his "listening relationships": *indicative* (correlating with Schaeffer's mode 1), *reflexive* (i.e. autocentric; has no Schaefferian equivalent) and *interactive* (correlating with Schaeffer's modes 3 and 4 as well as allocentric), and suggests that the first two are the most prevalent (ibid., 519–520). As introduced in the previous chapter, in Smalley 1997, he adds the term "listening to technology" (which has already also been called "recipe listening" and the *Sième écoute*), which has to do with listeners' paying attention to how a sound was generated or recorded and manipulated and eventually spatialized (Smalley 1997, 109).

In his first introduction to spectromorphology and spatiomorphology, Smalley employed the following five sections: spectral typology, morphology, motion, structuring processes, and space. One immediately discerns the Schaefferian heritage (the use of typology and to a slightly lesser extent morphology and motion) and Smalley's moving forward in terms of taking structure and space into account. Before continuing, one point of criticism needs to be raised. Like Schaeffer, Smalley tends to avoid empirical examples rather consistently. The one exception is in a focused article on sound transformations (Smalley 1993) in which every term he discusses is accompanied by an example. We will return to this article below. Fortunately, other writers are extending Smalley's terminology, and there are currently plans to carry out full analyses using spectromorphological and spatiomorphological tools. In the interim, it is difficult to ascertain to what extent these tools are relevant to different types of sound-based works, not to mention mixed and non-electroacoustic works. What is clear is that Smalley's approach can be applied to both real-world and synthesized sounds. He also suggests (in Smalley 1997, 109) that spectral instrumental works might also be investigated using his terminology.

Spectral typology can be reduced to three spectral types: notes, which are further subdivided into note proper, harmonic, and inharmonic spectra; nodes, "a band or knot of sound which resists pitch identification"; and noise. Smalley calls the "buffer zone" between note and noise "the pitch-effluvium continuum" (Smalley 1986, 65–67). Electroacoustic sounds are rarely stable; they evolve by way of temporal shaping or morphologies. Smalley, like his predecessor, uses a two- to three-phase envelope to describe such shapes, similar to the attack, sustain, and release (a/s/r—without the interim decay) common to synthesizers. Very common morphological shapes—Smalley accompanies his terms with graphic shapes whenever possible—are called "morphological archetypes." A more complete list is designated "morphological models." When these shapes occur in sequence, Smalley speaks of "morphological strings" (ibid., 69–71). These shapes can be heard in isolation (e.g., "separated attack-impulses"), along a continuum (e.g., "an iteration" where the movement of the sound is audible), or as a "grain" (where the impulses are no longer individually perceived). This sequence is called the "attack-effluvium continuum," similar to the sequence ranging from note to noise (ibid., 72).

Although Smalley's choice of motion is rooted in Schaefferian theory, it is much more detailed. This section of his article also introduces two of his key terms, the external contouring of a *gesture* and the internal behavior of a *texture*, terms we return to below. In discussing his "motion typology," Smalley introduces five basic motion analogies: unidirectional, bidirectional, reciprocal, centric/cyclic, and multidirectional. These five generate a host of more specific motion types (ibid., 74). These types are accompanied by what Smalley calls "motion styles," which are designated in Schaefferian fashion by opposing pairs: synchrony/asynchrony, continuity/discontinuity, conjunction/disjunction, and periodicity/aperiodicity accompanied by internal motion designs. Spectromorphological motion can thus be described through a combination of type and style descriptors. Smalley concludes this section with a trio of "pitch-space settings" for stable textures.[43]

In terms of structure, Smalley immediately acknowledges that a multilevel approach, whether hierarchical or nonhierarchical, is normally needed for spectromorphological investigation. The two key terms, gesture and texture, are introduced as the two fundamental structuring strategies. He defines them as follows: "Gesture is concerned with action directed away from a previous goal or towards a new goal; it is concerned with the application of energy and its consequences; it is synonymous with intervention, growth and progress, and is married to causality. . . . Texture, on the other hand, is concerned with internal behaviour patterning, energy directed inwards or reinjected, self-propagating" (ibid., 82). Gesture, "an energy-motion trajectory" (Smalley 1997, 111), is associated with surrogacies. These range from a "primal gesture," "on which sounding gesture is based, [and which] occurs outside music in all proprioceptive perception"; "first-order surrogacy," which "projects the primal level into sound, and is concerned with sonic object use in work and play prior to any . . . incorporation into a musical activity or structure"; "second-order surrogacy," which is related to "traditional instrumental gesture"; "third-order surrogacy," which "is where a gesture is inferred or imagined in the music"; and "remote surrogacy," where "[s]ource and cause become unknown and unknowable as any human action behind the sound disappears" (ibid., 112). Surrogacies can also be dislocated in terms of context. With all of this in mind, Smalley likes to speak of structures as either "gesture-carried" or "texture-carried" (Smalley 1986, 83). In discussing structural function, the a/s/r above are replaced by Smalley's onset, continuant, and termination. These as usual are embellished with nineteen more specific descriptive terms. Smalley also discusses structural relationships, which deal with "simultaneous and successive structural components" and which may be useful in describing "the internal workings of motion, gesture and texture" (ibid., 88), the key nodes of which he calls interaction/equality, reaction/inequality, and interpolation, which are further detailed at a second level. Elsewhere (Smalley 1994), Smalley's approach to macrolevel relationships is developed through various forms of discourse. In the first instance, he uses the terms *source-cause discourse* ("which is concerned with the bonding play of specific inferred sounding identities"—ibid., 46; Smalley uses the term "source bonding"), *transformational discourse* ("where an identity is transformed while retaining significant vestiges of its roots"—ibid., 43), and *typological discourse* (where "[i]dentities are recognised as sharing timbral qualities but are not regarded as being descendants of the same imminent identity"—ibid., 44).

Space is presented rather differently throughout his publications making a summary slightly more challenging. He has written: "I use the term spatiomorphology to highlight [the] special concentration on exploring spatial properties and spatial change, such that they constitute a different, even separate category of sonic experience" (Smalley 1997, 122). His starting point is the difference between composed spaces ("the space as composed onto the recording media") and listening spaces ("the space in which the composed space is heard," ibid.). The former can be further subdivided into external (which exist "outside and around spectromorphologies") and the less significant internal spaces ("when a spectromorphology itself seems to enclose a space"). The latter is equally subdivided into two: personal and diffused space variants which come into play only when the listener has heard a given work in more than one space and in more than one diffusion style.[44] Yet it is external space where we find the greatest level of spatiomorphological detail (ibid., 122–124). To create analogies, Smalley proposes the term *spatial texture*. Spatial texture "is concerned with how the spatial perspective is revealed through time"; it involves the notions of contiguous and noncontiguous spaces. To conclude his introduction to spatiomorphology, Smalley offers the reader guidelines "to help define the global spatial style" of a work (ibid., 124). Gesture is associated with spatial trajectories here, a foundational element of any sound diffusion.

In Smalley 1992a, the notions of *indicative field* as well as its plural form, *indicative networks*, are introduced. The term "indicative" is indeed associated with the above-mentioned indicative relationship in terms of listening: "The term 'indicative' signifies that the musical manifestation of a field refers to or indicates related experiences in the nonsounding world" (Smalley 1992a, 521). He introduces nine fields in this article, the first three of which are marked as being archetypal: gesture, utterance, behavior, energy, motion, object/substance, environment, vision, and space. "Gesture" has already been introduced; "utterance" is linked directly to the human body. Trevor Wishart, whose work will be introduced in subsection 5 below, has written extensively on this subject (see, e.g., Wishart 1985). Sonic behavior has been linked to causality, but it is also associated with relationships that exist among sounds that have been placed in a context. Smalley introduces related terms, including dominance (foreground)/subordination (background) and conflict/coexistence, to illustrate other behavioral aspects of sound. He also discusses energy and motion, both of which have previously been introduced and are associated with spectral textures and how they evolve. Object/substance is associated with "thingness" (Smalley 1992a, 529). In the acousmatic situation, material existence is neither necessary nor evident. "Objectness" therefore "can be attributed to morphologies without reference to real materials as long as there is some semblance of a plausible gestural origin" (ibid.). "Substance" is, on the other hand, more involved with textural motion. "Environment" is exactly what it suggests: the use of environmental sound in electroacoustic contexts. "Vision" is used here in the sense of images being created by way of sound, a kind of synaesthesia. "Space" has already been introduced, although in this particular article new terms including intimacy/immensity and confinement/vastness are presented.

This article also introduces Smalley's views on the notion of sounding models. Using his terminology concerning indicative fields, Smalley (1992a) investigates models based on nature (environmental and animal life variants),[45] native culture (human utterance and human agency are at the top level of a host of sounding models), and other cultures' models. Smalley also introduces another key concept: transcontextuality. This involves the dual nature of sounds in a given sound organization that possess both intrinsic (to a work, to an art form) and extrinsic (referring to the real world) aspects. He writes: "Where the sounds taken from cultural activity or nature are used as recorded, or where transformation does not destroy the identity of the original context, the listener may become involved in a process of transcontextual interpretation" (ibid., 542). Furthermore: "The concept of transcontextuality is a useful way of understanding an indicative process since it is obvious that something outside the musical context is indicated" (ibid., 543–544). To achieve this, one might be able to move beyond a purely reduced listening approach, as nonmusical associations are indeed being made. As in so many of his other spectromorphology discussions, Smalley acknowledges that indicative fields and sounding models are usually dynamic and that the study of indicative and model shifts forms part of any spectromorphological investigation.

In 1993, Smalley wrote an exceptional article entitled "Defining Transformations" that applied his descriptive terminology to the subject of sound transformations—in the sense of sound morphing—that appeared in an issue of *Interface*, in which Trevor Wishart also made a contribution on the same subject. Here Smalley combines an investigation of source-cause (or "source-bonded") relationships with purely spectromorpholigical ("source-freed") approaches. What is exceptional in this article is that in a large number of cases of terminological definition, Smalley cites a composition as an example. The following is a list of the transformations Smalley has identified. They are listed here simply to suggest how he has applied a terminology to this specific subject that is similar to the terminology he uses to discuss spectromorphology-based music: incremental, growth, continuous, unitary, noncontiguous, proximate, simultaneous, revelatory, crossing, gesture, instigated transformations, and transformations in parallel.

Spectromorphology is Smalley's personal means of approaching analysis. In an introductory article written with coeditor Lelio Camilleri for an electroacoustic analysis issue of the *Journal of New Music Research*, he notes: "If we can 'understand' our relationship to the wide-ranging sound-world of electroacoustic music, then we shall be better positioned to arrive at a more comprehensive understanding of music and listening as cultural practices; that is the longer-term ambition of an analytical agenda centred on electroacoustic music" (Camilleri and Smalley 1998, 4). They admit in this text that reduced listening is not the *modus operandi* for everyone: "[a]n important goal of analytical exploration is . . . to attempt to reconcile and relate the internal world of the work to the outside world of sonic and non-sonic experience," in particular through the identification of a work's and the genre's pertinences or salient features (ibid., 5).

So how have others in the field reacted to Smalley's work? Although this work dates originally from the 1980s and Schaeffer started constructing his theory some thirty years earlier, there seem to be comparable followings of both and, not surprisingly, they tend to congregate around linguistic strengths (hardly any Schaefferian scholarship is available in English, whereas most of Smalley's followers have published in English). In any case, it is interesting that some have applied spectromorphological thinking and terminology to works that are not done on a fixed medium— for example, Bowers (2003) on improvisation and real-time performance and Emmerson (1998a) on a mixed work of Smalley's.[46] Returning to fixed medium works, spatiomorphology is put to the test again with a Smalley composition by Lotis (2003).[47] Fischman (1997), in analyzing a piece by Michael Vaughan, uses spectromorphology terminology, although not exclusively. Paul Rudy remarkably puts spectromorphology to the test with the soundtrack of a Hollywood film (Rudy 2004), and David Hirst proposes in a short paper (2003) how spectromorphology ideas might be further developed into a methodology appropriate to the analysis of Smalley's works. One must assume that this methodology, when completed, would also be useful for others' compositions. Finally, Michael Casey acknowledges the influence of Smalley's and Schaeffer's theories regarding his research involving the capture and description of "acoustic lexemes," in particular by way of the Internet (Casey 2005).

Christiane ten Hoopen and John Young have also investigated Smalley's ideas, and by implication, Schaeffer's, along with those of Trevor Wishart (see subsection 5, below). In ten Hoopen's work, areas of particular importance are source and cause—how they are presented and how they are sometimes difficult to identify. For example, other than cases where source and cause are apparent (as in traditional-sounding work) and cases where neither is apparent (as in a more abstract sonic situation), combinations of an inferred or unrecognizable source with a recognizable, inferred, or unrecognizable cause lead to real or implied situations of human agency. As source recognition can become ambiguous, for those not using solely a reduced listening approach, it can also be difficult. One of her novel ideas is the distinction between re-presentation (of recorded sounds) and representation (ten Hoopen 1994, 1997) as introduced in chapter 1.

Young has investigated what he considers to be the ambiguity that "arises when a sound suggests more than one plausible physical origin" (Young 1996, 79). He proposes levels of "reality" and "abstraction." These levels can be tangibly articulated in electroacoustic music, namely through mediation and jux-taposition. Mediation is achieved through gradual shifts in apparent order of surrogacy,[48] which may be heard in terms of a progressive interchange of a number of distinct sound identities, or where a specific identity is heard to change its order of surrogacy or transformation. Juxtaposition involves the direct com-bination of sounds of typically quite polarised orders of surrogacy, either sequen-tially or simultaneously. In musical contexts these articulations are not mutually exclusive. Our attention may be shifted freely from one type of articulation to another within the same work. (Ibid., 84; see also Young 2004)

Elsewhere, Young has also added the terms *idio-morphology* and *exo-morphology* (Young 2002), defining them as follows: "idio-morphology —defining timbral features of sound identities that are nested within transformational sequences, and exo-morphology—a feature of a sound that is used to reshape some aspect of the structure of another" (ibid., 345). It is clear that Smalley's approach has found a reasonable amount of resonance from musicians and scholars alike.

Few words have been written in this section concerning the construction of music. This is because there has been surprisingly little written about compositional theory in general in terms of sound-based composition of the sorts discussed here. Frankly, most work fitting into this category is made from the materials upward, which is a large departure from most music, which tends to fit into a known form or convenient structure. Even Smalley's approach to structure can take place only when most of the detail at the sound-object level has been investigated, a logical approach given that that is also the way he composes.

A question worth posing at this point is: how much of what has been described in this subsection might be seen as relevant to today's sound artists (see subsection 9, below) and musicians working with real-world sounds in contexts that are not directly related to the musique concrète or reduced listening tradition? Many sound artists physically expose their sound sources or modify them only slightly, for example in installations. Others want the source to be recognized through the environmental aspects of where the work is being presented. The musicians and theo-rists (most of whom are also musicians) discussed above have taken an extreme position both in the dimension ranging from recordable to syn-thetic sounds (the Paris–Cologne divide in the early 1950s) and the dimen-sion ranging from reduced listening/acousmatic behavior to the worlds of anecdotal and soundscape composition (introduced directly below). Fortunately, more recent scholarship and musical composition take these surrogacies into account, turning all of the gray areas between the poles into acceptable places to visit in just about any given work employing any given approach. This is yet another form of convergence that is taking place. Still, it is interesting how, after more than half a century, so much interest still focuses on the end points of these axes as will now be illustrated.

(2) Real-World Music: From Acoustic Ecology to Soundscape Composition

It is the job of the artist to work in relation to existing (sonic) contexts to challenge them and thereby to challenge perception, listening, continually. And it is the role of the listener to be jarred, confused and challenged to find a new relationship with what he/she hears. If the artist's work exists too far away from a recognisable expression this chasm between recognition and unfamiliarity is too wide to be overcome by the listening activity. The listener feels alienated and abandons his/her engagement. (Voegelin 2004)

At one end of the sound spectrum, which ranges from found sound to abstracted approaches (Truax 2002, 6), we find real-world sounds including our everyday soundscape. Reduced listening is at most of secondary interest to those focused on the conscious use of real-world sounds, in particular those interested in what is known as *soundscape composition*. Here, source and context identification are of central importance. Katharine Norman, while accepting the value of Schaefferian terminology, adds two terms to contrast with reduced listening that are fundamental here: *referential listening* and *contextual listening* (Norman 1996, 2). The former focuses on the sound sources themselves; the latter involves the perception of activities taking place in a work being projected upon an individual's personal experiences, that is, placing sounds in a known context. Listeners participate in the aural experience by "making sense" (ibid., 9) of "an imaginative journey" in sound (ibid., 11). In consequence, "we have a need for a new kind of literature to explain works of art for sound, one that listens differently to what is going on and allows for subjective interpretation as a valued tool" (Norman 2000, 217). Listening may become reduced depending on one's concentration and focus; what is being discussed here, in contrast, is *heightened* listening, the contextual opposite of Schaeffer's *écoute réduite.* This allows for the creation of aural storytelling in which both the composer's and the listeners' experiences feed into an activity known in the social sciences as *collective memory.*[49]

Barry Truax, the key spokesperson for this subject, has worked closely with the father of soundscape composition, R. Murray Schafer. Both are composer/theorists who have contributed significantly to building the foundations of this area. Definitions of theirs, many of which appear on the EARS site, are presented here to introduce the relevant key concepts to those who may not be familiar with them.

Soundscape   Truax says the following about the term "soundscape":

An environment of sound (or sonic environment) with emphasis on the way it is perceived and understood by the individual, or by a society. It thus depends on the relationship between the individual and any such environment. The term may refer to actual environments, or to abstract constructions such as musical compositions and tape montages, particularly when considered as an artificial environment.

The study of the systematic relationships between humans and sonic environments is called *soundscape ecology,* whereas the creation, improvement, or modeling of any such environment is a matter of *soundscape design.* (Truax 1999)

Soundscape composition   On this term, Truax says the following:

The term "soundscape composition" refers to a kind of electroacoustic work [in which . . . [e]nvironmental sound recordings form both the source material and also inform the work at all its structural levels in the sense that the original context and associations of the material play a significant role in its creation and reception.

In other words, the soundscape composition is context embedded, and even though it may incorporate seemingly abstract material from time to time, the piece never loses sight of what it is "about." (Truax 2000, 124)

The principles of soundscape composition are:

1. listener recognizability of the source material is maintained, even if it subsequently undergoes transformation;
2. the listener's knowledge of the environmental and psychological context of the soundscape material is invoked and encouraged to complete the network of meanings ascribed to the music;

3. the composer's knowledge of the environment and psychological context of the soundscape material is allowed to influence the shape of the composition at every level, and ultimately the composition is inseparable from some or all aspects of that reality;

4. the work enhances our understanding of the world, and its influence carries over into everyday perceptual habits.

Thus, the real goal of the soundscape composition is the reintegration of the listener with the environment in a balanced ecological relationship. (Truax 1996b, 63)

This last sentence is key: "The reintegration of the listener with the environment" is but one way of articulating the formula that art is part of life. "Meaning is inescapably contextual" (Truax 1996b, 52); "[E]nvironmental sound[s] . . . are not only source material that is rich in acoustic complexity, but also rich in a variety of levels of meaning, both personal and cultural, and possibly even cross-cultural" (ibid., 60). As we have already discovered, meaning can include emotional responses as well as reactions that involve identification and other forms of experience. In the current case, the goal is a combination of the artistic with the ecological. This combination, according to Truax, "is potentially disruptive and even subversive to the established norms of the [music] field. . . . It points to a blind spot in the dominant paradigm of nearly every discipline which can be related to electroacoustic . . . music" (ibid., 49). For example, musicology is generally focused on the primacy of pitch relationships, not to mention the increasing interest in grammatical formalisms that are normally abstract.[50] Furthermore, virtually all associated fields have difficulty with the concept of timbre. Psychoacoustics, for example, has hardly demonstrated interest in real-world sounds (ibid., 49–50). One alternative, at least as far as the study of music is concerned, according to Truax, is the notion of psychomusicology he attributes to Otto Laske, the study of musical process as opposed to artifacts (ibid., 52).

The soundscape world is not only associated with music. It is also associated with the fields of acoustic communication, acoustic ecology, acoustic design, and the like, disciplines of study that focus as well on environmental issues.

Acoustic communication is an area interested in supporting greater understanding of "the intricate system of meanings and relationships that sound creates in environmental context" (Truax 1996b, 58), that is, "understanding the acoustic environment through listening" (Truax 1984, xii).

Acoustic ecology   (also known as *soundscape ecology*) is an area related to the field of acoustic communication that investigates the impact of increasing levels of sound on our environment and makes proposals to improve certain acoustic conditions.

Acoustic design   "A[n] interdiscipline requiring the talents of scientists, social scientists and artists (particularly musicians), acoustic design attempts to discover principles by which the aesthetic quality of the acoustic environment or soundscape may be improved" (Schafer 1994, 271).

Schafer's and his colleagues' goal is to achieve improved "hi-fi" environments, environments "in which sounds may be heard clearly without crowding or masking." In contrast, in "lo-fi" environments, "signals are overcrowded, resulting in masking or lack of clarity" (Schaefer 1994, 272). Lo-fi environments often suffer from noise pollution, according to Schafer; many current forms of background music ("moozak" for Schafer) are society's way of reacting against such noise pollution, a form of "audioanalgesic" (ibid., 96). Truax introduces two listening strategies for this very reason: *analytical* and *distracted listening* (Truax 1984, 147).[51] He has also launched what he calls a paradigm shift in music in which: (a) "the end of the Fourier era" is called for, that is, a shift away from linear acoustic models to multidimensional, nonlinear ones which are more pertinent in terms of environmental sounds; (b) "the literate composer" (of art music) is becoming obsolete, that is, there is no need of traditional musical literacy to create sound-based work; and (c) the "abstract work of art" is coming to an end (Truax 1994, 177–178):[52] "[g]iven that abstract music has virtually no audience outside of its practitioners, and if not supported by the academy would probably not survive on its own, it would seem that such questions should be uppermost in composers' minds today" (Truax 1996b, 13).

All three points may have been overstated for effect; nevertheless, Truax has clearly identified under his first point one form of antithesis against traditional music's thesis in terms of sound-based music's development. Truax notes in another publication that "the tension for the electroacoustic composer . . . comes from balancing Schaeffer's 'reduced listening' with Schafer's expanded 'soundscape awareness'" (Truax

1996b, 14). Luke Windsor has similar views in calling for an ecological framework for sound-based music analysis that involves location, identification, and the eventual interaction of sounds (Windsor 2000). Consequently, many followers of music that contains real-world references are devising methods to create new forms of musical narrative.

Returning to the notion of acoustic design, Schafer suggests that "[its] principles . . . may . . . include the elimination or restriction of certain sounds (noise abatement), the testing of new sounds before they are released indiscriminately into the environment, but also the presentation of sounds ('soundmarks'[53]), and above all the imaginative placement of sounds to create attractive and stimulating acoustic environments in the future. Acoustic design may also include the composition of model environments, and in this respect it is contiguous with contemporary musical composition" (Schafer 1994, 271). And so we come full circle, as artistic endeavor goes hand in hand with aural ecological concerns according to Schafer, Truax, and their many followers. It should be said that works of "phonography" (the aural equivalent of the photo) and of "anecdotal composition" belong in this category regardless of the reservations some artists may have who adhere to these concepts.

Anecdotal composition   "is the name given to the genre inside electroacoustic music that employs recognisable sounds more for their 'anecdotic' or narrative aspect than for their abstract potential" (Caesar 1992; see also EARS).

Clearly there is no small dose of idealism as far as acoustic ecologists are concerned. That said, today's awareness of sound pollution far exceeds that of, say, three decades ago when Schafer was writing many of his key works in the field.

This awareness can easily be applied in education. In 1976 Schafer published *Creative Music Education*, containing a number of previously published booklets. This compilation includes important terms such as:

Ear cleaning   "A systematic program for training the ears to listen more discriminatingly to sounds, particularly those of the environment" (Schafer 1994, 272).

Clairaudience   "Literally, clear hearing . . . exceptional hearing ability, particularly with regard to environmental sound" (ibid.).

Soundwalk "A key aspect of soundscape studies is the sensitisation of citizens to their acoustic surroundings and the educational imperative of assisting in the development of the individual's listening skills. Sound-walks are an aspect of this, comprising periods of time when one listens with greater attention than usual to one's sonic environment (i.e. sound-scape). Soundwalkers may even let their ears determine the route of the walk. A soundwalker may at the same time be recording material for further use in soundscape composition" (EARS).

In these texts, Schafer proposes interdisciplinary curricula for sound-scape studies. It is fascinating how many of these ideas have been inte-grated into many contemporary electroacoustic or music technology curricula and communication programs with acoustic ecology special-izations. It is also interesting that two key figures in acoustic communi-cation, Truax and Andra McCartney, are situated in communication departments despite their music/soundscape specialization.

Truax's two key publications elaborate enormously on Schaferian con-cepts. His (1984) book *Acoustic Communication* is the most complete description of the field available. His (1999) CD-ROM *Handbook for Acoustic Ecology* is to this field what EARS is to sound-based music studies, and also kindly provides illustrative sound examples. His other work, which we return to in subsections 4 and 5 below, concerns granu-lation and what he terms the *inner* and *outer complexities* of music.[54] McCartney's analytical work on soundscape composition was introduced earlier in chapter 1. Her work on gender in sound-based music, especially its technology-driven areas, has deservedly gained international respect beyond these analytical studies (see, e.g., McCartney 1995, 1999, 2003).

Returning to Schafer, his most cited term seems to be the word "schizo-phonia." This term refers to the dislocation involved with any record-ing, that is, its being played back at another time and, most likely, in another place than its original recording. It is an aural equivalent of Walter Benjamin's reproducible artwork, Schafer (1994, 90) writes:

Related to schizophrenia, I wanted ["schizophonia"] to convey the same sense of aberration and drama. Indeed, the overkill of hi-fi gadgetry not only con-tributes generously to the lo-fi problem, but it creates a synthetic soundscape in which natural sounds are becoming increasingly unnatural while machine-made substitutes are providing the operative signals directing modern life.

Perhaps there is something contradictory in Schafer's objection, as he has produced many recorded compositions throughout his years. (Nam June Paik also often declared that John Cage should never have sold his scores or recorded his indeterminate works.) What rings throughout these notions is an acute desire for sound organization, soundscape composition in this case, to be linked to our own world implying a conservationist (as opposed to conservative) attitude in the world of acoustic communication. Even today's urban world can provide inspiration for these studies and applied artistic work (see, e.g., Rocha Iturbide 1995). Clearly this radical, idealist movement has proven invaluable in terms of redirecting people's attention to their own day-to-day experience as an available resource for innovative sound-based art making.

Some of Schafer's theory parallels or at least reflects that of Schaeffer and his followers. In some cases, this is done to set up a contrast, but not all the time. For example, Schafer offers the term *sound event*.

Sound event   "Like the sound object [in the sense of Schaeffer, the sound event] is defined by the human ear as the smallest self-contained particle of a soundscape. It differs from the sound object in that the latter is an abstract acoustical object for study, while the sound event is a symbolic, semantic or structural object for study, and is therefore a nonabstractable point of reference, related to a whole or greater magnitude than itself" (Schafer 1994, 274).

Schaeffer might have worded his interpretation of the *objet sonore* slightly differently, but the related roots of these two terms are nevertheless clear. For Schafer, however, source *and* context are part and parcel of the sound event.

Schafer also uses the Schaefferian terms "typology" and "morphology," yet again with a soundscape twist: "Applied to soundscape studies [morphology] refers to changes in groups of sounds with similar forms or functions when arbitrarily arranged in temporal or spatial formations. Examples of acoustic morphology might be a study of the historical evolution of foghorns, or a geographical comparison of methods of telegraphy" (ibid., 272). He also uses the terms "gesture" and "texture," words many associate with Smalley (even though his writings appeared later). Here are Schafer's definitions: "There are times when one sound is heard; there are times when many things are heard. Gesture is the name we can give to the unique event, the solo, the specific, the noticeable; texture is the generalized aggregate, the mottled effect, the imprecise anarchy of conflicting actions" (ibid., 159).

In terms of visual representation Schafer is interested in what he calls *sonography*, the art of soundscape notation. He is not against the use of technological means such as the sonogram, but tends to use other means himself. As part of his approach to sound classification, he uses a two-dimensional grid. On one axis, he investigates what he calls, attack, body, and decay. On the other, he looks at durations, frequency/mass, fluctuations/grain, and dynamics. This is in a sense a simplified although otherwise comparable approach to Schaeffer's *Tableau récapitulatif du solfège des objets musicaux* (TARSOM).

So where do works with real-world sound references—*audio vérité*, as I called it earlier—fit? That *audio vérité* is sound-based music goes without saying. In terms of the language grid, these works tend to be found in the box where mimetic discourse and abstracted syntax meet. The emancipated view that this book subscribes to is that it belongs to both sonic art and electroacoustic music, not to mention its own, narrower subgenres. It is the relationship here with musique concrète and acousmatic thinking that is of interest. As composers who believe in clear source recognition are by definition non-Schaefferian, it is predictable that some participants prefer not to be grouped with the French school. Hildegard Westerkamp called for this separation in a recent issue of *Organised Sound*, as has John Levack Drever (Westerkamp 2002; Drever 2002). In Drever's case, his view is that soundscape composition has more to do with ethnography than with acousmatic thought.[55]

Soundscape works do tend to have one thing in common with their acousmatic counterparts, namely that they are normally built from the bottom up using chosen source material rather than being based on formal constructs (though environment modeling is an exception). Sounds recorded and eventually manipulated and/or placed in layers and sequences to create a structure is the normal work sequence, just as in the French school, although some soundscape and anecdotal work is also offered in its "as is" state, an extreme instance of real-world composition. But this is where the comparison ends, as their attitudes to the source/cause question are polar opposites regardless of the fact that they share their approach from material to structure.

In considering soundscape works, Norman points out that we are now finally able to realize Luigi Russolo's dream to "orchestrate sounds" (Norman 1996, 2). Yet many listeners are unaware of the subtlety of soundscape composition techniques. Westerkamp has admitted that she is "continually worried that nobody notices that I'm composing!" (in Norman 2004, 80). Norman calls this type of montage the "stylisation of nature" (ibid., 94). More formal approaches can also be integrated into real-world sound composition whereby the relationship between sources and context is not necessarily lost. Even more radical sound manipulation, such as granulation (see subsection 4), can be integrated into a soundscape approach as long as one doesn't wander too far from the source's recognizability. In discussing a Luc Ferrari composition, Norman notes that ambiguity can be achieved in such works. Discussing his *Presque rien avec filles*, she writes: "At many levels *Presque rien avec filles* draws attention to the several boundaries it fails to respect: those between music and sound, between coherence and confusion [e.g, the spoken text is not easy to follow], between subjective and quasi-objective analysis—and between listening and being bored ... [it is] deliberately opaque and alienating" (Norman 2000, 229). She mentions, for example, that a (processed) gunshot is heard and yet the birds keep singing (ibid., 236).[56] Whatever the case, an aural tale connected with our lives is clearly being told.

Soundscape scholarship differs in general from musique concrète scholarship in that it leans away from phenomenological philosophy, leaning instead toward ecological and other sociocultural concerns and thusly demonstrating the difference between *époché* (musique concrète) and clairaudience (soundscape composition). Soundscape scholars, however, often deal with several categories of study, as do their reduced listening colleagues. These include the classification of sounds and contexts, the listening experience, modes of discourse, analysis and representation, organizing sounds, interdisciplinarity (that is, working with other disciplines of study), and, although not discussed above, new means of presentation. Soundscape works are often presented outside of the standard concert space, sometimes in site-specific contexts. The associated scholarship considers the implications of the use of these alternative venues.

(3)   Appropriation: Convergence (1)

Digital technology can be applied within any of the genres and categories discussed in this chapter. Analog technology can be used for most as well. What is particularly interesting about digital technology is that the traditional "high art versus popular music" (*E* vs. *U*) gap has diminished in many cases. Most of the specialist equipment used in sound-based music in the early days was made for art music pioneers. As soon as certain equipment seemed of interest to popular musicians and could possibly be used in live performance, their design began to take into account the general needs of popular musicians. By the time the digital Yamaha DX-7 was invented, the *E* composers had more or less been written off by the digital instruments industry, though the Fairlight and Synclavier music computers were perhaps very expensive exceptions. The CSound program and the like were for the *E* team, while MIDI was primarily for the *U* team. However, with the appearance of the sampler and the many hardware and software advances that followed, one form of convergence started to occur: tools and equipment began to be produced for a wide variety of users.

The sampler was probably the key catalyst of the drive to offer popular musicians the potential to incorporate real-world sounds into their real-time environments. The ever-decreasing prices and the success of the MIDI protocol made the technology accessible to a large pool of potential users. "Appropriation" became a musical term. Copyright lawyers face a huge new task of defining not only what is borrowed and what stolen in terms of composing music but also in terms of sampling.[57] New music trends began to develop. In an increasing number of cases, the line separating high and popular, *E* and *U*, became fuzzier than ever. Terre Thaemlitz, in describing his own work, has claimed to search for "'empowering' audio images which are different from, but not free of, associations with their roots. It is not universal or timeless, it is entirely contingent upon today, with the possibility of being recontextualised by other people now and in the future to serve their own agendas"

(Thaemlitz n.d.). This statement is interesting for a number of reasons. In particular it fulfills Emmerson's criterion that sound-based music incorporates "common codes." Elsewhere in the same interview Thaemlitz clarifies that he is equally interested in both the academic and the commercial aspects of sonic works. Although his music is not timeless, he is nevertheless concerned about the future. I would venture to guess that Thaemlitz finds the *E* and *U* music separation of no relevance to his work.

Paul D. Miller (aka DJ Spooky that subliminal kid) has written, "Sampling is a new way of doing something that's been with us for a long time: creating with found objects. . . . The mix breaks free of the old associations. New contexts form from old" (Miller 2004, 25). He adds: "Sampling plays with different perceptions of time. Sampling allows people to replay their own memories of the sounds and situations of their lives . . . sampling is dematerialized sculpture" (ibid., 28–29).

Tara Rodgers describes the sampling phenomenon as follows: "sampling functions as a postmodern process of musical appropriation and pastiche, often filtered through modernist conceptions of authorship and authenticity" (Rodgers 2003, 313). Writing about John Oswald, she believes that samplers deserve their own instrument "family" classification similar to that of woodwinds and that "[s]amples themselves must be analysed as highly aestheticised digital bits with a specific music function within the context of a particular sequence or mix. The historical and cultural circumstances of a sample's source, and the politics of its reconfiguration into ongoing, evolving sonic environments (such as DJ mixes or remixed recordings) are likewise essential to how sample-based music is interpreted" (ibid., 319). In short, samples may be used for their musical as well as their cultural referential qualities (ibid., 313). Sound classification and analysis meet social impact.

Kodwo Eshun holds a different view. He has coined the term "sampladelia," which he sees as representing the mythology of samples. He notes: "In HipHop headmusic, R. Murray Schafer's schizophony has become premonitional. Sounds have detached themselves from their sources and are reaching you before their causes do" (Eshun 1998, 47). Here reduced listening is brought into the world of a form of popular music. Continuing on the subject of (un)identifiable samples, Eshun adds: "Sampladelia is both the reality-effect of samples you recognize and the Origin Unknown effect of samples you don't. These Unidentified Sonic Objects can suddenly substitute themselves for the world, eclipsing it, orphaning you, washing you up on its shores. There's a powerful sensation of deletion as samples trigger successive waves of synthetic defamiliarization" (ibid., 57; I would suggest that the word *decontextualization* might make more sense). He is placing himself somewhere along that axis between *écoute réduite* and clairaudience, as do many of today's artists who come from a drum 'n' bass background.

Simon Waters is of the belief that sound-based music has moved from what he calls an acousmatic culture to a sampling culture (see, e.g., Waters 2000a, 2000b, 56). He claims that the former culture is largely self-referential, whereas the latter is more concerned with context. Like many of the authors cited here, Waters finds that sampling catalyzes recontextualization and, by implication, transformation, which in his view is a sign of the times, similar to the currently popular concept of morphing in terms of image (2000b, 64). One of his most interesting insights in terms of today's sampling culture concerns cultural placement: "Sampling has an uneasy relationship between tradition and innovation incorporating the archival instinct of the former and the speculative and exploratory influence of the latter" (ibid., 71). In his view, as modernism concerns itself with the rejection of the past and postmodernism with a rejection of innovation, sampling becomes difficult to pigeonhole (ibid., 70). He suggests that one of the most intriguing aspects of sampling culture is the ambiguous relationship between authorship and ownership (ibid., 68). Similar to the soundscape theorists, Waters never loses sight of the sociopolitical dimension of sound-based music. The field of cultural studies deserves to be added to the sister disciplines relevant to sound-based musical study. It provides yet another angle with which to investigate an aspect of sound-based music that is indeed ubiquitous. However, the amount of analytical scholarship on acousmatic composition has not been reflected in the scholarship on our sampling culture.

These issues lead us to a particularly useful example, *plunderphonics* (see, e.g., Oswald 2001). This word is highly associated with the artist John Oswald and the CD that was "absolutely not for sale" bearing the new genre's title.[58] His choice of music to plunder on that CD, ranging from the Beatles to Beethoven to Webern to Bing Crosby, not to mention a recording of Pygmies, demonstrates an unusually broad eclecticism.[59] Of course, whether he treats all of his source material with due respect is for the listener to decide. His enormous talent for microsplicing appropriated music is on display on this and subsequent plunderphonic recordings. Chris Cutler describes the genre as follows: "Plunderphonics is the opposite of music *ex nihilo*. It begins and ends only with recordings, with the already played" (Cutler 2000, 90). It is a genre of "microsamples," "electroquotes," and "plunderphones" (Oswald's smallest recognizable sonic quote level; see Igma 1986, 4). "[P]lunderphonics as a practice radically undermines three of the central pillars of the art music paradigm: originality (it deals only with copies), individuality (it speaks only with the voice of others), and copyright (the breaching of which is a condition of its very existence" (Cutler 2004, 143). I would slightly reword this sentence, as Oswald's and others' originality is clear in the finished product—it is a combination of that of the maker and the plundered. Kevin Holm-Hudson likes to think of this work as a means of construction of new pieces by deconstructing the past (Holm-Hudson 1997). As far as appropriation is concerned, in quoting Oswald, Cutler notes: "If creativity is a field, copyright is a fence" (Cutler 2004, 103).[60]

Larry Polansky claims that Oswald's key interest is not so much source material, it is the process of transformation that plunderphonic composition catalyses. It deals with "Music as verb, not noun" (Polansky 1998). Reflecting Rodgers' view, Polansky notes: "Plunderphonics' aesthetic might be called post-modern in its recontextualization and juxtaposition of popular, often pedestrian sonic materials. But Oswald's compositional ideas . . . are also modernist and highly formalist" (ibid.). Katharine Norman suggests: "In the groove between 'Is this homage?' and 'Is this ridicule?' there's some room for comparison. It takes a moment to decide" (Norman 2004, 178). This wonderful statement underlines not only the nonuniversality of music, but also the presence of the potential double entendre in so much of today's appropriated music from bootlegging to plunderphonic works. Her analysis of the track "Crackle" on the original plunderphonics CD—a recording of the sound of a turntable stylus bouncing against the end of a record side—

is a highly insightful discussion of the genre and the issues that it raises (Norman 2004, 186–191).

So where does Oswald's music fit? He's definitely on the fringe of the popular music scene, and thus not a popular musician in the traditional sense, but he is pioneering a new area of what some might consider as a form of experimental popular music.[61] He is equally at home with E, "high art" music. In fact, he lends the impression that he is not at all interested in this E/U split simply but rather is creating his genre for anyone interested. He is, in this sense, similar to Thaemlitz and many other current musicians. Also, this is a form of music-based music, that is, a form created by (ab)using an existent musical structure (the original piece), filling it in or playing with it using music-based plunderphones. The form is not generated through a formalized structure (see subsection 6 below); instead it is a point of departure, something already known to the listener. The aural experience, however, is a sound object based on many examples of appropriation in a sound-based music context.

This in-between attitude of ignoring categories is by no means unique. More and more festivals, whether annual or one-off events, are appearing in which the atmosphere seems to adhere more to one associated with popular culture than to an elitist "in the know" culture, where work belonging to or somehow associated with popular music coexists comfortably with other forms of live, audiovisual, and audio-only music ranging from works of Bernard Parmegiani,[62] a GRM composer with a user-friendly approach that has been adopted in certain popular music circles, to the latest laptop performers combining sound-based and experimental note-based music.[63] In fact, some events seem to have neither E nor U roots. In either case, E sound-based music is taken out of the ivory tower, which is not necessarily a bad thing. The serious aura that forms part of the tower's reputation is also less extreme at such events. Sound-based music seems to have penetrated a public of an increasing number of younger listeners who enjoy work ranging from sophisticated audio improvisation to new media art and acousmatic composition. Although Kim Cascone has every right to complain about the split between academia and the rest of the world (Cascone 2000), it would appear that given the universal availability of so many tools and programs, this gap will diminish. Innovation will take place both within academia and outside it, and such eclectic performance opportunities will allow people from a wide variety of communities to discover what is being developed. Plunderphonic composition is an excellent example of the *E* and *U* split becoming a nonissue as it fits comfortably into eclectic sound-based events like the one described above.

Returning to Waters, one key question remains. Picking up where Jacques Attali leaves off in his well-known book, *Noise*, Waters asks: "is the sampler—and the culture it signals—the harbinger of a new political economy of music in which music is stored everywhere, in diffuse, virtual space, accessible as material for the performing out of individual preferences?" (Waters 2000a). Indeed, a new set of concepts for the entire process of creativity will be needed in tomorrow's sampling culture, again raising the question whether our current systems of categorization are appropriate.

I contend that this change of atmosphere is primarily due to the two forms of convergence, the wide application of tools and the *E* versus *U* distinction becoming less relevant in certain circumstances as described above. Enthusiasts regardless of background slowly but surely seem to be becoming increasingly aware of others' work. This change is due to the affordability and availability of works and creative tools that are potentially of interest to people of all ages, experiences, and taste. Any child who has enjoyed a computer game could very well be interested in attending such an event and be amazed by the recontextualization that Thaemlitz clearly described that holds so much of this music together. Whether it has a beat or not is no longer the issue; the issue is how people are touched by the sound worlds of artists of all kinds. Appropriation has catalyzed change and much of it not only has far-reaching manifestations, but is also supporting our interest in access and accessibility.

(4) New Sounds: From Synthesis to Microsound to Noise

The following paragraphs consider works which focus on the discovery of new sounds within a musical context. There are many paths leading to Rome when it comes to the search for new sounds. In instrumental and vocal contemporary music, the developments in extended techniques have led to the discovery of hundreds of new sounds. In musique concrète, processes of sound manipulation have led to radical new sounds as well. In electronic music, excluding work by those interested in the synthetic creation of existent sounds or the creation of new sounds to be used in more traditional musical (i.e., note-based) contexts, most generated sounds are intentionally made to be perceived as new.[64] One path followed by many in search of the new is that of various forms of microsound, creating sounds from very small sound particles. One form of microsound, granulation, when applied to synthesized and real-world sounds, will provide an example here.[65] The use of noise as musical texture will be presented alongside granulation as a more abbreviated second example.

Timbral results in works within the category of new sounds range from the highly alienating (e.g., the continuous presence of noise is found to be alienating by most listeners other than those who appreciate what is known today as industrial or noise music) to the aesthetically warm (e.g., the granulation of real-world sounds tends to provoke such a reaction). Where the source is not a major concern, works focused on new sounds tend to be abstract as are virtually all formalized works, discussed in subsection 6 below. Nevertheless, those involved in the search for the new can be at least as spectral as formalist in their approach; it is a question of whether priority is given to the sounding result or the structure, or, eventually, both.

A problem with this particular subject area's publications is that they are much more focused on technological than theoretical points of view (see Roads 1996a for the most comprehensive technology-based overview). The amount of theoretical study given to today's new sounds is in fact quite modest. The Cologne school of new serial electronic music is an obvious exception in its development of concepts that could be applied toward the generation of new sounds. These will be introduced under formalism. Studies attempting to valorize works focused on new sounds have not come to my attention. The situation is not dissimilar elsewhere, but it seems particularly ironic in this adventure land of sound. At least the field of cultural studies has been open to the discussion of noise, as we shall discover below.

Approaches to new material are as broad as can be imagined. Charles Dodge is well known for taking the inadequacies of the technology of voice synthesis of the time and exploiting them within a musical context (e.g., his well-known *Speech Songs*). John Cage has said that he "wanted to elevate the sound effect to the level of musical instruments" (Cage 2003, 164, in discussion with Richard Kostelanetz) noting that "the tape normally goes past the head horizontally, but if you cut it and splice it back diagonally . . . you could get beautiful sounds by putting it at an angle to what it should have been" (ibid., 168). Alvin Lucier, "poet of electronic music" according to Pauline Oliveros (Lucier 1995, 10), is, like many in the field, a sound hunter. James Tenney has summarized Lucier as someone who deals "with virtually the whole range of natural acoustic phenomena as follows: sound transmission and radiation, reflection, diffraction, resonance, standing waves and speech," and adds that "in most of his pieces, the sounds we hear result from the complex interaction and mutual interference (convolution, confrontation, collision) of two or more systems—mechanical, electrical, or biological, . . . often natural (brain, voice, conch shell)" (ibid., 12–14). Iannis Xenakis was obsessed with the new. He told Gerard Pape that he did not want to be weighed down by history (Pape 2002, 18). Although his electroacoustic works formed a minority of his compositions overall, his evolution from musique concrète works to his later creations of stochastic synthesis always entertained the notion of inventing new sounds and noises. He is considered one of the fathers of microsound[66] for his investigations of acoustical quanta in the late 1950s. The terminology he introduced, including "sound masses," "clouds," and "screens of sound," reflects this search for the new. With microsound came microstructure, implying again that the interrelationship between new sounds and new structures is quite important to Xenakis.

The above selection does the breadth of the field no justice. What can be said is that, in general, the act of searching for new sounds *an sich* has not led to the creation of many genres, and those that do exist tend to have to do with either microsonic and/or noise-based investigations.

Some ideas behind microsound   The work of Curtis Roads and Barry Truax will be used to create the framework for this discussion for it is they who have written many key texts in this area, Roads primarily although not solely from the technical point of view, Truax more from other points of view. Truax, who played a major role in the previous section, has found a link between soundscape and microsound composition (Truax 1992a) in creating the differentiation between "music within the soundscape" and "soundscape within the music," something he also calls its "inner world" (ibid., 374). What holds the two together for Truax, ideally, is that each represents a paradigm shift.[67] I have already presented Truax's idea that nonlinearity, that is, a shift away from linear (such as Fourier) models in acoustics, plays an important role in soundscape. It is also essential to his views on microsound (Truax 1992b), as such short sounds will never be reducible, at least audibly, to their constituent parts of frequency, loudness, and duration; he is much more interested in timbre and timbral development.[68] He is fascinated by "the triviality of the grain vs. the richness of the layered granular texture that results from their superposition" (Truax 1992a, 390) and notes that "if a granular synthesis texture is played backwards it will sound the same"; it also exhibits time invariance, allowing it to be slowed down with no change in pitch (ibid., 391). This leads Truax to what he calls *models of complexity* (ibid., 29).

Truax links the soundscape world to the world of microsound through the investigation of three areas of interest: physical (context), social (external influences, such as political music), and psychological (emotional) (Truax 1994, 179). This forms part of a personal plea for meaning and against overabstraction. Even while creating works of extreme complexity, Truax believes that the pieces should have a context, a relationship to real-world experience and the ability to trigger emotion. In his early granular work, *Riverrun*, the sound material was generated electronically, but between the title and the tidal behavior of the sound, he was able to fulfill his own criteria. In later works, his sound material has been derived from real-world recordings in a manner in which source identification is possible.

Truax has shown me examples of his own and his students' analyses on CD-ROM describing the processes involved in the making of some of their works, including those applying granular techniques, at Simon Fraser University. Such initiatives are praiseworthy; it is to be hoped that they become available in traditional published form or over the Internet, as we lack examples of composers speaking about their work from their approaches to construction (which may include classification analytical aspects), to intention and other dramaturgical aids, to issues of performance. The dissemination of such studies allows the user to try out some of the constructional approaches (by way of patches, algorithms, etc.), and interactive learning can take place as a result, all of which is relevant to sound-based music studies.

Roads is associated more with the technical side of things. He also makes the occasional contribution to other discussions. For example, he has written: "More than ever, electroacoustic compositions must prove themselves on musical terms; abstract ideas cannot be counted on to impress in and of themselves" (Roads 1996b, 86), a statement which could be the slogan of this book. His approach to microsound, which given the nature of his approach is more wide-ranging than granulation (see Roads 2001, *Microsound*, for the key publication in the field), includes a study of the place of "micro" within the context of different time durations (Roads 2001, chapter 1; Roads 2000). His list ranges from the infinite to the infinitesimal:

infinite

supra (years)

macro (minutes-hours, a miniature composition to the "Ring" cycle, the notion of macroform)

meso (phrase or sequence level)

sound object (note or *objet sonore* level, 100 ms to several seconds)

micro (transient audio phenomena from "the threshold of timbre perception" [several hundred microseconds] up to "the duration of short sound objects" [ca. 100 ms, from 20 to 20,000 Hz]; sounds under 2 ms are perceived as a click)[69]

sample (e.g., 1/44,100 of a second or unit impulse)

subsample (where nanosonology of the future may take place)

infinitesimal

Grain is but one name of a microsound unit; Roads identifies thirty terms in his book in a list that he claims is incomplete (Roads 2001, 21). He also suggests that music's vocabulary can be expanded owing to microsonic possibilities:

We can now shape sonic matter in terms of its particle density and opacity. Particle density has become a prime compositional parameter. Physics defines density as the ration of mass to volume. In music this translates to the ratio of sound to silence. Through manipulations of density, processes such as coalescence (cloud formation), and evaporation (cloud disintegration) can occur in sonic form. Opacity correlates to density. If the density of microsonic events is sufficient, the temporal dimension appears to cohere, and one perceives a continuous texture on the sound object level. Thus by controlling the density and size of sound particles we have a handle on the quality of sonic opacity. Coalescence takes place when particle density increases to the point that tone continuity takes hold. An opaque sound tends to block out other sounds that cross into its time-frequency zone.

Going in the opposite direction, we can cause a sound to evaporate by reducing its particle density. A sparse cloud is transparent, since we can easily hear other sounds through it. A diaphanous cloud only partially obscures other sounds, perhaps only in certain spectral regions. (Ibid., 332–333)

Roads also challenges some accepted notions. He states: "Even such sacred notions as tone continuity and simultaneity reveal themselves to be illusions. The micro time scale defrosts these frozen categories into constantly evolving morphologies" (ibid., 330). Roads, like Schaeffer and Bayle, uses word pairs to assist in finding means to describe microsound works. As in the structure of this chapter, Roads makes a distinction between formalism (see subsection 6 below) and intuitionism (a key foundation of musique concrète), between coherence and invention, between intervals and morphologies, and between spontaneity and reflection, all of which can be applied within a microsonic compositional context (ibid., 336–341).

Roads investigates the opportunities for formalism ranging from the microsound level to the macro-level. Agostino di Scipio puts this type of approach as follows. Using the terms "microstructural time modeling of sound" and "micro-time sonic design" (di Scipio 1994), he speaks of " 'sound synthesis' and 'music composition' becom[ing] one and the same," in, for example, certain works of Xenakis and Brün (di Scipio 2002, 23). What di Scipio is describing is neither bottom up nor top down, but instead is more integrated. There are composers who take this approach to an extreme, Stockhausen with his use of the term *Formel* being the currently best known. These composers apply one and the same formalism at the micro- through (multicompositional) macro-levels. However, Roads is uncertain about the possibility of generalizing formalisms. He turns to the famous musicologist Carl Dahlhaus for his argument: "As [Dahlhaus] wisely pointed out, serial methods that are already barely decipherable on the level of notes and phrases disappear into invisibility when applied on the micro-level of tone construction" (Roads 2001, 78). This brings up a key question that is pertinent to the entire discussion of formalism: if one cannot hear it (the formalism, that is), what then is the importance of that tool? Although Roads acknowledges later in the book that formal approaches to microsound can be valuable (even though they are not necessarily audible as such), he questions the usefulness of the application of a formalized approach, such as an algorithm or a series, at several compositional levels simultaneously.

Phil Thomson has remarked that in the Roads volume, no example is taken from outside the known establishments of music research, be they universities or large subsidized centers (Thomson 2004). Kim Cascone has become one of an increasing number of voices representing independent artists who have access to tools that are just as powerful as those used by institutional composers and developers. Clearly very powerful sound tools can be downloaded from the Internet today or purchased for very little money. Cascone is a spokesperson for today's "glitch movement" and others related to microsound. What holds these independent artists together is what he calls "the aesthetics of failure" (Cascone 2000) and the third definition of the word "electronica," the one regarding laptop performance and glitch. The word "failure" is included here because these artists use what might be called technological detritus as their sound sources, such as a CD click when it loops.[70] In fact, none of the terms used by Cascone can be found on Roads' list cited above, so he was correct that the list was incomplete; nevertheless, there is a great deal that links such artists to the work of artists whom Roads has cited. This art music/independent artist split is synthetic to a large extent. Some institutions, such as the University of East Anglia in the U.K., are very interested in the work of such laptop microsound artists. *Contemporary Music Review* recently focused an entire issue (22[4], 2003) on laptop music.[71] One ironic aspect of microsound-based laptop music raised in this issue is that many of its advocates believe that it has appropriated the practice of acousmatic listening and transplanted its listening strategy, demanding active reception (Cascone 2003, 102, 104) through a rediscovery of "aural performativity" (Stuart 2003b). Stuart feels, however, that tape music "is culturally distant from current audiences for contemporary laptop musics" (ibid., 61). Although there may be audiovisual add-ons to a laptop performance, the performance as such is of little to no visual importance (as most anyone who has attended such an event would conclude; see Jaeger 2003).[72] As Cascone has identified, this issue poses very important questions about the visual element of performance.

Janne Vanhanen has introduced another question related to laptop microsound music, suggesting that the laptop producer's role is paradoxical as it in fact overlaps with both academia and experimental popular culture. "One could make a general distinction between the 'tools' of laptop music, which are mainly derived from the academic community, and the 'methodology' of laptop music, which takes its cue from the low-budget, do-it-yourself production values of the bedroom community" (Vanhanen 2003, 45).[73] This is yet another form of convergence where neither the overtly "academic" or "high art" nor the overtly "popular" is being sought. In terms of our genres and categories discussion, Monroe (2003) states that it is the instrumentation that holds laptop work together, work that consists of a cluster of styles based mostly on improvisation. This may be so; however, although the laptop can play any sound, Monroe adds, the surge of glitch and similar movements has led to at least one significant cluster: "now, in an increasingly digitised everyday, when dance music is a mass youth cultural phenomenon and synthetic sound is part of the fabric of reality, perceptions of threat and, critically, of coldness repeatedly attach themselves to unmediated electronic sound presented as music" (ibid., 35–36). Laptop music's "aesthetics of failure" combined with this sense of coldness form an appropriate bridge to our next subject: noise.

The art of noise A noise texture is not necessarily a new sound, although when placed into a musical context, it would normally qualify as such. Murray Schafer reminds us that there are four types of noise: unwanted noise, unmusical sound, any loud sound, and a disturbance in any signaling system (such as static on a telephone) (Schafer 1994, 182).

Rob Worby, a noise proponent, has suggested that "noise may well prove to be the most appropriate metaphor for the twentieth century" (Worby 2000, 138). So where does noise fit within sound-based music? The futurists introduced noise into music at the turn of the twentieth century, signaling the need to reflect industrial society in art. Today there exist entire genres of noise-based music emancipating the noise—as often suggested by Stockhausen—in a similar manner to Varèse's search for the emancipation of the sound and Cage's search for the emancipation of silence within a musical context. An interview with Merzbow (1999) is entitled "The Beauty of Noise." Its introduction emphasizes his being inspired by Dadaism, surrealism, and futurism, leading to a "musical genre composed solely of pure, unadulterated noise." Paul Hegarty considers Merzbow to be the epitome of Japanese noise, or Japanoise artists, artists involved with "'noising' inspired by free jazz, progressive rock, 'improv,' traditional Japanese musics, punks, throw[ing] these together in different combinations, taking the old genres to extremes. 'Japanese noise' represents a diverse take on the interaction and furthering of Western contemporary musics" (Hegarty 2001, 195). He therefore considers Japanese noise to be a nongenre owing to its diversity: "So, the term might not be of any obvious utility—but the development of a cross-genre, cross-category, ultra-amplified and often ultra-processed music is something specific (in its breadth and range at least) to Japan" (ibid.). Merzbow "is the pursuit of noise, as if it were music, and *vice versa*" (ibid., 195), rejecting sound source recognition to support the noise's otherness. Today, "the term, 'noise music' [has been] incorporated into Industrial Music and . . . includes the outer edges of techno and other popular genres" (Worby 2000, 161). So, here again, we have something that covers a category more than a genre (despite noise being placed on the potential genre list earlier in this chapter) owing to the breadth of possibilities it offers. This is typical of something being named after either its technology or its sound source. As John Richards pointed out in a recent paper entitled "Getting Beyond the Medium" (Richards 2005), "lowercase sound," a current (quiet) form of music that uses microsound and often involves noise textures, is one of very few category or genre terms that cites neither the source nor the technology.

Noise has found its way into a number of prominent titles. Jacques Attali's *Noise* is one of the most often cited books concerning the place of both music and noise in late-twentieth-century society (Attali 1985). Douglas Kahn's surreal title *Noise, Water, Meat* is a very personal view of twentieth-century music primarily from a cultural studies standpoint including discussions on the roles of noise in artistic developments (Kahn 1999). For our purpose the key noise issue is its relationship to music. Katharine Norman writes: "In the fold between 'Is this music?' and 'Is this noise?' there's some room for manoeuvre. It takes a moment to decide" (Norman 2004, 178), a variation on her comment on the ambiguity between homage and ridicule above. Bernd Schulz, aware of Stockhausen's objective of emancipating noise as musical material, believes that in sound art at least, there is "a dissolution of the border between sound and noise" (Schulz 2002, 14). Hegarty suggests that Attali offers a form of polemic where he "argues that noise is an attack on established forms of meaning, but one that brings something new" (Hegarty 2001, 193, paraphrasing Attali 1985, 33). Attali suggests that music reflects the need for order in the face of the violence of noise (Attali 1985, 85, cited in Truax 1992a, 378).

So how does one react to music based on what Schafer has called "unwanted" audio? Stan Link takes a positive view. Citing popular music examples, he writes, "Noise . . . is not just a particular sound or type of sound; it is an aesthetic and technical approach to the work as a whole. . . . As part of this process, noise thus acquired a value centered largely on its phenomenal character rather than its prior relationship to music" (Link 2001, 41). He suggests further that "Noise thinly and seductively partitions perception and meaning, recognition and understanding. . . . Noise is a style of distance—a distance that can be meaningfully confused or exchanged with location, memory, presence, absence, temporality, and experience" (ibid., 47). In contrast, Alistair M. Riddell comes straight to the point: "By definition, [noise] will never substitute for music," regardless of the fact that he is nostalgic for the noise heard on old LPs (Riddell 1996, 160). Reinhold Friedl, in a quirky presentation on sadomasochism and musical pleasure, relates the odd situation concerning the lot of contemporary music to noise: "The rise both of compositions that equal a set of technical instructions and of perhaps impossible requirements upon performers can be seen to make the act of taking pleasure in their execution a form of masochism. The audiences of increasingly intellectualised musical styles could be said to enjoy a similar relationship to performance. And in the more physical 'noise music,' the intended effect is often not auditory pleasure but suffering" (Friedl 2002, 29).

These remarks regarding new sounds have differed to an extent from what we have encountered in the first three subsections. Cultural studies and sound construction have presided above analytical theories. Some classification work has been done on the production aspect of microsound, but others involved in new sounds tend to avoid the search for cohesion. Although I have had students attempt to analyze noise music, I am not aware of published analyses thus far. I find this unfortunate, for we seem to be postponing gaining knowledge about music that is currently innovative.

(5)   An Interim Summary: All Sounds Are Sound Objects

We are near the golden mean of this lengthy chapter, a good time to take stock.[74] (In fact the remaining four subsections consist of different types of musical themes.) The first four subsections have delineated a large space of musical opportunities. Added together, they offer the possibility for any sound to be used within a sound-based composition. On their own, they tend to be exclusive—the avoidance of identifiable or electronic or synthesised sounds in musique concrète, coinciding with the absence of concrete sounds in early electronic music; the preference for the identifiable in soundscape composition; the use of existing sounds when appropriating and the avoidance of known sounds when searching for the new. We have a couple of theses and antitheses here; but fortunately many have moved beyond this and feel they have the freedom to use identifiable and nonidentifiable, real-world and synthesized, new and previously existing, possibly appropriated sounds—in short, all the resources available to sound-based music. Although composers have quietly acknowledged this reality for years, today people are writing about it more and more.

Important authors on this type of music in which all sounds can be used include Denis Smalley, Trevor Wishart, and Simon Emmerson, all based in Britain. What is being discussed in this subsection is primarily music composed for concert presentation and everything that this implies, based mostly on recording and some form of sound diffusion—that is, what most people would call electroacoustic music recorded on a fixed medium. For purposes of the present co-hear-ence discussion, live performed works, such as live electronic, mixed, or real-time works, will be treated separately. This may come across as a contradiction at first glance, but we are dealing with forms of classification, and these works will be viewed by many as performed works before they are rightly categorized as possessing the "sound" discussed here. I hope to demonstrate in the subsection on live performance that a significant part of that repertoire could equally have been covered in the present discussion. Furthermore, another largely overlapping area, sound art, which also includes acoustic works, will also be presented separately in subsection 9 below.

I have often spoken of sound-based music as representing a form of emancipation in music similar to other forms of emancipation in contemporary society (although it is the sounds that are freed; we are emancipated only in the sense of our ability to acknowledge sounds as potential musical material). This is similar to the realization of a choreographer that it is possible to utilize any movement material in a contemporary choreography, whether it be the artist or any material or object.

The ability to combine any sounds within a given work has led many composers toward what we may call their own sonic signature. We have determined that a great many have sought signatures that represent different languages, reflecting the awkwardness of our map. That said, even in art music, there have been cases of clustering from time to time. I used to call one such cluster, a fairly large one in this case, the "Bourges sound" in the 1980s and 1990s, reflecting common aesthetic tendencies heard in works presented at the Bourges Festival of Electroacoustic Music (and elsewhere around the globe[75]). This sound is generally, though not always, deeply rooted in E culture. It tends to avoid lengthy rhythmical passages, although in recent years exceptions are on the increase. Any sounds can be used, but there are commonalities in the aesthetic approach of many of the pieces, in the technical tools used, and, to a lesser extent, the choice of source material. Narrative discourse as opposed to rigorous structure is the more common choice. I have over-heard colleagues speaking of this type of music's becoming more for-mulaic (in this sense of discourse) without further specification. The German composer Michael Obst has even gone so far as to suggest that there now exist "electroacoustic clichés" (Obst 1996). It is interesting to note that he presented this argument at the small conference that accom-panies the festival in Bourges. Certain sound sources seem to become popular, such as the treatment of the rainmaker in the early 2000s. There are specialist labels, for example, the Canadian empreintes DIGITALes iMED series of Jean-François Denis (see Daoust 2002), focusing prima-rily on music that adheres to what is being described here (as well as soundscape works to a lesser extent). So, some cohesion can be found despite the large pool of potential source material, the "Bourges sound" representing a well-known example.

Nevertheless, although there have been many adherents to a specific sound, I do not want to suggest that sound-based music has become largely homogeneous. This would contradict directly with the previously suggested map of large-scale fragmentation. But this broad category of composition does represent one of the more identifiable clusters from the listener's point of view. Beyond this, national and regional approaches do exist, often related to one or more of the first four subsections above.[76] For example, two articles in the Australasian-themed issue of *Organised Sound* specifically addressed musical qualities that a number of com-posers shared within New Zealand (see Dart, Elmsly, and Whalley 2001; Norris and Young 2001).[77] Music making that involves sound organiza-tion is a global phenomenon. Inevitably there will be some points of intersection and others of diversity; there will be regionalist composers and universal ones, not to mention individuals who attempt to avoid any known descriptor. A trip to most contemporary electroacoustic music festivals will provide the reader with a clear picture of the pattern of behavior described above.

(Un)identifiable sounds and structures   There have been a few recurring themes in this section thus far. One has to do with the types of material used in a given sonic artwork. Another would be discourse, and, to a lesser extent, a third deals with the factor of newness so important to many contemporary works. The most important theme, one particularly important in terms of accessibility, is that of the predominant use of abstract or identifiable sounds, gestures, and structures (this is not unrelated to Emmerson's language grid). Douglas Kahn relates a story dating from his student days that is relevant to this particular distinction. He found that "academics were against sounds being signified" (Kahn 1999, 17), preferring an electronic, nonreferential universe; this is an interesting, possibly unintended parallel with Schaefferian ideals. Rebelling against this notion, he adds, "In the course of trying to hear what was muted, the actual abundance of historical moments of sound became evident" (ibid., 18). Here, Kahn is combating the rather popular view of sound-based music having no past; instead, he prefers to search for experiential links inherent in any identifiable sound.

Kahn has chosen here an extreme view, one that could also be applied within soundscape composition. It is certainly an understandable view from the standpoint of accessibility, as the sharing of the history alluded to by Kahn is one of the strongest things to hold on to in any work of sonic composition.

The "something to hold on to" factor can be relevant to certain abstract works, for example, those in which audible elements are treated with some form(s) of consistency. Barry Truax has provided us with a pair of terms that are related to Kahn's ideal, suggesting that those works of sound-based music in which "the materials are designed and structured mainly through their internal relationships" display what he calls "inner complexity." He is referring to relationships at the note/structural level within a formalized context, not necessarily subtle relationships at timbral level as one might find in, for example, Japanese shakuhachi music. Works in which musical relationships engage with the (extramusical) context of the materials used possess "outer complexity" (Truax 2000, 119–120). Works displaying inner complexity are more Western in Truax's view and consequently more abstract. When works with inner complexity contain at least one element that can be perceived as creating a form of aural cohesion, then the "something to hold on to" factor applies. The axis ranging from the most abstract approaches including those of inner complexity to the most contextual works at the other end of the spectrum is an important one when establishing coherence.

Regardless of Obst's remark concerning clichés, the fact is that sound-based music is now a "broad church." We would therefore assume that its underlying theory would have developed much further as well. As far as this accompanying theory is concerned, Schaefferian terminology does not seem to be evolving much in recent years. Spectromorphology-related discussions seem to be a bit more dynamic, although, as said, it seems a bit odd how rarely this theory has been applied within empirical analytical contexts. One hopes that this situation will improve. There seem to have been relatively few new terms of note introduced into the theoretical vocabulary of sound-based music; only a small minority of these terms have been widely applied or even used by others than their authors.[78]

We therefore have an inheritance of theory for bottom-up composition, much of which has been generated at the Groupe de Recherches Musicales in Paris, by people associated with the GRM and its ideals, or in isolation. The formalists, introduced below, have spent most of their efforts composing in such a different manner that their theories seem to work largely independently of the Parisian school's and are normally more construction-orientated than related to any reception questions. With time at least some forms of convergence would be desirable.

Trevor Wishart's contribution   Trevor Wishart has created a fairly unique position for himself in terms of theory. Where Schaefferian theory is very much from the listener's point of view, Wishart's work focuses both on construction and reception. There are two areas in which his interest is at best limited: formalism and what he calls lattice-based thinking. The former implies that he, too, is a bottom-up composer. The latter suggests that he is more interested in continua than in discretely defined musical parameters. For example, he criticizes a good deal of algorithmic and traditional electronic composition as being more based on traditional musical values with discrete pitches, fixed durations, dynamics, and so on than with the new opportunities in which all pitches, timbres, and complex morphologies are made possible. Wishart has provided theory on both musical construction and the listening experience, as well as software for electroacoustic musical production techniques, particularly in the area of sound transformations. His publications contain models for the discussion of sonic art (his term) in which the various continua can be placed. His two key works, both originally self-published, *On Sonic Art* and *Audible Design* (Wishart 1985,[79] 1994), are important resources for anyone interested in theoretical concerns; the latter is focused primarily on applying his theory to techniques of production and manipulation.

In contrast to Schaeffer, whom he clearly respects, Wishart is much more open minded, allowing his sounds and spaces to range from the "real" to the "unreal," the quotation marks allowing for the listener to ascertain what appears to be real or not (Wishart 1986, 48). He notes that in one particular combination, "real sounds/real space"—what he calls with nod to John Cage imaginary landscape[80]—an opportunity is created to realize a form of surrealism, that is, the "bringing together of normally unrelated objects in the virtual space created by loudspeakers" (ibid.). With this in mind, Wishart represents a growing number of sound-based musicians who have become critical of Schaefferian reduced listening as a goal in itself. His landscapes therefore involve the disposition of any sound objects in time and space (Wishart 1985, 79).

Wishart offers intriguing, sometimes metaphoric statements that occasionally make links to the fine arts. In one text (Wishart 1992, 575), he speaks of his art form as being similar to plastic art: "Sound materials become like clay in the hands of the potter." In other texts (Wishart 1993; 1994, 11), he speaks of music evolving "from architecture to chemistry." This latter metaphor has been used in discussions focused on sound transformation. His view is that music no longer relies primarily on structure (architecture) but instead on moulding (chemistry), supporting his antiformalist position. He illustrates his view through the image of a beach filled with unique pebbles. He suggests that in the past, one would seek out all the pebbles of one color to build an instrument (he includes typical CSound instruments in this category); now any pebble is usable. This picture reflects the idea of any sound being a potential sound object as well as the notion of building music from its smallest elements upward.

In fact, *Audible Design* commences with a credo that illustrates the above concepts directly: "This is a book about composing with sounds. It is based on three assumptions. 1) Any sound whatsoever may be the starting material for a musical composition. 2) The ways in which this sound may be transformed are limited only by the imagination of the composer. 3) Musical structure depends on establishing audible relationships amongst sound materials" (Wishart 1994, 1). As far as our discussion of terminology is concerned, it is clear that Wishart is a proponent of sonic art as a form of music.

Recognition of sound sources can either take place intrinsically, in cases where a source is recognizable regardless of its context, or contextually, in cases where a context can assist in identification or in contrast mask it. It is here where music and fine art separate, as the recognition of objects in representational painting is generally immediate (ibid., 81–83). Wishart's notion of "masking" is crucial to his theory. He is one of the key figures involved in the developments that have led to today's possibilities of creating sound transformations, or "morphs" in current jargon, and masking represents a significant tool for Wishart's transformation protocols. As early as his key analog work, *Red Bird* (1973–77), Wishart was experimenting with means of creating transformations. In 1991 he told me that there was no obvious means to create a straightforward transformation. The trick was to find a means of masking the sound's source, which allowed the effect to come across as naturally as possible. In cases where he restricts himself solely to sound elements from the beginning and end state sounds, he speaks of a technique he calls "inbetweening," finding an appropriate balance of these sounds to create a convincing interpolation between one and the other (Wishart 1994, 98). Sound transformations, in turn, are related to Wishart's interest in what he calls "dynamic morphologies": "sounds in which the perceived pitch spectrum, amplitude envelope, etc., etc., all evolve through time" (Wishart 1985, 37). It is no wonder he favors the notion of sound continua as opposed to the traditional lattice approach, including discrete pitch, time duration, and dynamic symbols, which is more or less inapplicable here.

One means of classifying sounds proposed by Wishart is along the axis ranging from discrete to iterative to continuous sounds (Wishart 1985,

97), his three basic categories. Here his views do not differ significantly from those of Schaeffer or Smalley. Alongside this axis, he also speaks of the difference between sounds that possess intrinsic morphologies and those where the morphology is imposed, something he relates to causality as well as the "gestural structure of sounds" (ibid., 98). He also makes an important distinction between an apparent or physical origin of a sound and an imagined one (Wishart 1996, 19). In the latter case, the imagination can be called on when synthetic or masked sounds are present or where sounds have been modified (such as in the early GRM experiments in which an instrument's attack was cut out or one instrument's sound recording was manipulated by the dynamic envelope originating from another instrument).

This classification scheme by no means implies a lack of interest in pitch and the like. Particularly in *On Sonic Art*, Wishart spends a good deal of time investigating relationships between pitch and timbre, introducing his interpretation of multidimensional timbre space. He also makes a clear distinction between harmonic timbre (timbre determined by a sound's harmonic components) and dynamic timbre (where the sound's dynamic curve is more important to timbral perception than its harmonic content) (Wishart 1985, 36). He, like Stockhausen, favors descriptive words pertaining to timbre (e.g., scraped, struck, and the like) although in Stockhausen's case these were used for composition, not description. Having introduced his approach to timbre, Wishart provides a rather remarkable definition in the glossary of *Audible Design*: "Timbre—A catch-all term for those aspects of a sound not included in pitch and duration. Of no value to the sound composer!" On the other hand, he defines texture as the "[o]rganisation of sound elements in terms of (temporal) density and field properties" (Wishart 1996, 134–135). The primacy of the ear is the call of the day in a book that is essentially a "how to" book of sound design.

Wishart logically avoids any discussion of form or structure as leading elements in sound-based composition. Yet in *Audible Design*, a chapter is dedicated to new approaches to form. One key sentence stands out: "The distinction made between 'structure' and 'expression' is in fact an arbitrary, ideological divide" (ibid., 104). He goes on to elaborate this concern: "All the changes to the sounds can be traced to structural properties of the sounds and the control of those structural properties. The distinction structure/expression arises from the arbitrary divide created by the limitation of notation" (ibid.). There are two points to be made here, one hardly relevant to this book. Traditional notation does, indeed, represent far less than half of the musical whole. More relevant is Wishart's interest in expression and structure both emanating from the treatment of sound object, much in line with the procedures associated with the GRM school; still, there are some bottom-up formalists who come to the same conclusion, though for very different reasons. The structure debate in sound-based music is not well developed at this point. This is partially the result of the bottom-up approach of so many of its composers alongside the proliferation of individual languages. It is also a result of the infinite possibilities at our disposal. As many formalists are also interested in individual languages, this makes the subject even more complex. The relative lack of debate on structure does raise the question of whether our art of emancipation has somehow lost its way. If we do not take structure into consideration in an art that possesses so many possibilities, are we not contributing to our own marginalization? Structure is yet another potential thing for listeners to hold on to in sound-based music and Wishart, despite his rhetoric here, is very aware of this as can clearly be heard in his compositions.

Trevor Wishart occupies a unique place in terms of sound-based music studies. His two restrictions aside, his theory and sound design ideas cover a huge area of sound organization relating a variety of concepts to the specific means of sound production and manipulation. His writings present issues ranging from basic classification of sounds to the listening experience, discourse and representation, new virtuosity, and new means of presentation, a very broad spectrum of interest. He shares two major concerns with Denis Smalley, namely that of the musical gesture as well as spatialization and, one also shared with virtually all the writers presented thus far, that sound-based music starts with the sound itself and develops into structures by means of definable sonic relationships.

(6)   Formalized Works: From *Die Reihe* to All Things Algorithmic
Pierre Boulez wrote in *Die Reihe* in 1955: "Considering the logical developments which are bound to come about, we will have to approach the

two domains, the electronic and the instrumental, in radically differing ways . . . from a world undifferentiated in its timbre, pitch, intensity and duration, we are required to create a composition which is coherent not only in its internal structure but also in the constitution of its actual sound material" (Boulez 1958, 19). Such music might also be considered spectralist, but in fact those who were invited to contribute to this important postwar journal were more interested in formalizing the construction of works at every conceivable level, picking up where Anton Webern had left off. It is here where formalism was launched in early sound-based music history. Reading through the *Die Reihe* (or the row, as in a 12-tone series) issues, one notes famous names in postwar serial composition speaking about the potential of parametric thinking as a means of formalization in this new world of *elektronische Musik*, including Herbert Eimert, Mauricio Kagel, Gottfried Michael Koenig, Werner Meyer-Eppler (responsible for a good deal of the new terminology at that time including parameter, statistical, and aleatoric; see Eimert 1958, 6; Ungeheuer 1999), Henri Pousseur, Karlheinz Stockhausen, and Hans-Heinz Stuckenschmidt. Its proponents have indeed included sound construction as part of their theories and, in consequence, compositional approaches, Stockhausen not being the least of them. However, and in particular in the early period, the link to a Cartesian (or lattice) approach to organizing sound was an imperative for this group, with the exception of noise textures. Perhaps the music was not formed of quarter notes and eighth notes, chromatic pitch, and so on; still, sound events were often perceived as contemporary electronic equivalents of notes and were, therefore, less sound-based than the work of their "rivals" at that time in Paris.

Although it did not take terribly long before Karlheinz Stockhausen included concrete sounds in some of his electroacoustic works as did another formalist composer, Iannis Xenakis, their main focus was to become the generation of electronically generated sounds. As suggested above, in the case of Xenakis, the discovery of new sounds was essential.

The concepts of formalization that were simultaneously evolving on both sides of the Atlantic in the 1950s and 1960s, in particular in Cologne, at the Darmstadt summer school in Germany, and on Ivy

League campuses in the United States, helped to extend the reign of serial thought that originated in Vienna in the 1920s. It was Xenakis' reaction to the serial restriction that extended the world of formalism into more sophisticated branches of mathematics, architecture, and the like. Mappings involving extramusical data became increasingly sophisticated.[81] These crucial developments led to the vast world of formalization in music today that ranges from fractal theory to cellular automata, genetic algorithms, and neural networks, all acting as potential bases for sound organization.

The fact that in the early years new timbral possibilities were seemingly not quite as significant to many as the new forms of potential orderings of sounds, including notes, within formalized contexts led to some criticism. As Eimert complained about the haphazard nature of musique concrète, many of the French school complained conversely about the sterile or clinical nature of the new electronic works. For example, Michel Chion has written: "the sounds obtained [in electronic serial music] possessed neither color nor personality" (Chion 1991, 30). This was of course partly true because of the relatively inflexible equipment present at the time. Guy E. Garnett has a more specific worry: "Too often an implicit assumption exists that if a formula generated it, and the formula is coherent, then the resultant music is not just coherent, but somehow, and usually thereby, aesthetically valuable" (Garnett 2001, 30). His view, which goes to the heart of one of the few debates today on valorization, is that being new or being unique is not sufficient for a work to be appreciated. Of course this remark is pertinent to any header listed in this section on genres and categories. What Garnett is implying is that a great number of formalized works, including those in the early period of sound-based composition, represent complex, abstract results. This in many ways works against listeners' being able to perceive coherence in this new corpus of works, often because of the complexity issues, making the works in general that much more inaccessible. Granted this is a generalization; several works based on formalist approaches, including the early *Gesang der Jünglinge*, which will be returned to briefly below, have become central to the late twentieth-century repertoire partially as a result of their being more accessible than other formalized works.

Quite relevant to the present discussion is the fact that many of the theories of formalization have been applied to instrumental and vocal contexts at least as much as within electroacoustic frameworks. This raises the question: to what extent do particular formalisms have to do with sound-based composition? Although there is a great deal of literature to be found on individual approaches to formalization, as far as current theoretical development is concerned, this subject will prove to have had less impact on sound-based music studies than many other topics regardless of the fact that this subject is exceptional in that it is often focused on ordering procedures and structure unlike those thus far introduced. Perhaps if developers and artists presented their arguments more frequently concerning the "why" element related to formalization in sound-based contexts, or their thoughts concerning the listening experience, this would change and our understanding of the musical experience of formalized sound-based composition would increase.[82] Although the electronic sound is a common denominator in many electroacoustic formalized works, the diversity of approach is such that one can only speak of coherence in this group because of an interest in formalizing constructional principles, not from the point of view of the sonic result. Neither the word "formalization" nor the formalization protocols determine the sonic result of a piece. For example, there have been instrumental (a)tonal fractal pieces and electronic fractal (a)tonal pieces created, as well as electroacoustic fractal works ignoring both tonality and atonality.

In 1987, I wrote an article with the somewhat cryptic title, "Comp(exp. ♩) = $f_t\Sigma$'parameters'(~)" (Landy 1987; also summarized in Landy 1991, 11–16). Deciphered, the title reads: the composition of experimental music is a function (over time) of the sum of sound parameters. Parameters presented in that article, although only a sampling, included:

pitch

duration

tempo

dynamics

timbre (a "combination parameter")

sound types

space

density

simultaneity (also known as harmony)

(dis)order

energy (another "combination parameter"—density + order)

freedom (from controlled to indeterminate)

compositional bearing (rationalized to intuitive)

form/structure

Formel (from Stockhausen, referring to a "super-parameter" capable of organizing the very small to the very large)

It would be pointless to try to create an exhaustive list, as many parameters are created by composers for a single work and often borrow from an extramusical system or environment mapped onto the musical field.

The fact is that everything mentioned above can be projected both onto a vocal/instrumental field as well as an electroacoustic one, albeit in different ways. There are parameters, of course, that can only be used in sound synthesis contexts. If timbre could be generalized to sound morphologies—which would be a conglomerate parameter—then a great deal of electroacoustic sound manipulation techniques could easily be incorporated. In any case, if one adds the terms "models" and "analogies" to "parameters," the potential for formalization becomes truly vast.

In those early German works alluded to above, the technology of the day did not allow for sophisticated sound manipulation and transformation techniques. Thus Stockhausen was able to devise only relatively simple lists for sound synthesis in the early years, and he clearly did take timbral manipulation into consideration. For example, in *Die Reihe* 2, Stockhausen speaks of the eleven electronic sound types used in *Gesang der Jünglinge* (Stockhausen 1958, 46) that are pertinent to sound-based composition:

sine tones

sine tones in which the frequency modulates "periodically"

sine tones in which the frequency modulates "statistically"

sine tones in which the amplitude modulates "periodically"
sine tones in which the amplitude modulates "statistically"
"statistical" combinations of both sine tone modulations
"periodic" combinations of both sine tone modulations
colored noise with constant density
colored noise with "statistically" varied density
"periodic" sequences of foltered "beats" (*Knacke*)
"statistical" combinations of foltered "beats" (*Knacke*)

The accessibility of this work is due to the finite character of this list and the consistent use of this restricted set of sound types.

In his famous article ". . . how the time passes . . ." (". . . wie die Zeit vergeht . . ." Stockhausen 1958), sophisticated relationships are formed between duration and (sub-)harmonics of pitch. Interestingly, this article is oriented primarily toward instrumental music although the electronic potential is at least as pertinent. Regardless, Stockhausen, Boulez, Koenig, and others serialized timbre in these early days, including the new notion of timbral interpolation (see Decroupet 1994) and Stockhausen's *Klangfarbenkontinuum* (allowing for the continuous change of timbre; see Ungeheuer 1994). In the early 1970s Stockhausen introduced his concept of *Formel* whereby the construction of sounds, structure, and even series of works can be linked together by using the same "formula" (*Formel*) to generate micro- and macro-level entities.

During the postserialist period, university composition students started submitting composition dissertations complemented with explanatory essays. Curiosity about extramusical phenomena as part of the new world of algorithmic composition took off in the latter half of the twentieth century, quickly evolving to the wide spectrum of approaches formalization represents today. Clearly there was already some interest in quantifying aspects of a musical approach on university campuses internationally. What transpired was that the majority of the works' write-ups consisted of explanations of formalisms. One wonders to what extent the reason this practice evolved was that it is easier to write about the quantifiable than the qualitative. For our purposes, two questions are of great significance. (1) To what extent is a given formalization more important than how a work sounds as a result? In other words, to what extent is the reception of a formalized work taken into account and to what end? (2) To what extent is the formalization specific to a given electroacoustic context? These are not loaded questions; still, few people find it easy to discuss them. As most publications are focused on the minutiae of the particular formalization, these reports represent some of those "upper-floor rooms" alluded to in the introduction of this book. Answering such questions is of foundational importance.

Those who have used environmental factors as part of their mappings seem to combine their formalized work with one or more of the aspects of the genres and categories previously introduced. This exceptional case exemplifies an attempt to take our understandings of bottom-up composition and apply them within more formalized contexts, a step toward convergence among our first five categories and this sixth one.

Clearly there are some tools that have been created for use by more people than just the individual who developed them. For example, IRCAM researchers have developed software called Formes. This is a tool that was developed for musicians who share a desire to formalize aspects of a composition's structure. Today's most powerful and most often applied programs that are able to serve as an excellent formalization tool are MAX-MSP and its cousin, PD (although they are also used with other goals in mind). They are to formalization what the combination of Pro-Tools and GRM Tools and the like are to those making works from the materials upward, for example, those adhering to the acousmatic and soundscape schools of sound. That said, these programs are in a way like the subject of formalization itself: able to be used for virtually any approach to sound-based music, and therefore not necessarily identifiable with a specific genre, category, or sound, but instead more adaptable to individual need. Therefore, they serve the diversity of the worlds of formalized music; their use is less obvious in terms of this chapter's aim of seeking common denominators in works of organized sound.

Let's look briefly at a publication by the composer and theorist Jean-Baptiste Barrière, once associated with IRCAM's interest in developing new means of formalization:

I consider timbre to be the set of material/organization interactions leading to the elaboration of a form. Given this framework, the goal is to formalize constraints through a process of unifying control over these interactions by exploiting the theory of formal systems: composition is considered first as the action of composing symbols, combined into propositions which are mutually generated through the application of reference rules. In addition, the emergence of new structures is explored through materials produced via simulation methodology, in the evolving processes of modelling, hybridisation, interpolation, extrapolation and abstraction. There then arises the question of a theory of references which can describe centripetal and centrifugal elements, controlling and structuring them. The critical and selective process of arriving at discrete structures can be performed in a heuristic fashion as a function of causal determination based on the classic distinction between excitation and resonance modes. In this context, the representation with which (and on which) one can operate becomes a key issue. The ambition is to develop a grammar of formal processes, a morphogenesis. The conceptual graphs and semantic networks thus developed can be considered as veritable generators of forms, offering control over the trajectories and paths along which musical material can be elaborated, diverted, transformed. (Barrière 1989, 117, abstract)

Barrière is one of many who have constructed very sophisticated formalized systems, within both electroacoustic and instrumental contexts. What is discussed here does not sound like something that is destined for use by a large group of musicians. Nevertheless, the author in no way is claiming any territory for himself; on the contrary, he is creating a potential framework for formalist approaches. Still, it may come as a bit of a surprise after reading the preceding paragraph that elsewhere he discusses the importance of his systems' being audible and how this aids understanding (Barrière 1992). This is a fairly exceptional opinion, however. The author Martin Supper supports this when he states his view that it is rare that these processes are intentionally made audible (Supper 2001, 48). Yet where are the podia where such debates are carried out, where these systems are evaluated?

Musical terminology has increased only modestly owing to the opportunities offered by formalization other than borrowed extramusical words used for mapping purposes. Klarenz Barlow has been known to create new terms for his specific approaches to pieces, such as *Spektastik* ("spectastics," spectral stochastics) and *Schwellenreiten* ("riding waves," cross-synthesis applied algorithmically), just to name two (Barlow 1999).[83]

Other approaches worthy of mention include Eduardo Reck Miranda's use of techniques from artificial intelligence to help create timbre in instrument designs where the timbre is "unknown" or "abstract" (Miranda 1994).[84] Formalization does not only occur in sound-based music for fixed media. Robert Rowe is one of many who concentrate on formalization within an interactive context (see, e.g., Rowe 1993, 2001), a context in which more and more activity is taking place whether formalized or not (see subsection 8 below). The diversity of interactive contexts is huge, so it again refers to a category, not to the creation of aural coherence. With this in mind one can conclude that formal approaches have led to an enormous diversity of performance contexts, means of construction, and sonic results.[85] Therefore, it is neither desirable to attempt to delineate this area nor useful to attempt to create a survey of selected individual contributions in this context, as the selection would most likely be piecemeal. When individuals' concepts begin to resonate within others' creative work in this field, that is, where clusters of activity evolve relevant to this co-hear-ence discussion, relating formalization to the potential listening experience, the important developments in this area will finally receive the credit they are due. It is unfortunate that so few writers seem comfortable working in the areas represented in subsections 1 through 5 above as well as this subsection, linking objectivity in terms of construction with the more qualitative experience of reception. Very few authors I have discovered have published that they were open to investigating links emanating from these worlds of thought and none has discussed this possibility at any length.

Fortunately time moves on. The tension between the pure spectralists and the pure formalists has diminished somewhat. At the 2000 International Computer Music Conference in Berlin I heard a work composed by someone I had known since the late 1970s whom I had always liked but whose work did appear somewhat clinical to me. I feel pretty awful when I am unable to reconcile someone's personality with his or her artistic work. He presented a new work at this conference which was much more accessible, not to mention appreciable, at least to me. Its sounds seemed to have been molded from clay and, not to my surprise, the piece was algorithmically composed. I went to him immediately after the concert, shook his hand and said, "At last." His reply was similarly to the point: "It's converging and it's about time." Architecture was meeting chemistry in sound-based composition.

(7)   The Popular Dimension

Most, but by no means all, popular music that employs electroacoustic techniques, and which could be said to belong to or be associated with sound-based music, is driven by a beat. As far as beat-driven music is concerned, Bob Ostertag rightly points out in his article, "Why Computer Music Sucks" (1996), that the computer is ideally suited to deal with absolute regularity of tempo in combination with automated mixing, effects, and so on. His conclusion is that some of the most exciting innovations in sound-based music can be found in today's club scene.[86] Most music described thus far avoids the presence of a beat. It might be said that the presence or absence of a driving beat has been the decisive factor in separating *E* and *U* sound-based music; my view is that the *E/U* separation is not as important today and perhaps could even rest in peace, but things are not that simple. Another type of convergence is slowly taking place. The inclusion of this subsection is to emphasize this evolution, not to celebrate separate histories.

In 1998 a former Ph.D. student of mine, Martijn Voorvelt, completed an analytical thesis entitled *British Post-punk Experimental Pop (1977–1983)*. In his thesis, among other issues, he took a close look at works by, for example, Art Bears and Brian Eno. These are clearly not hit parade musicians, but they are not entirely anonymous either. Eno has produced and participated in some very successful recordings. He has clearly crossed the traditional *E* and *U* cultural divide through his audiovisual art works that have been displayed in contemporary galleries and museums, if not through his music. One of the fascinating discoveries that arose during Voorvelt's study concerned the separate existence of communities related to what he defines as experimental popular music on the one hand and certain manifestations of experimental art music on the other. He was able to conclude that synergy was developing across the divide, sometimes knowledgeably, sometimes independently where sounds, structures, and a rebellious attitude were present in both. In short, he concluded that people who appreciated one group (or individual) on one side of the divide could and probably would appreciate work that they might not be aware of on the other (Voorvelt 2000).[87]

Voorvelt's point concerning the perceived divide is extremely important here. Most experimental popular music artists (there are exceptions) neither consider themselves mainstream artists nor want to be associated with the more commercial and entertainment aspects of the popular music world. These artists have their own smaller—perhaps more optimal—audience, one that is interested in elements associated with music with popular roots treated in new and innovative ways. A good deal of the music Voorvelt studied fits within the topic of this book. One might say that the more experimental the electroacoustic techniques employed in popular music might be, the more likely the work is focusing on sound-based methods and therefore might be classified as sound-based music. In any event, most of these artists see as much of a divide between themselves and more commercial, entertainment, and fashion-based pop industry as they do between themselves and the art music world. This is also true to varying extents as far as musicians are concerned who are associated with electronica in the popular music sense of the word.

Electronica is a term that brings together recent popular genres that evolved from dance music. We will have to use the term carefully as it is by no means synonymous with the current electronica scene associated with Kim Cascone and many others described in subsection 4 above. Furthermore, we seem to be missing a term for the innovative practices from other decades, such as relevant works from Kraftwerk, Soft Machine, Pink Floyd, and so on, in which a good deal of attention was given to sound organization.

There is sadly a lack of literature dealing with the sound organization side of relevant genres. Take trance as an example. The online reference, Wikipedia, defines trance as follows: "Trance music is a subgenre of electronic dance music that developed in the 1990s. Perhaps the most ambiguous genre in the realm of electronic dance music (EDM), trance could be described as a melodic, more-or-less freeform style of music derived from a combination of techno and house. Regardless of its precise origins, to many club-goers, party-throwers, and EDM enthusiasts, trance is held as a significant development within the greater sphere of (post-)modern dance music."[88] The one sign that this music may be relevant to our study appears in a neighboring chart on the website indicating that its typical instruments include the synthesizer, drum machine, sequencer, keyboard, and sampler, most of which are able to treat audio samples.

The only means of creating coherence in those types of sound-based music associated with pop music currently is through their (sub-)genre names. Wikipedia and the *All Music Guide to Electronica: The Definitive Guide to Electronic music* (Bogdanov et al. 2001) provide more than most other books and articles that were consulted in preparation for this book. In Wikipedia, the subheads under Electronic Music Genres (excluding their inclusion of musique concrète) are: ambient, breakbeat, downtempo, electro, electronica, hardcore, hi-NRG, house, industrial, intelligent dance music (IDM), jungle, Miami bass, new age, noise, nortec, rave, synth pop, techno, and trance. Hip-hop and turntablism are listed separately, that is, not under electronic music genres.

The Definitive Guide also includes several genres or, in the terms of the editors, styles of "electronic music." There are sixty-one styles defined in the book. Of these, eleven are given a more complete historical treatment: house, techno, electronica (which is the editors' umbrella term within popular music), jungle/drum 'n' bass, trance, trip-hop, ambient, electro (the 1980s phenomenon, not the francophone catchphrase), garage, hardcore techno, and acid jazz. The useful influence maps in this book demonstrate how much crosstalk there is among these eleven categories, electronica representing more a hub than a higher-level style denomination.

It is fascinating how different the two sources' lists are. The borderline between electronica and electronic remains somewhat unclear. Electronica is, according to the book's editors, "a suitably vague term used to describe the emergence of electronic dance music increasingly geared to listening instead of strictly dancing" (ibid., x). This implies clearly that the beat is no longer a must, especially as ambient music is included on their list. "Electronic, on the other hand, spanned the space from Cage and Stockhausen to The Can, synth-pop and techno" (ibid., ix–x). One might conclude that in their sense electronic includes *E* music whereas electronica does not. Ambient music qualifies as dance music only to the extent that it is often present in chill-out rooms in clubs. Brian Eno, Mr. Ambient himself, suggests that this genre is "music to swim in, to float in, to get lost inside" (Eno 2004a, 95).

Connoisseurs will know about most if not all of these. Others are referred to these sources and the EARS site[89] for further detail. Ned

Bouhalassa is one of the first to have done the inevitable and extended such lists to include glitch and other forms of microsound (Bouhalassa 2002), but then his interest was not in the *U* and *E* music boundary. It is clear that much research needs to be done to place these genres in broader contexts and, as stated, much more analytical work is needed that would aid our understanding of the content and innovation of the wide variety of sound-based forms associated with popular music that have been developed over recent decades. As part of that work, the points of view of the musicians should be investigated to discover how they position themselves with respect to being a popular artist, dance artist, and/or electronica artist. As we can see, terminology here is just as messy as it is elsewhere.

Another Ph.D. analytical project, this time by Sophy Smith on turntablist teams (Smith 2005),[90] has taken on this challenge. She has developed a detailed scratch notation (not the first of its kind, but the only one created thus far for analysis) for turntable team performance that can be used for comparative analysis of multiple performances of a single work, or various works of the same team or between different teams. She has also documented the evolution of works following how the devising process takes place within these teams. Finally, she interviews her musicians about the music, its process, and how the musicians position themselves within music culture. Most see the link with hip-hop culture as much more important than any connection with the more general pop culture. This is similar to many of today's drum 'n' bass artists not feeling part of the high-powered, high-volume commercial world of entertainment. If similar research projects were to take place focusing on other relevant styles or genres, we would learn more about how sounds are chosen, sampled, manipulated, and used in studio and performance contexts as well as where the artists feel their music belongs within broader musical contexts.

Similarly, these genres' evolution deserves greater attention. Élie During recounts: "It is the task of the musicologists and music historians to define the borders where new genres find themselves, by observing the relevant vectors (tempo and color, bpm and rhythmic intensity, timbre and granularity), or by discovering the elements of the technological needs and social circumstances which make the genre's practice possible" (in Gallet 2002, 223). Bastien Gallet takes dub under the loop and decides that it can be a subgenre of anything given remix culture's ability to take anything and turn it into anything else (ibid., 22). It is here where the new field of studies for sound-based music offers important investigative opportunities. However, currently most writing on these subjects is journalistic, often lacking depth; most scholarship deals with cultural aspects and with lyrics, hardly touching on musical and technological content.

Simon Emmerson once suggested that in a way popular music, world music, and electroacoustic influences are merging (Emmerson 2001a), and that ambient music is an excellent example of that convergence. Toop and Prendergast have already been singled out as writers deserving recognition for their initial exploration of the horizons that go beyond separate *E* and *U* worlds of the art of sounds. The more who study the music in detail, the more understanding we will have of how fuzzy these boundaries can be. Fusion composers such as Frank Zappa, who have been at home on stage as much as in the studio, in the experimental popular music worlds as well as in the contemporary music concert hall, illustrate this spanning of the perceived divide excellently.

And then there is DJ culture, already alluded to in terms of turnablist teams, which is pertinent to a good deal of the above discussion. Christoph Cox and Daniel Warner have articulated their thoughts on this music as follows:

> From Schaeffer onwards, DJ Culture has worked with two essential concepts: the cut and the mix. To record is to cut, to separate the sonic signifier (the "sample") from any original context or meaning so that it might be free to function otherwise. To mix is to reinscribe, to place the floating sample into a new chain of signification. The mix is the postmodern moment, in which the most disparate of sounds can be spliced together and made to flow. . . . DJ Culture also describes a new modality of audio history and memory. No longer a figure of linear continuity that, ideally, could be recalled in its totality, musical history becomes a network of mobile segments available at any moment for inscription and reinscription into new lines, texts, mixes. In short, musical history is no longer an analog scroll but digital and random access. (Cox and Warner 2004, 330)

Reflecting this, Paul D. Miller (DJ Spooky) has written: "DJ-ing lets you take the best of what's out there and give your own take on it" (Miller

2004, 17). He adds: "The best DJs are griots, and whether their stories are conscious or unconscious, narratives are implicit in the sampling idea. Every story leads to another story to another story to another story. But at the same time, they might be called 'music before the impact of language,' or pre-linguistic stories" (ibid., 21). He summarizes: "Give me two turntables, and I'll give you a universe" (ibid., 127). Gallet's basic premise in his book is that the cut is the defining notion, that is, that which makes things hang together in remix culture, binding samples together in infinite combinations. This is as close to a discussion of sound-based music techniques (other than basic "how to" books) as one seems to get these days.

What is fascinating about all of these remarks is how similar they are to many ideas introduced in the appropriation section above, a category where for many the *E/U* music discussion is of no interest. The techniques of most of the genres discussed above are generally no different from those discussed in subsection 3. In fact most of these genres work to a large extent with appropriated sounds, whether of the environmental type or, more frequently, ones associated with popular music instruments; some of their techniques have been derived from analog music, in particular from musique concrète, and have established themselves in a different guise within these more recent genres.

So where has this subsection led us? I believe that, with some exceptions, most sound-based musicians with roots in popular music perceive a divide between their work and the commercial pop world that is in fact similar to one they tend not to think about, namely the one between themselves and the sound-based worlds that are not associated with popular music materials. Where I can easily imagine the former separation, the latter one is more peculiar. I would agree with Voorvelt that the more sound-oriented and experimental this work becomes, the more interesting the work will appear for currently separate sound-based music communities and that, in fact, a subsection in this chapter on popular music was only a means to an end linking the more sound-based practices here with ones introduced elsewhere, whether convergence has already taken place or is simply something to be expected in the not too distant future.

(8)   The "Split" between Fixed Medium and Live Electroacoustic Performance: Convergence (2)

It has been a long time coming. We are almost through the list of sub-sections and finally arrive at one where live performance comes to the fore, although it has been a feature of a good deal of the music in the previous subsection. This is because a reasonably large percentage of sound-based work created has been in recorded form and neatly fits within the umbrella of *musique sur support* (music on a fixed medium). Musicians who create works on a fixed medium are comfort-able in the studio, perhaps more so than on stage. Their works are recorded and then disseminated on the radio and on CDs (and modern equivalents such as the Internet and the DVD, some able to present multitrack spatialized versions of works). These means of presentation normally reach more listeners than those reached by the finite number of concerts works often receive. Larry Austin and Rodney Wachka believe that the CD is the definitive venue for sound-based music (Austin and Waschka 1996). They have led the publication of a series of computer music CDs, one of a number that have been established internationally.

In a sense, it might be said that for these artists performance takes place in the studio. Mark Prendergast, in discussing Brian Eno's work, has stated: "One of his essential contributions was to highlight the importance of the recording studio as an essential part of the musical experience; a veritable instrument, which in the hands of the right person could work wonders" (Prendergast 2000, 115). Eno has written an entire article entitled "The Studio as Compositional Tool" (Eno 2004b). Studio-based musicians belong to one or more of the categories that have already been presented. We will discuss the notion of virtuosity in the studio in section B5 in the next chapter.

Granted, in many cases the concert presentation of a pre-recorded work includes spatialization that one cannot normally reproduce at home. However, the performance atmosphere of a concert hall with someone diffusing a piece behind a mixing desk is an acquired taste for many. After nearly sixty years of fixed medium presentation, there are still many people who claim they are unable or unwilling to acquire that taste. Nevertheless, some writers, including Robert Normandeau (2002), a fixed medium composer, still feel something special about the ritual function of the concert even without performers on stage.

Taking the step to live performance, the reaction to a physical gesture translated into sound unambiguously is of course immediate. The protagonists of staged electroacoustic performance often discuss the need for corporeality in music or people's desire to view effort as part of the musical experience (see, e.g., Bahn, Hahn, and Trueman 2000, 46; Ostertag 2002, 11–14; Waisvisz 1999, 119–120).

Fundamental to our thinking about sound-based music and performance is the word "gesture," a word with several meanings that range from the physical gesture to the musical one. A CD-ROM publication edited by Marcelo Wanderley and Marc Battier (Wanderley and Battier 2000) focused specifically on gesture, in particular gestural control within live musical contexts, and is a useful reference here. Claude Cadoz and Wanderley's joint contribution to the publication offers a broad diversity of definitions of gesture ("Gesture—Music," ibid.). Fernando Iazzetta's contribution investigates how movement can express meaning in live contexts ("Meaning in Musical Gestures," ibid.). He cites Simon Emmerson's two terms that relate to gesture, *local* and *field* (see Emmerson 1994b) as being highly pertinent to meaning. Emmerson presents these two terms as follows: "Local controls and functions seek to extend (but not to break) the perceived relation of human performer action to sound production [while] field functions place the results of this activity within a context, a landscape or an environment" (ibid., 31). This has to do with Emmerson's plea, which will be treated below, concerning the relationship between what is seen on stage and what is heard. "Local" clearly refers to causal relationships, and "field" involves an aural context. The local relationship can be real (i.e., real-time and transparent) or imaginary (prepared in advance to suggest causality). Emmerson suggests that local/field relationships can be mapped on to Wishart's real and unreal objects and spaces introduced above. One of Emmerson's concerns here has to do with the placement of sound coming out of loudspeakers, that is, diffusion regardless of context. For example, displacing the sound of a live performer is something he questions. He therefore believes that one could use the local and field notions linked to specific loudspeakers. To achieve these goals, he is interested in the development of better performance control over the mobility and directionality of modified sound sources and suggests that particular algorithmic treatment of local and field sound placement may be the best way forward.[91] This theory is one of very few cases in which theoretical issues are posed before technological development takes place, and thus it belongs to the categories of new virtuosity and new means of presentation to be discussed in chapter 3.

Using old-fashioned terminology, a differentiation will be made in this subsection between (a) mixed music, that is music for live performer(s) using traditional instruments and recording; (b) real-time performance (live electronics, interaction[92]); and, as a separate subject, (c) the presence of organized sound in audiovisual contexts.

Mixed music   I have written elsewhere that I see mixed music as a midpoint between traditional concert practices and sound-based music, an "in-between" category bringing together the traditions of both worlds. My experience in terms of this practice of presentation has involved works' being placed along an axis which, at one extreme, includes compositions where the recorded part consists of sounds derived from the performing instrument, an approach commonly associated with works by Horacio Vaggione, and works where the recorded sounds clearly contrast the sounds made by the live performer(s), such as the *Synchronism* series by Mario Davidovsky. There are works, of course, that can be found between the two extremes of fusion and contrast (Landy 2006b; see also Menezes 2002). Works on the homogeneous end of the axis often involve extended techniques that are more timbral than pitch-based, thus allowing the work to lean more toward a spectralist sound universe than others.

Although the technical processes taking place are different when interactivity is involved, not least owing to the fact that the performer can lead the interaction whereas he or she is normally led by a pre-recorded "tape part" in a mixed instrument plus fixed medium performance,[93] mixed real-time works follow a similar story in terms of the listening experience to what has been described above. It is a category. Such works can sound like any type of sound organization; the cohesion in terms of this chapter's goal of finding forms of co-hear-ence is much more in the form of presentation than in the sound of a given work. It is the combination of the music's influences and where it fits along the mixed music axis that defines the placement of a given performance work in terms of content and listening experience.

Real-time performance   With live electronic performance, there is no assumption that the performer is making traditional instrumental sounds. In fact, in its early days, the sounds were all electronic and performances often allowed for improvisation (not that all instrument plus pre-recorded sound works avoid improvisation). For decades, the idea existed that most electronic musicians were either studio musicians or stage electronics performer-composers, not to mention instrument developers. With our ever-faster computers and processors, this distinction is due for redundancy soon, but we have not quite reached that stage yet. This is illustrated by the fact that, for example, the Chemical Brothers have offered studio and live mixes of some of their works, such as their *Meat Ball Manifesto*, as they were, by definition, different in terms of the possible rigor of the end result. Jean-Claude Risset is one of many who has considered the lack of rigor or complexity to be a drawback of real-time situations (Risset 1999, 33–35). One wonders, given the developments of speed of today's and tomorrow's digital equipment combined with ever-improving means of control, how long Risset's historically correct view will remain valid.

Risset also believes that composition is not a real-time process (ibid., 37). This remark will not please any improviser. John Bowers is one of many artists inside and outside of sound-based music who have made statements concerning their belief that improvisation should be seen to be synonymous with composition (Bowers 2003). In one of the few theoretical works concerning performance that involves technology, *Improvising Machines: Ethnographically Informed Design for Improvised Electro-acoustic Music*, he suggests that the listener "should know something of the technology to understand the improvisation and what goes on, fails, etc." (ibid.). This does raise the accessibility level to that of a knowledgeable public, but I would assume this to be true in many musical genres when listeners attempt to understand when and how something special is occurring. Bowers believes that Smalley's spectromorphology theory, normally used for studio-based works, can be applied to what he calls electroacoustic timbral improvisation. His thesis on real-time sound-based improvisation focuses on five key issues:

1) The importance of understanding the contingent practical configurations which interrelate technology, musical materials and form, performance practice, the specifics of setting and occasion, and different understandings of improvisation. 2) Variable sociality: noting the different social interactional relations that are worked through in performance. 3) Variable engagement and interactivity: noting the different and varying relations that performers have with respect to their instruments and technologies. 4) Musical materials: noting the range of musical materials which have been experimented with and their different interactional features. 5) Along the way, I develop a sketch of a potential aesthetics for improvised electro-acoustic music which seems idiomatic for the analytic approach of this chapter and the design orientation of the next. (Ibid.)

These points are notable as they demonstrate a cross-section of musical investigation along with the technological as well as the social and aesthetic sides of his work, an exemplary study.

Like mixed music, live electronic performance has been as diverse as one can imagine and, if anything, that breadth has grown with time. Calling a group of people "laptop performers" says nothing about content which can range from instrumental sounds, to appropriated sounds, to transformed sounds of any type, to synthetic ones including noise or any combinations thereof in any combination of styles to which the group adheres. We are therefore again dealing with sound-based music's categories.

Then there is the subject of *interactive systems*. The two books previously cited by Robert Rowe typify research in the area, that is, more focused on particular developments, particular protocols than particular types of music, related theories, or reception. Rowe does acknowledge that such systems are becoming increasingly dependent on interdisciplinary research, specifically involving music theory, music cognition, and artificial intelligence (Rowe 1993, vii). It is not all "development speak" though. At one point Rowe cites Parales who comments on the stiffness of some interactive music systems works: "Perhaps the best we can hope for is that someone will come up with a way to program in some rough edges, too" (ibid., 262–263). In his second book, he explains that: " 'Machine Musicianship' is both an exploration of the theoretical foundations of analysing, performing, and composing music with computers, and a tutorial in writing software to pursue these goals. The theoretical foundations are derived from the fields of music theory, computer music, music cognition and AI" (Rowe 2001, 1). He adds: "The need for better musicianship in music processing is relatively self-evident when contrasted with the aesthetic and ethical questions surrounding the use of automated composition and performance programs. Computers in music have made possible new kinds of creation at the same time that they have caused upheaval in the social and cultural practice of music making" (ibid., 3). With this openness, I look forward to future publications on this subject taking the areas of appreciation and reception into account.

One distinction that can be made in these contexts is whether what you see is what you get, or not, as the case may be. It is primarily Emmerson[94] who has observed that he finds music dissatisfying in performance contexts in which physical gesture is not reflected in the sound result, where dislocation occurs. Marc Battier refers to this as the "paradox of electronic instruments" (Battier 1995). This can be caused by a number of things. In days past, one reason could have been the time required to calculate the translation of a gesture into audio or even simply caused by MIDI or audio latency. Today that is much less the issue. Instead, composers/performers create situations whereby what you see can influence what you hear, but owing to issues of complexity or whatever other reason, this is not perceived as such nor understood in terms of how things are working by listeners. In such cases the instrument is used primarily as a complex, opaque interface or controller.

Emmerson believes that we will reach the point where the divide between event and signal processing will disappear (1991, 135). A consequence of this would be the ability to incorporate signal-processing instructions into the "score." His worry, at the time at least, was that too many people were focused on complexity, in particular concerning structure at the expense of complex sound objects; that is, there was too much interest in syntax and too little, therefore, in phonology. His recommendation here was: "(a) to extend the human gestures of the composer and performer and their immediate choice of and control over: sonic materials, signal processing and treatments; (b) to manage, under the control of the performer, score systems in the broadest sense including systems configuration" (ibid., 138).

Clearly, Emmerson agrees with me that Risset's complaint concerning the lack of rigor of real-time music is one that is due to become redundant. Using Smalley's terminology, Emmerson states a preference for first-order surrogacies in live performance as opposed to more remote ones (Emmerson 1994a, 97), preferring more apparent causal relationships (ibid., 98). In a later article, he focuses on Smalley's nine indicative fields (adding two more, natural and cultural fields) and relates them to live electroacoustic performance (2000a, 195–198, 200). He and Guy E. Garnett are therefore seeking "more human . . . modes of musical behaviour" (Garnett 2001, 32). Emmerson rightly suggests that we need new terminology and approaches to the analysis of live electronic music (1996a); in particular there is a need for evaluation criteria and methodology for analysis, taking the aspects introduced above into account. One of his ideals is an "agreed paradigm" (1996b, 51). Another of his desires is the investigation of new forms of human agency in areas ranging from sound installations to the Internet, and also including DJs and plunderphonics (ibid., 210–213). In any event he is one who believes in wysiwyg live electronic/real-time performance, articulating the view of many potentially interested sound-based music listeners that understanding gestures in a sound-based context is yet another thing to hold on to. His views on performed sound-based music are an extension of views introduced elsewhere and fall under the categories of the listening experience (audiovisual in this case), modes of discourse, and new means of presentation.

What musicians in this area are looking for is well summarized by Bowers: "An aesthetic specific to improvised electro-acoustic music [. . .] in terms of exhibiting the variable relations people can have to technologies and each other in a machine world" (Bowers 2003). Today's interactive music, as diverse as it is, can achieve exactly this and has its own public. Bowers' work, linking social aspects of performance to technology and to content, represents a new, important area of focus as far as sound-based music studies are concerned.

Audiovisual presentation   The subject of audiovisual manifestations of sound-based music forms an interesting bridge between the current subject of live electroacoustic performance and the next one, sound art

→ sonic art. It has been my experience that inexperienced listeners tend to find sound-based works more accessible when introduced in a convincing manner within audiovisual contexts regardless of what they are. We are indeed living in the era of the image culture. This is in no way a criticism of audio works. It simply recognizes the fact that masses of people, when exposed to sound-based material in films, documentaries, even advertisements, seem to digest it without any difficulty in general. Similarly, I have discovered that when presenting sound-based music in video, theater, performance art, dance, and installation contexts, the number of viewers is normally greater than what I would reach within music, with the possible exceptions of radio broadcasts and CD recordings. In other words, those who might find the staid atmosphere of the "tape concert" challenging will tend to have much less difficulty if their eyes are engaged. Furthermore, successful collaborative works or works by intermedia artists often create situations whereby the sound "lifts" the image or vice versa. Therefore, video works or today's new media audiovisual opportunities involving sound-based music represent ideal media for supporting accessibility and important environments for sound organization. For those interested in mappings, the medium of visual music, where the image and the sound are interrelated, has provided an ideal opportunity for innovation as well as a means to offer viewers things to hold on to.[95] It should be mentioned that again, here, the fact that sound-based music is being presented in an interdisciplinary context says nothing about how a work sounds. It is yet another category.

There has also been a great deal of work undertaken in recent years concerning movement tracking (mainly of dance) using sensors for audio, and sometimes, lighting application. The literature, again focusing primarily on development work, is vast. One project has attempted to interpret emotional and expressional information as well as pure movement data (see, e.g., Camurri, Trocca, and Volpe 2002). Movement-conducted performance of sound-based music is a much awaited discipline. It can and will have those rough edges alluded to above; many experiments thus far have demonstrated great promise.

Another area that is highly relevant to this book, in particular the following subsection of this chapter, is that of interactive sound installations, which is something that possesses a live element in cases where the spectator is also performer. Frank Popper makes an important distinction between participation and interactivity. Participation represents "an involvement on both the contemplative (intellectual) and the behavioural level," a new ritual ceremony, while interactivity "refers to a still more comprehensive involvement" with "important social implications" given the fact that the participant is raised to the level of co-composer and performer (Popper 1993, 8). Garth Paine is very supportive of Popper's point of view as he sees a clear difference between reactive sound installations, that is, installations that literally react to a trigger command and digital interactive installations where the installation's program develops according to the participant or participants' behavior, learning and reacting to the information generated and received, that is, involving intelligence (Paine 2002, 304). Within the category, new means of presentation, Paine represents one of a group of artists highly involved with technology who prefer that the technology be hidden so that one is engaging mainly with the installation or the performers and not with the technological equipment (Paine 2003). Agostino di Scipio describes this notion of moving from responsive to interactive behavior as a development from "interactive composing" (as in the pioneering work of Joel Chadabe and other composers in the 1970s) to "composing interactions" (di Scipio 2003, 270). We will return to sound installations below as part of the sound art discussion. The fact that these installations tend to be placed anywhere other than inside concert halls is something to keep in mind.

This subsection has focused on three new means of presentation. What holds all of the live areas together is the fact that they are slowly but surely offering the same opportunities for "chemistry" as Trevor Wishart likes to call it that traditionally have occurred as part of studio-based work. It is indeed the highly skilled improviser or new music technology performer who can mould with the same finesse as the studio artist. This being the case, another form of convergence is taking place.[96] This subsection has rightly made no comments concerning *E* and *U* influences, as the act of performance is not the distinguishing factor although how the performance is presented might be. More important, the implication of Wishart's chemistry being applied in these contexts raises the question to what extent this subsection really needs to be kept separate from the first six. The performance dimension is important, but the act of performance itself is not necessarily the distinguishing factor. The sound of studio and performance works is converging as our processors become more sophisticated and performance opportunities continue to grow. This is not necessarily a bad thing.

Our next stop in this section investigates a final example of convergence. I would like to demonstrate that sound art is intimately associated with what is known as sonic art and that sonic art is related to everything we've discussed in this section thus far under our chosen term, sound-based music.

(9)   Sound Art → Sonic Art: Convergence (3)

"Only recently have individuals begun to describe themselves as sound and sound installation artists, audio and radio artists. Only recently have they been self-identified with projects such as the radicalisation of the sound/image relationships, or of acoustics in architectural, environmental, or virtual space." These are the words of Douglas Kahn (Kahn and Whitehead 1992, 1). Add sound designer to the list and one sees a major step in terms of the strong relationship between everything described thus far in this chapter and music's being discarded as the art form of sound-based music's practitioners. In fact it is rather amazing when one takes the time and discovers how many innovative musicians and sound artists were trained in the fine arts, Brian Eno being an important example.[97] Having made my statement about "is it music?" in the preface, I will not return to it here. The point that Kahn makes is important nonetheless, as it implies that sound has become the driving force for certain practitioners who have created these designations to represent this stance professionally.

We discovered in the introduction that sound art is a subset of sonic art. Both use sound as a point of departure. Sound art tends to be heard in nonconcert situations, whether in art galleries, public art exhibitions, through radiophonic broadcast,[98] or on the Internet. Sonic art can be heard in the concert situation as well. That said, I have seen work, which was originally designed as sound art installations, having been transformed or adapted for the concert situation, and so I prefer not to make the distinction so black and white.

Sound art   It should come as no surprise that, given fine art's greater public acceptance than contemporary music's in general, sound art is more publicly available as well. During the period in which this book was written, Bruce Naumann created a sound installation for the Tate Modern in London. It consisted of the simultaneous presentation of twenty-two single human voices, each one heard on an individual loud-speaker in the huge entrance to the Tate Modern. I can remember only a handful of contemporary composers' works drawing nearly as much attention as this one. Although it was in a museum, there was virtually nothing to look at. Does this make Naumann's work that much better or more important than any other major contemporary sonic art work? He is not on the U side of the fence, so that argument cannot be used. Granted, a Jean-Michel Jarre *son et lumière* city work gets headline exposure as well, but that accompanies the huge investment and spectacle status the work receives. This was, instead, just a sound installation at a museum entrance.

Is its interest and popularity a result of the fact that the primarily non-time-based fine arts are lending support to one of its time-based relations, the sound installation? Or is there something more to it? I believe the truth can be found in some combination of the two. Sound artists are most often interested in the context of their work; many are specialists in site-specific settings, not only aware of the community (or communities) that will receive their work, but also taking them into account. If a work is truly taking context on board, by definition the viewer is provided with something to hold on to, namely the work's successful or unsuccessful relationship with that space. This way of reacting to sound art is equally valid in non-site-specific situations. Context or some other inspiration is on offer and is normally communicated to those present. In short, dramaturgy is virtually a *sine qua non* of this art form. This in itself distinguishes sound art from its more overtly music-based cousins that often demonstrate a fairly lax attitude toward dramaturgy.

But to what extent can these two be separated? Within a single book, two slightly different opinions have been offered. Barbara Barthelmes eloquently shares her personal confusion concerning the relationship between sound art and its relatives (Barthelmes 1999) by leaving open whether *Klangkunst* is a category or genre or whether it should simply be added as a subgenre to something already existent based on the history, characteristics, and style of any given work. Ulrich Müller, on the other hand, is adamant that *Klangkunst* should not be classified as a form of music. In presenting his argument, he uses as an example that of the performance artist clarifying that he or she is not making theater while being fully aware that theater has informed a great deal of any performance art presentation (Müller 1999). He is inferring therefore that sound art is beyond music, its own art form, yet he diplomatically concludes that the borders are simply fuzzy.[99] And as stated in the introduction, there are those who do not believe that sound art qualifies as music as if it were a lesser art form, and there are those who do not believe that sound art qualifies as music because of the contexts of its presentation, its ritual function as it were. Similarly, a good deal of (although fortunately by no means all) publications concerning sound art is coming from arts publishers, the high quality series from Kehrer Verlag in Germany being a well-know example. However, even this series is including the work of trained musicians making sound art and the work of musical writers to underline the hybrid nature of the work involved.

Even at a smaller scale within sound art there are problems. Jacques Rémus argues, in a recently published article, "La sculpture sonore, pratique artistique en recherche de definition" (Rémus 2004), that finding a useful definition for sound sculpture poses problems. In fact he finds it easier to suggest what it is not, for example, a sculpture in which music based on the tradition of notes is diffused. Obviously this has something to do with the fact that a sound sculpture might not involve sculpture at all or that there is a tension here between fine art, music, and even performing arts (ibid., 71). His list of potential terms is similar to our search in the introduction of this book. Sound sculptures have been made for decades and yet the term remains vague.

At this point, I could simply rally around the cry that our terminology is rather useless; but I believe that Müller has got it right by accepting the notion of unclear borders. What is perhaps more of interest is the attitude of the artist in question and, one hopes, the resultant artwork.

Sonic artists, other than those who prefer the name electroacoustic musicians, tend not to be focused on concert presentation as a key mode of disseminating work. Still, those sonic artists who do make *musique sur support* are often just as happy to have their works performed at specific sites, in alternative spaces, or simply at people's homes. Having said that, some sonic artists, like this author, will not distribute stereo reductions of multichannel pieces. The governing logic is that a stereo reduction is a document of a piece, not the piece itself, and the person who is listening to the document is not listening to the piece. In short, there are different agendas at work and the classification can be slightly awkward here. What is clear is that the concert hall is not sound-based music's sole performance space; fine arts venues represent another, perhaps more welcoming home for this medium. My personal view is that our relationship with the performance venue is due to be emancipated in a manner similar to the sound being emancipated within music. Specialist or purpose-built venues have been appearing more frequently in recent years such as those at IRCAM and the Sonic Arts Research Centre in Belfast. This offers the artist a complete choice of technology and is seen by many as an ideal venue. However, a few concert-focused composers are giving this issue some thought and looking for further options. For example, Simon Emmerson has shared his dreams of a more holistic "Sound House," a multipurpose arts venue for sonic art and the like (Emmerson 2001b).[100] He supports this notion with remarks he made three years earlier (Emmerson 1998b) in an article entitled "Acoustic/Electroacoustic: The Relationship with Instruments," in which he suggests the need for new opportunities and directions for "post-acousmatic" music. His remarks include the investigation of "a mature relationship of sound art to visual art" in which there is an "[e]vocation of a sense of being and place" which is related to visual experience (ibid., 135)—that is, something to hold on to. New, hybrid forms of art making, such as musical theater using new digital means, offer one pathway, but clearly what Emmerson is seeking is a step away from the world of reduced listening and toward the more contextual, community-orientated vision that sound art represents. Whether an audio-only, multimedia, or interdisciplinary artwork is involved, context and content ideally should be linked.

Installations and site-specific works   Site-specific pieces in local areas normally attract the local population to try out and experience a work, people who would not go out of their way to see a similar work in a concert or perhaps even gallery or museum environment. Some are "won over" if a work communicates to them particularly well and they subsequently occasionally seek out means to appreciate similar works. This is a key strength of successful public art. It caters to the community interested in public art as well as the community interested in the specific site. Proposals to create public artwork often come from nonprofessional artists. What better way to increase access is there than to take the steps from avoidance to appreciation to creativity?

Installation artist and musician Robin Minard's story is worth relating in this context. He was brought up in an urban environment and became disenchanted with the prevalence of noise pollution. It is perhaps not surprising that he is Canadian born, coming from the home of the acoustic ecology movement. However, he is not in favor of industry's means of attacking this noise, that is, by providing a "functional" sound mask, muzak or the like (Minard 1991, 23). Instead, his interest has become a search for the "integration of new sounds and new musical forms in public spaces," something he has called "environmental music" (ibid.). Sound spatialization is crucial in his case as his installations simulate nature in many ways; in nature, sounds are all around us, of course.

Interactive works in this context are perhaps the greatest catalysts of increasing access. We have already discovered the perceived distinction between pre-recorded music and music in which there is some form of live presentation. Within the latter area, interactivity is playing an ever-increasing role. Similarly, in the installation world, interactivity is becoming increasingly common. When people experience that they are in fact "conducting" an installation and are fairly clear about what their movements represent in sound (and image), they feel empowered within the installation, another example where wysiwyg is a reality when there is no perceivable latency.

Xavier Berenguer has suggested some guiding principles for such inter-active systems: " 'richness,' that is to say abundant information elements and paths, . . . the 'ease' of use . . . '[c]onsistency' . . . [and t]he user must be able to guess meaning and purpose from any element . . . its 'self-evidence.' " The fact that he also includes the word "predictability" comes as no surprise (cited in Waters 2000a). This formula, according to Simon Waters assists in the development of "aesthetically significant" interactivity (ibid.). This is a form of language rarely used with tradi-tional electroacoustic music. I continue to wonder, after years of working in the discipline, why this is the case. Here appreciation and the audio-visual experience meet in terms of the formulation of ideas.

Radiophonic art and other areas related to sound art   Sound art is said to have its own history and, in fact, some of its influences, including musical ones, predate the term. Radiophonic art making certainly belongs to this list as does a good deal of text-sound poetry. Although there was some experimentation before the Second World War, the latter half of the century provided an extraordinary opportunity for the radio play to evolve in many different ways. Musique concrète was one of them, so-called audio art another, and so on. Although the fidelity of the listening experience is based on the equipment present as well as the lis-tening space (a car radio, a small transistor radio, an excellent hi-fi system in the home, etc.), this in no way stopped artists open to this medium from experimentation.

Along with Schaeffer, a hero of this history is Klaus Schöning of the WDR broadcasters in Cologne, whose Hörspiel Studio was one of the great laboratories in the history of sound-based art making. His guest list, that is, list of commissioned artists, is an exceptional roster of sound experimentalists. His audience, although it was not to be compared with the regional pop stations or even the traditional soap opera–like radio plays, was still quite substantial, in particular when compared to broad-casts of more traditional contemporary music. Many of his commis-sioned works, regardless of the presence of a given language, have been rebroadcast around the globe, although possibly reaching more modest audiences than that of the regular German listeners. The range of the works put out by the Hörspiel Studio is substantial and, in consequence, in some cases experimentation has ventured beyond the accessible. Still, many of Schöning's artists have fully appreciated the fact that they were working with a potential audience with little experience in her or his area. This has led to a huge bouquet of experimental works for radio, often taken off the air and onto the Internet in many countries these days. A revival of interesting radiophonic work with things to hold on to for a public broader than the "in crowd" is long overdue and, with its ever faster speeds, the Internet will clearly be its future home.

Internet music   We have already discovered that some communities are virtual ones and that sound art and many other forms of music are developing quickly on the Internet. Although there are many Internet sites for music for individual users, reflecting what many fear is the individualization implicit within digital culture, what shall be introduced here is collective Internet performance. Clearly either can involve sound organization.

Sean Cubitt is rather outspoken about global culture and sees the Internet as a means of protecting cultural diversity as small communities become better able to share specific interests (Cubitt 1998). New communities include those involving sound organization, which, when formed, discover and develop new "network sound aesthetic[s]" (Cubitt 1997, 45). He also has suggested that Internet music is to the arts what Internet chat lines are to the communities in question. People seem to lose certain inhibitions when they communicate virtually (think of the international popularity of the CB radio on roads a few decades ago). This supports my view that tomorrow's folk music will take place at least partly online. This view is taken on by many others who see the computer as a means of democratizing music now that things have become relatively affordable for a reasonably large percentage of people around the globe.

Alvaro Barbosa has classified network systems for music creation into a 2 × 2 grid—its y-axis (synchronicity) focusing on synchronous and asynchronous interaction and its x-axis (location) ranging from colocated[101] to remote. He coins the term "shared sonic environments" to describe the quadrant where synchronous interaction is combined with remote location. He describes this as: "used in organised events for groups of multiple remote performers/users, displaced in space, improvising and interacting synchronously with a set of musical instruments (or virtual musical instruments). In this case sonic interdependency is affected by network latency. Telepresence (remote unilateral participation) is a particular case of this set of applications" (Barbosa 2003, 57–58). Its orientation is toward "[t]he creation of community-oriented shared virtual environments, where users dynamically join and leave, supporting collaborative ongoing sonic performance based on the simple manipulation of sound objects in a soundscape or on the creation of musical structures. This approach goes beyond the enhancements of existing acoustic communication paradigms, focusing on diverse Internet collaboration" (ibid., 58). He concludes: "Just as similar paradigms oriented towards visual or textual communication (Multi User Dungeons [MUDs], Object Oriented MUDs [MOOs], Internet Relay Chats [IRC], Active Worlds, etc.) tend to lead to new mechanisms of interaction not usually seen in 'real life,' a similar result can be expected in paradigms oriented towards music or sonic art, suggesting the sonic outcome of such systems could express interesting new artistic results" (ibid.).

Gil Weinberg recently (2005; see also 2002) published a useful survey article entitled "Interconnected Musical Networks: Towards a Theoretical Framework." His approach is multidimensional. Historically, he divides networked music into four periods: analog electronics, the PC, the Internet, and alternative controllers. Internet music is subdivided into what he calls the server approach (interaction by a single user with a server), the bridge approach (multiuser domain), the shaper approach (multiuser as well, but in this case the computer generates materials that are shaped collaboratively by the online users, who often use algorithms), and the construction kit approach (with a higher-level multiuser domain where participants can contribute their own music or structures to any given session). Alternative controllers are divided simply into small- and large-scale local systems. He goes on to make a separation between process- and structure-centered musical networks in which the former seems to allow for much more user input and flexibility, and is less goal oriented than the more "traditional" structure-centered ones that lead toward composition and/or performance. He understandably looks into the social organization of musical networks, distinguishing between centralized and decentralized networks, adding a second dimension of equality/inequality among users. For example, inequality in a centralized system is deemed a monarchic approach, whereas equality is a more democratic one; in decentralized systems the range is between anarchy and decentralized organizations. Finally he offers a selection of potential architectures or topologies to complete this theoretical survey. Examples are given throughout leading to a publication that represents in terms of networked systems that which Simon Emmerson's language grid represents to electroacoustic material and structure approaches. However, musical content is not dependent on this classification, only system structure and attitude.

These are very useful descriptions, but the theory available today does not go much further than that which has been described. Cubitt offers a cultural theory approach; Barbosa and Weinberg offer useful means of categorization. Most discussions, and the number is growing rapidly,[102] review technological developments or individual systems designed for individual or collective use (see, e.g., Greshem-Lancaster 1998 on the history and aesthetics of the Hub, Duckworth 1999 on the *Cathedral* project, and Jordà 1999 on the *F@ust 3.0* project [an example of Weinberg's construction kit approach]).

What is noteworthy in this brief introduction to Internet music is that any type of music including sound-based varieties can be part of an Internet music system. Internet music can be seen to form part of the world of sound art, but it can equally relate to classical music, jazz, or any improvised music, and so on. Interfaces vary greatly as do the approaches and sound material. Therefore, this category entry is a bit similar to formalized types of sound-based music as formalization can apply to a host of vocal-instrumental types of music as well. What I find particularly exciting about these still fresh developments is that they may lead to the formation of all sorts of new communities and artistic practices. Visual art and sound may converge in some systems, sound-based music and science in others. New hybrids and new genres will be formed, supporting the notion of convergence. The word "hybrid" is very important here. The concept of hybrid forms an important foundation of Simon Waters' writing; therefore, he will lead the final discussion in this subsection of chapter 2.

Hybrids   A number of times in this chapter we have discovered areas of convergence. There is one that has not yet been presented that forms the focus of a good deal of recent writing by Simon Waters, namely his concept of "hybridization," one of his two key terms in a paper published online (Waters 2000a), "hybrid thought," and "digital aesthetic." Beginning with the latter, Waters writes that he is interested in "current identifiable aesthetic tendencies [which] can be understood as responses to digital technologies." Unlike some writers cited in this book, he believes "that responses to digital technology indicate a development and continuation of existing aesthetic concerns." And yet he admits that there is also a great deal of innovation taking place owing to our digital culture in terms of content, approach, and even art form. For example, Waters notes that "there's [a] debate—that the discrete sensory organs we have for sight, sound, and so on are in some way indicative of essentially separate modes of engagement with sensory input in those areas—whereas our experience strongly suggests that we function as synthesisers of these multiple inputs" (Waters 2003). This synthesis is reflected in recently developed interfaces which "make use of identical concepts—frame, freeze, copy, paste, loop—as controlling strategies, and this is already resulting in a commonality of language between practitioners who were previously unaware of conceptual connections between their fields of activity" (Waters 2000b, 60). Alain Thibault agrees with him by suggesting that a good deal of sound-based music has a much closer relationship with the media arts than with other forms of music (Thibault 2002, 54). As Waters' interest is indeed innovation in the arts, he writes that his concern is "placing the 'margins' at the centre" (Waters 2000b, 60) of his investigation. He is also pleased about the relatively universal availability of relevant technologies alongside the fact that one need not be either "professional" or highly skilled to become involved with many of these technologies. He suggests: "This is a threat to those power élites who have relied on such characteristics [skill, intelligence, 'professionalism'] to justify their privileged status. It has resulted in rapid shifts of 'aesthetic' criteria, as specialists attempt to keep distance between their situation identified by many authors (for example, Born 1995), in which the criteria of aesthetic success have become synonymous with those of technical innovation" (ibid., 67). Georgina

Born has been known to call this attitude "science envy" (Born 1995, 166).

Waters sees other borders breaking down, as well. As processing speeds become faster, the split between formalist and spectralist is no longer needed in his view. More important, perhaps, is Waters' discovery that the hierarchical system known to most *E* and some *U* music is evolving more toward a collaborative devising model (although Waters does not use that specific term) involving mutual ownership of digital sound-based music (Waters 2003). He also joins Pressing and many others in the call for the reintroduction of human presence in art making.

Waters is very much against the threatened continued individualization often associated with digital technologies. He abhors the notion of "'walkpeople' isolated in their personal portable acoustic space, [who] are indicative of a practice which has become primarily non-participative, desocialized, and exists predominantly to placate its audience, rather than to excite, challenge or stimulate them" (Waters 2000b, 60). Similarly, he is wary of a notion concerning institutions that is "too easily overlooked. Institutions can protect individuals, on a temporary basis, from the pressures to conform which come from everyday socializing and conditioning, and from the demands of the marketplace. In this respect they can be important islands of refusal, resistance and critical 'noise'" (Waters 2003).

Instead, Waters believes that hybridization is taking place. This is revealed by the fact that intradisciplinary and interdisciplinary shifts toward "collaborative and collective working practices are becoming more prevalent." Furthermore, "informal networks" are evolving which are synonymous with the forming of new communities, which lead to more "'ensemble' working practices" including new forms of (networked) connectivity (Waters 2000a). "It may be that, as in the sciences, some of these 'new' or hybrid activities, unnamed as yet, will evolve into new disciplines" (Waters 1994b, 26).

He believes that three main categories of interdisciplinarity can be identified: "One in which practitioners within an existing field batter at its boundaries, trying to extend the nature of the practice. Another [is one] in which two or more fields of activity pool certain concepts and strategies in the hope of allowing cross-disciplinary work. The third is a radical tendency which rejects as unhelpful much previous practice, and in which artists (or students) work with problems and strategies which might be realized in any way, with any means at their disposal, irrespective of medium or idiom. In practice these three approaches frequently coexist" (ibid., 48). The goal is to find new means of authorship that will lead to increased empowerment of any creative artist (ibid., 26). The types of experimentation listed above can lead toward the discovery of new hybrids.

In this culture of convergence that exists within the realms of the art of organized sound, some new types of fusion are also evolving. Simon Waters explains (see, e.g., Waters 2000b, 56–57) that we are living in an age of hybridization, where combinations are discovered, things are recontextualized, and radical activity is less common. Using traditional tools to seek coherence may not be ideal in this type of environment.

So Waters has offered us yet another form of convergence, one that potentially does link art and life, for as he has suggested, his culture is a sampling culture in which sounds are recontextualized. To recontexualize an original (known) context is a *sine qua non* for the listener. His culture is also as much an audio culture as an audiovisual culture, one that has been more accessible to the world at large for several decades now.

Before moving on to the conclusion of this section, the reason for this subsection's peculiar title, sound art → sonic art, needs to be revisited. Sound art seems not only to be a subset of sonic art; its horizon is as wide as the one related to sonic art, although sound art more often takes the context of performance into account. Perhaps our means of classification should focus on these differences of attitude rather than use two separate terms that, in my view, demonstrate a significant overlap.

We now have reached the point where we can leave this wide-ranging section on families of approaches to and works of organized sound. Yet, how many families and approaches have we been able to clearly delineate? Far fewer have been identified than categories. There is no easy formula to capture the wealth of today's sound-based music within a single clear-cut system. The following paragraph summarizes different ways of approaching coherence in terms of the relevant body of artworks.

Co-hear-ence summary   One main thread above has been (i) the axis between reduced and heightened listening. This is a most useful axis, with the caveat that there is a good deal of gray in between so that many artists involved with sound like to jump around this axis within a single work. It is perhaps this axis more than any other that identifies approaches in this field. Then there is the decades-old question concerning (ii) the presence of a pulse. Clearly, there was a great deal of avoidance of any sense of beat in much electroacoustic E music throughout the decades. This is diminishing in time as it has in much instrumental contemporary music. As in so many such situations, the understanding of the axis ranging from an audible beat to beatlessness is important as emancipation occurs when the known and the unknown are both appreciated, where synthesis takes over from thesis and antithesis. Even in the world of club culture the beat is strong on the dance floor but much less so in chill-out rooms. This only signifies how far that musical world has evolved in terms of this particular axis. A third area of interest has been the (iii) formalist/spectralist divide, one that is becoming fuzzier with time and, more importantly, less audible. However, the (iv) abstract versus dramaturgy-based distinction—as in contemporary music and other art forms—is alive and well and an important one in terms of any coherence investigation. Although there are abstract forms of discourse that are highly accessible, works dealing with intention and involvement with context are simply different. In contrast, as processing speed increases, the divide between (v) studio-based composition and live performance has diminished enormously. Laptop composers have just as much ability to mold sounds as anyone working in isolation. To what extent do any of these aid in term of classification? Although categories seem to have reigned supreme over these pages, we have several dimensions now through which we can discover clusters of works. They might not have a genre designation, but the works can be characterized by using criteria ranging from (vi) Emmerson's language grid, (vii) the "things to hold on to," (viii) salient sound characteristics, and even (ix) the type of artwork (e.g., installation, audiovisual new media work, improvised laptop performance), and so on.

So where does this leave us? I recently visited and participated in the NewMix Festival at the Palais de Tokyo in Paris (December 2004). This two-day mini-marathon festival was put together to celebrate the tenth anniversary of the Electronic Music Foundation. Each night's performance lasted well over five hours. Audience members could come and go whenever they pleased. What made this event so rewarding was its eclecticism. No two pieces in a row were similar. Many were audiovisual, some involved traditional instruments, some newly devised instruments, some were on a fixed medium; the majority consisted of live electronic or mixed works. The sound ranged from timbral tonality to text-sound poetry. There were real-time VJs and laptop performers. There was sound sculpture and there was singing. Some pieces had four beats to the measure, others had no audible pulse. What held the event together was that all pieces were sound-based to a greater or lesser extent; they were sonic artworks or sonic art-influenced works. Although inevitably the works' quality varied—and how could it not?—interest was sustained throughout given the great wealth of sound-based music and its diversity. This raises the issue of whether these works are currently categorized ideally to reach their optimal audience. This question will form part of the subject of the concluding section of this chapter.

It must be admitted that, in today's society, trying to create a reasonable amount of cohesion in terms of sound-based works was always going to be a challenge. We are nowhere near where we should be, but again, this early twenty-first-century landscape had to be extremely diverse, did it not? There is currently no single obvious means to improve our genre classification; however, the desire to create co-hear-ence among the repertoire and to start doing so with the theories has succeeded to a reasonable extent in this chapter. Improving this genre classification is work for the future; investigating how the theories might be brought into some type of order is the subject of the final chapter.

Under the nine broad subheads introduced above, how many have a substantial amount of theory (be it cultural, musical, or otherwise) supporting them? In preparing this book, one of the most painful experiences was to discover that which I had always feared, namely that the amount of foundational and even advanced theory supporting these various genres, axes, means of presentation, and so on is indeed quite low, especially given how much innovation, development, and content exist. Of that theory, a huge bias is due to the efforts of a unique individual, Pierre Schaeffer, who was, similar to other modernist pioneers, aware that creating a musical revolution without a supporting theory would have been an error. He provided us with a wealth of theory, too little of which has been developed (Smalley being the worthy exception) or even *mise en question*, for example, made more empirical and thus more applicable than it is. Theories concerning the soundscape, appropriation, and new sounds are developing apace. It comes as no surprise that the prize for most eagerly awaited theory goes to the formalists, who more than the spectralists have an opportunity to evolve their current how-to theories.

Today much sound-based work remains not terribly well understood. Without a greater wealth of supporting theory the exciting forms of convergence introduced above will not be properly appreciated for their potential impact and social relevance. As long as this convergence is not understood and embraced, the less than ideal situation in terms of appreciation will continue.

(B)   A Return to the Classification Debate: In Search of a Paradigm

It is now clear that one consequence of today's awkward state of terminology is that classifying a good deal of work into neat genres is quite problematic. For example, it would be too simple, not to mention wrong, to suggest that electronica is *U* and electroacoustic is *E*, that sound art is for artists and sonic art for musicians. Some may believe this, but there is simply too much work that goes across several boundaries and, equally, there is work that is made in total ignorance of traditional boundaries. This may delay the creation of more universally used terminology and genre names, or, alternatively, it could be helpful once acknowledged. It all supports my belief in the need for a new paradigm for sound-based artwork in the sense of a "supergenre" as proposed in the preface.

Many writers have articulated their views concerning whether sound-based music is a separate entity or simply an evolution from existing forms of music and other arts that need to be treated as such. Jean-Claude Risset has been apprehensive about disconnecting electroacoustic music from music (Risset 1996, 82). He was, of course, reacting to the views of many of his colleagues who were calling for greater autonomy. Supporting Risset's view, Rosemary Mountain believes that we must look forward in sound-based music while embracing the past, making boundaries between separately categorized forms of music more malleable (Mountain 2001, 99). A few years later she expressed her concern about how this music has been (mis-)marketed, suggesting that one should be more interested in listeners' aesthetic preferences and serving them regardless of whether music is electroacoustic or not, popular or not (Mountain 2004). I sympathize strongly with these ideas of malleability and preferences that cross genres, but I believe that this in itself cannot aid the cause for greater recognition of the art of sound organization in general or its artistic placement in particular.

For example, and returning to one of the issues raised in section (A) above, how have writers felt about the separation of *E* and *U* in terms of our musical corpus? Although open to change, Joel Chadabe and Simon Emmerson believe that merger has not yet taken place (Chadabe 2000, 9; Emmerson 2000b, 1). Both imply that they will converge and take on new forms in the future. What is needed, according to them, are new musical languages and an associated terminology. Chadabe (2004) does suggest that electronic music, as he calls it, has evolved from being elitist to being more or less ubiquitous, both in terms of the presence of electroacoustic sound virtually anywhere you go and of the availability of electroacoustic tools.

But there exist other views. In a recently published book, *Audio Culture: Readings in Modern Music*, editors Christoph Cox and Daniel Warner write in their introduction: "Over the past half-century, a new audio culture has emerged, a culture of musicians, composers, sound artists, scholars, and listeners attentive to sonic substance, the act of listening, and the creative possibilities of sound recording, playback, and transmission. The culture of the ear has become particularly prominent in the last decade" (Cox and Warner 2004, xiv). They continue: "It will have been noticed that what we are calling 'contemporary music' or 'modern music' has a peculiar character. Though it cuts across classical music, jazz, rock, reggae, and dance music, it is resolutely avant-gardist in character and all but ignores the more mainstream inhabitations of these genres" (ibid., xvi). They exemplify this much later in the book in their discussion of minimalism: "[T]hough composed for marimbas and bongos instead of samplers and sequencers, the kind of layered, modular repetition later fostered by Reich and Glass is the stuff of which Techno is made" (ibid., 287–288). It is this type of diachronic discovery of relationships that cross or ignore the *E/U* border that is taking place too infrequently.

I have a great deal of affinity for Cox and Warner's point of view. When Martijn Voorvelt was writing his dissertation on experimental popular music, introducing me to works that I had never heard, I wanted to hold a blindfold test for learned members of the public using many of his chosen artists to see whether they were perceived to belong to either the *E* or *U* musical world, both, or neither. I am certain that the results would not clearly reflect existent appreciation patterns. Similarly, there are many sonic artworks that would probably be unknown to many a listener of experimental popular music that might be considered to "belong" to their repertoire or at least to be found of interest. These works straddle or ignore a boundary that was determined by the musicians' intention or background or, more likely, today's marketing structures in general. Clearly, there are fusion works that consciously belong to both domains. It is the work that leans one way or the other or is hard to place that is of interest here. The question is whether the common element of the sound ties these diverse works together in a more distinct manner than the gap that separates a good deal of, but by no means all, works of instrumental art and popular music. My contention is that it does. In fact Cox and Warner's view sits well with Mountain's remarks.

In this chapter's conclusion I would like to focus on the proposal of sound as a common denominator while attempting to bring together two seemingly opposing views, the hybrids concept introduced above by way of its spokesperson, Simon Waters, and the notion of the electroacoustic paradigm, a term coined by François Delalande in his book, *Le son des musiques: Entre technologie et esthétique* (Delalande 2001b, chapter 2). Delalande believes that we have experienced three historical musical paradigms: oral tradition, written (meaning by way of a score), and electroacoustic (music recorded on a fixed medium). He even suggests that the historical importance of the invention of the studio to music is comparable to that of the ability to write down a score (Delalande 2002). Delalande offers a separate musical paradigm, a more general one called "technological music," which includes mixed music, interactive music, and music with live electronics, but he never seems to be able to define this to any level of detail. This is a shame, but music technology, similar to studio-based fixed-medium works, focuses on technology over material. I would suggest that material as well as the use of material might be a better binding source.

I sympathize strongly with the approach launched by Delalande, but believe that history has superseded his separation of music recorded on a fixed medium, as has been illustrated above. Delalande has spent most of his career documenting work at the GRM and extending the musicological foundations for work made there and work associated with GRM principles. It comes as little surprise that throughout his rather large oeuvre of publications, little attention has been given to non-GRM sound-based work, such as the creative projects of sound artists. It is here where his well-meaning concept loses strength. Furthermore, again given the GRM's roots in the acousmatic, reduced listening approach, Delalande has never pursued multimedia work to the best of my knowledge, unlike his former colleague, Michel Chion. But there is reason to look at Delalande's proposal in a positive light.

One sometimes needs to step back and gain distance from one's main area of concentration to reach a new perspective. Normally when this takes place, a bit of one's rhetoric is softened. An example of this within contemporary music is the late Peter Schat's means of dealing with atonality, something that entered his life as a student. He established a need to combine atonal methods with the notion that his music needed some sort of center. He introduced the term *tonicality* as a result. Here Schat reaches a synthesis from the thesis (tonic-centered music) and antithesis (tonic centerless atonal music). If François Delalande had done the same during the period in which he coined these paradigmatic designators, he might have been able to move beyond the GRM world, one that, according to Alain Thibault, is aging, becoming more classical in a sense. He compares the electroacoustic music on a fixed medium being made by known institutions to jazz, which he believes has lost its dynamic and relevancy to an extent (Thibault 2002, 54). Thibault's alternative is for electroacoustic music to see itself as part of the wider scheme of media arts. "This medium does not escape from cross-overs with other disciplines, leading toward the birth of transdisciplinary and multidisciplinary works integrating music, video, digital animation, robotics, performance, etc." (ibid.). He concludes that electroacoustic musicians' hesitation to evolve is holding them back in terms of innovation and their becoming more accessible. His solution: "A new, more open term should be discovered, better expressing the new realities embracing the fact that the field's principle is one of perpetual evolution linked to new technological developments" (ibid.). Although he does not offer this term, Thibault is clearly a supporter of Waters' notion of hybridization.

Taking these two concepts and adding the fact that in this book a choice has been made for sound-based music above electroacoustic music or sonic art as its key term, it is my firm belief that a *sound-based music paradigm* could very well exist regardless of whether a work is audio or audiovisual. Again, here the focus would shift from Delalande's studios of sound organization to the breadth of sonic materials and related knowledge concerning artistic aspects of sound organization. If a sound-based music paradigm (or a different term if Thibault or someone else finds one) were to be found, a large amount of work in this chapter and in the "Genres and Categories" section of the EARS site would be able to be rethought, and appropriate terms would slowly but surely become available.

It is here that the questions concerning malleability return. Some sonic art and a reasonable number of electroacoustic music works do seem to have deep roots in what Trevor Wishart called "lattice-based" music. Many of these works might be found to fit only partially into the sound-based music paradigm. These works will fit more easily in Mountain's scheme of aesthetic preference than in one of genre classification. That is perhaps a downside of this effort. The upside is that works based on the art of sound organization, most of which utilize technology as well, would find a home, albeit one housing a wide diversity of approaches reflecting the epoch in which we live.

Thibault has discovered a contradiction linked to the notion of clichés being found in electroacoustic compositions, namely the genre's raison d'être of being dynamic. The world of sonic arts needs a field of study to investigate the validity of a sound-based music paradigm and, in consequence, the best means of classifying, not to mention valorizing this body of artwork, and of finding a solution to Thibault's dynamic versus cliché issue. During this journey, a reappraisal of its terminology would be necessary and similarly a delineation of its subareas needed, for it would be in this careful developmental stage that "holes in the market," that is, underresearched areas, would be discovered and more scholarship undertaken, which would lead toward greater understanding of this artistic field. How this field of studies might look is the subject of the next chapter.

3

Toward a Framework for the Study of Sound-based Artworks

You have sound, the sound has a meaning, and no meaning can exist without a sound to express it. In music, it is the sound element which takes over.
—Claude Lévi-Strauss (2002)

This third chapter offers a potential framework for the study of sound-based artworks. It is influenced by the structure that has been created for the EARS site. It also seeks to describe why this structure has been chosen, how its areas and subareas are interwoven, and which issues might deserve being prioritized in terms of future research.

Of course, creating a framework is a challenging exercise as it is always fascinating to try to design a logical system from several loose yet inter-related strands. Doing this has indeed been rewarding, but there was a purpose in doing so. Given that there is still too much fragmentation in the studies of sound-based music and, furthermore, that most of this work is occurring at higher levels, it is rather tricky to deduce after the fact how the foundation of the field should look and, in consequence, how to facilitate the creation of greater coherence among the existent theory. Yet this is exactly what this chapter aims to achieve.

(A) To Start

Before introducing the key elements of the framework in section (B), a few issues relevant to the framework will be presented. The highest level of the structure of the EARS site will be introduced and one of the six EARS categories will be further discussed, namely the "Disciplines of Study" category, to demonstrate how interdisciplinary this field is. The focus on interdisciplinarity leads to the third subject in this section, namely the view that the best road to greater knowledge concerning works of organized sound is through a holistic approach that relates historical, theoretical, sociocultural, and technological aspects of a given issue instead of treating them in isolation. Today's scholarship is filled with single aspect treatises. This type of concentration has led to important insights; however, it has also led to a paucity of debate concerning, for example, the impact of sound-based music and its related technology on our culture and, in consequence, the contextualization of its repertoire. A holistic, interdisciplinary approach is therefore suggested as a *modus operandi* wherever appropriate.

(1)   A Return to EARS

The ElectroAcoustic Resource Site is very much a product of the new dynamic of our online era. What is introduced in this chapter may very well have been altered to some extent by the time the reader looks for it on the Internet. The logic behind the site, however, is not likely to undergo many radical changes.

Here are the six highest-level category headers and their abbreviations:

Disciplines of Study (DoS)

Genres and Categories of Electroacoustic Music (G&C)

Musicology of Electroacoustic Music (MEM)

Performance, Practice, and Presentation (PPP)

Sound Production and Manipulation (SPM)

Structure, Musical (Str)

MEM is the centerpiece of EARS as it is of this book. In fact, this chapter demonstrates how all other categories contribute to MEM. It is also important to note that EARS was originally constructed and funded with electroacoustic music as its focus. To represent the field delineated in this book the EARS team has added relevant information concerning, for example, acoustic sound art, that is, work that is not electroacoustic but which is sound-based including sound-based sculptures, performances, and installations solely employing acoustic sounding objects.

The complete EARS index at the time of this book's publication can be found in the appendix. The current one is also available online. The remainder of this chapter is based on the index as it has been published in the appendix. What is at least as important as the state of the index is the ever-growing bibliography of resources under most index entries that is intended to serve all readers interested in any subject introduced in this chapter. All EARS bibliographic citations include brief abstracts, relevant index terms, and, where relevant, hyperlinks. Index entries contain lists of all associated citations that have been entered thus far. Clearly, not all citations listed at a low-level entry are repeated at the higher levels, so the more specific the query the better the bibliographic citations will be. Citations are also listed by author and, where relevant, by periodical, and all terms are defined in the site's glossary section.

(2)   Interdisciplinarity: A Brief Survey of Disciplines Relevant to the Study of Sound-based Works

Music has always been interdisciplinary; it has also always been influenced by technology, although at times in the sense of technologies that do not have to be plugged in. Students of instrumental music normally learn the basics of acoustics and of physics to gain awareness relevant to their performance. Music has also often been part of interdisciplinary art forms involving text, acting, and movement. Therefore the statement that sound-based music is an interdiscipline comes as no surprise. What is important here is that the extent of interdisciplinarity is greater than in traditional music. Jörg Stelkens writes in his foreword to the proceedings of the KlangForschung '98 (Sound Research) symposium: "KlangForschung is an interdisciplinary symposium series where interdisciplinarity is treated in a very broad sense. It is not our intention to simply involve interdisciplinary exchange within the ivory tower disciplines, but instead an ambitious attempt to gain recognition, appreciation and understanding of artistic writings, concepts and works. Two way influences between the arts and sciences are by no means excluded" (Stelkens 1999, 7).

As part of this chapter's introduction, it is perhaps useful to be aware of areas that are related to sound-based music studies. The following list, taken from the highest-level items listed under the EARS site's Disciplines of Study, is not exhaustive by any means,[1] but it does indicate the breadth of areas that can prove of relevance to sonic artists and those studying aspects of sonic artworks. It excludes musicology, as it is the central subject of section (B) of this chapter.

- Acoustic communication
- Acoustics
- Audiovisual theory
- Cognitive science
- Complex systems
- Computing
- Critical theory
- Cultural theory
- Cybernetics
- Interactivity
- Interdisciplinary studies
- Linguistics
- Media theory
- Music cognition
- Music education
- Music perception
- Music psychology
- Philosophy
- Probability theory
- Psychoacoustics
- Semiotics
- Signal processing
- Virtual reality

This list excludes some areas that are pertinent to hardware development such as electronics. This is a risky omission as, for example, instrument making is relevant to people studying music. However, despite the fact a reasonable number of artists are DIY (do-it-yourself) instrument makers, most electronics discussions remain scientific and do not address artistic or music-theoretical issues. Therefore the following rule is applied: only discussions on development-based research that discuss theoretical aspects of the subject are included on the EARS site and are seen to be pertinent to this volume.

This restriction aside, the fact is that the interdisciplinary world of sound-based music is quite diverse. Hardly anyone involved with, say, electroacoustic composition is unaware of important notions from cognition and psychoacoustics, not to mention the fundamental knowledge of acoustics that is a *sine qua non*. How these relevant fields intersect and are related to sound organization is worthy of a book on its own.

(3)   Holism—How History, Theory, Cultural Impact, and Technological Development Are Interrelated

I once suggested (Landy 1999) that the musicology of sound-based music, similar to the musicology of any music, has a historical dimension, a cultural dimension, and a systematic dimension, the latter being a potpourri of subject areas, some clearly systematic, others (semiotics and aesthetics, for example) perhaps less so.

Finding a paradigmatic publication in the field tying these aspects together is difficult.[2] This state of affairs is by no means novel. Classically trained musicians, especially conservatory-trained artists, may specialize in interpretation without being offered much contextual study. We should keep in mind, however, that ideally any music student who has been classically trained will not have learned of a given composer without finding out about how his or her music fit into the greater musical developments of the time, how his or her aesthetic was interwoven with the work of predecessors and contemporaries, and how later composers were influenced by that composer's own original contributions to music making. This implies learning about the grammars of the music of the day, how the composer and contemporaries followed them, developed them, and abused them. This also implies that one needs to be aware of art music developments in the composer's country (or region) and its surrounding areas at that time to gain a holistic understanding of the composer.

Perhaps our composer of the previous paragraph did not need to know as much about perception and the application of number as artists do today, not to mention all of those fields that did not yet exist; nevertheless, his or her music in no way existed in a vacuum. Better musical scholarship takes these sister disciplines into account wherever relevant regardless of how focused the main subject of the research may be.

As sound-based music is thus more interdisciplinary than any music in the past, it should be studied and introduced in this manner as well. History books offer well-organized overviews of general tendencies. However, there have been two problems with many of these publications. First, they tend to focus on either art music, sound art for alternative spaces, or popular music; rarely do two or all three appear in one reference. More important, it is most unusual to discover a history combined not only with discussions of technological advancement, which most histories do include, but also with discussions of aesthetics, theoretical developments, analysis, and cultural contextualization. To this end, more rigorous holistic methodologies should be developed.

The cultural dimension of sound-based music has, without question, received much too little attention within our area of studies. The most often cited source that partially covers this area is a very specific case study, namely Georgina Born's "fly on the wall" investigation of IRCAM in the mid-1980s. The book is an anthropology thesis, an in-depth ethnography of the structure, cultural position, and internal dynamic of the European center of new music research directed at the time by Pierre Boulez. Fascinating for its insights regarding IRCAM's vision, its achievements during the period of study and conflicts within the organization and with the outside world, the book is a unique document concerning this significant organization. It does not, however, discuss musical content very much, restricting musical discussion to general placement within the broader scheme of new musics.

So, again, the in-depth investigation of cultural issues related to this institution is praiseworthy, but this has been achieved with marginal discussions of analytical and related contextual issues. Many studies that have been published in the area of cultural studies discussing music technology and/or sound-based music similarly tend to ignore or, at best, superficially discuss these other subjects whether historical or theoretical, in particular avoiding any musical analysis. This is unfortunate, as the highly important subject of the social impact of sonic artworks seems most often to be treated with little regard to essential questions concerning content and aesthetics although they would seem to be so clearly interrelated.

Let's briefly return to the example of the Bourges Festival. Their annual colloquium has existed for years. Papers covering a broad range of topics have been published. Yet who at this colloquium has been investigating questions that engage with the appreciation of today's sound-based music? Studying particular forms of sound-based works whether at Bourges or elsewhere with no or little regard for their relative lack of acceptance seems foolhardy. They have only published the occasional remark on this subject. The investigation of types of sound-based works other than those normally associated with festival concerts— electroacoustic art music—seems also to be uncommon. Such contributions would open up the colloquium to include a more holistic approach to sound-based music and might even influence the festival's (and other similar festivals') coordinators in terms of their curatorial approach.

(B)   The Proposed Framework

The framework that appears below is by no means the first attempt to devise some sort of taxonomy for sound-based music studies. For example, in 1996 Stephen Travis Pope published a short and useful overview entitled "The Taxonomy of Computer Music."[3] Pope has used the term *computer music* as the focus of his taxonomy; therefore, a much wider area is being treated than the one we are discussing here. The themes of the annual International Computer Music Conference parallel the wide-ranging fields Pope presented.

Pope's main sections are: (1) music theory, composition, and performance; (2) music acoustics, psychoacoustics, perception, and cognition; (3) musical signal and event representation and notation; (4) digital control and sound signal synthesis and processing; (5) hardware support for computer music; (6) computers in music education and computer music education; and (7) computer music literature and sources.

Within the first section, Pope separates the "composition of electroacoustic music" from "algorithmic and computer-aided composition," therefore implying that a given composition can obviously fall under two categories, although the choice was clearly one supporting a spectralist/

formalist divide. It must be emphasized that we are not particularly interested in computer-generated algorithmic composition scores for traditional instruments as far as this book is concerned. The umbrella term "computer music" covers a good deal of music outside of our scope just as sound-based music covers music that is made without computers. Pope's taxonomy is therefore recommended for those who place any digital application as the focus of their work. In our case, delineating the ideas and practices associated with sound-based music is our goal, reflecting a plea from Michael Vaughan in which he is critical of "foregrounding" technological theory (Vaughan 1994). It is with this type of attitude in mind that the EARS project's structure was built.

In support of a foundation for sound-based music studies, the EARS site offers an extensive glossary with an accompanying structured index that provides the means to find sources of relevance on the site's ever-increasing bibliography. The framework was laid out during a short and intense project funded by the then Arts and Humanities Research Board (now Council) and executed by Simon Atkinson and myself. During this six-month project, the original glossary was created as well as the site's initial index. In the following years, we have received useful feedback from the many users of the EARS site which has helped the research team to update and expand these two areas of our resource. Finding an ideal structure for the index, one that would assist greatly in articulating the framework introduced below, was very much the largest pattern-matching exercise I had ever undertaken. The day when the highest-level names were decided upon was a moment of celebration for us. The remainder of this chapter takes us through those areas of the EARS site that have not yet been formally introduced. They have been ordered as follows:

(1) Classification: from sound to work level

(2) The listening experience

(3) Modes of discourse, analysis, and representation

(4) Organizing sound from micro- to macro-level

(5) New virtuosity

(6) New means of presentation

(7) Achieving interdisciplinarity and holism

How do these relate to the main subjects on the EARS site? All of these subsections headers (the final one only indirectly) were called upon several times in chapter 2. Clearly, the Genres and Categories (G&C) section was the key focus of the previous chapter. It also reappears under subsection 1 in this chapter. The header Disciplines of Study (DoS) has been briefly glossed over earlier in this chapter. It will return in subsection 7 below. The leading subject header is the Musicology of Electroacoustic Music (MEM),[4] but the final three: Performance, Practice, and Presentation (PPP), Sound Production and Manipulation (SPM), and Musical Structure (Str) will all be introduced and placed within this delineation. MEM can be found throughout all seven subsections below; PPP plays a role in subsections 5 and 6; SPM and Str are the focus of subsection 4, but are also relevant to subsections 5 and 6. MEM's main headers (as well as secondary headers under Music Theory) are divided as follows: aesthetics (subsection 7 below), analysis (3), archiving (1), classification of sound (1), discourse within electroacoustic music (3), history (7), the listening experience (2), music criticism (7), philosophy of music (7), Schaefferian theory (1, 2, 3), sociocultural aspects of electroacoustic music (including access issues in 7), and textuality (3).

(1) Classification: From Sound to Work Level

To an outsider it might seem surprising that of the subsection headers chosen, this first one seems to be the least documented. However, with terminology in the state that it is, it is understandable that sound classifications relevant to sound-based music are not only few but also as rudimentary as work classifications. The situation also supports the premise that although there is a reasonable amount of high-level research taking place, the foundation does not seem to have been adequately laid. The classification paradox follows chapter 2's lead, demonstrating that although there are significant theoretical concepts available, there are still too few means on offer for the creation of greater theoretical coherence in our field. What is likely, and this is quite understandable given the vast variety of sounds and compositional approaches we are dealing with, is that no single classification system will be universally applicable.

We do not, despite Schaeffer's and others' (e.g., Thies 1982) well-meant attempts, have any reasonably accepted *sound classification* system for use beyond the systems that have been created for a specific purpose. Schaeffer made a valiant attempt at creating a comprehensive system for sound classification. It works at the level of the sound object within a reduced listening situation but cannot, for example, deal with real-world identifiable sounds adequately, or with brief musical gestures.

An initiative that is worthy of praise is that of the research group, the Laboratoire de Musique et Informatique de Marseille (MIM), which has created the Unités Sémiotiques Temporelles (UST—time-based semiotic units) system. This system offers a tool for analysis that works at three levels: the global morphological level, the semantic description level, and the level at which other characteristics that are found to be relevant are formulated (see Frémiot 2001). Its focus and its ability to be applied as a tool for classification are clear. Although not based solely on sound-based music analysis—it also covers the traditional forms of music—it has potential to be used to group perceived aural characteristics. Like Schaeffer's work, it relies on descriptive terminology to a large extent. It is a significant project, one of very few.

A more recent GRM/Ircam initiative takes the sound classification notion one step further and, moving beyond the Schaeffer–Bayle heritage, acknowledges sounds from the real world. The Ecrins ("jewelery cases"; it is an abbreviation for Environnement de Classification et de Recherche Intelligente des Sons) collaborative project not only involves sound classification in a dynamic manner as users enter their own descriptions of sounds, but has also been created as an system providing access to a sound sample database (see Geslin, Mullon, and Jacob 2002). In this project, causality, morphology, and semantic content as well as "genetic conditions" (of production) are all encoded. Sadly, this project has been evolving a bit slowly in recent years.

With sample data banks, "freesound" archives (see, e.g., http:// freesound.iua.upf.edu) and the like evolving, new improved sound classification systems will be needed to aid users' data selection as they will be useful for both artistic and analytical applications. Beyond this, those involved in technological development have been seeking protocols for machine-based analysis of various types of music and of sounds (see, e.g.,

Casey 2001 for a description of MPEG-7 being used for sound classification). Such researchers are dealing with traditional forms of music or with real-world sounds in general. This is a first step toward computational advances that might be useful to sound-based music, as these advances might be applied regarding sound sources (real and synthesized) and morphologies, musical gestures, and repertoire characteristics. At the time of writing this book, EARS has unfortunately found relatively few terms (and bibliographic citations) to place under the "Classification of Sound" header: abstract sound, referential sound (which are antonyms), sound event, sound source (and related terms), and *typomorphologie* (which is the link with Schaefferian theory).

Sound source material and sound production and manipulation techniques (the SPM header on the EARS site) are relevant to this subject. It is difficult to imagine how one can discuss approaches to sampling and their musical application without some basis in terms of sound classification. Similarly, sound synthesis, analog and digital, and resynthesis have led to the creation of new sounds. With so many new sounds evolving, new sound types will inevitably also be introduced. Physical modeling, for example, is not solely applicable to the reinvention of the wheel as it were. Research concerning how to resynthesize *and* alter real-world sounds will lead to greater knowledge in a fascinating area that is inextricable from sound classification. Yet where are the texts that combine developments and theory? Take, for example, an article by Välimäki and Takala (1996) on physical modeling,[5] one offering a historical survey and bibliography including a comparison of approaches to physical modeling, but one where neither musical nor musicological investigations are present. Similarly, when it comes to convolution,[6] Zack Settel and Cort Lippe offer an excellent example of a "how to" approach in "Real-time Timbral Transformation: FFT-based Resynthesis" (1994), but how it may influence musical behavior or reception is simply left undiscussed regardless of their wealth of artistic experience applying convolution in performance. This is true in terms of most presentations of sound generation and sound shaping. The lack of discussion of musical application forms part of the work that still needs to take place that in turn would serve the betterment of our classification systems.

Between the level of sound and the work, there are other levels that could qualify as candidates for classification systems. Using the terminology that is currently applied in the field, gesture would provide an excellent example. There has been far too little music analytical work done in this midpoint are between the small and the large. Further study would allow us to develop analytical tools (perhaps some borrowed from more traditional forms of music) that would be useful for segmentation as well as comparative analysis.

The *classification of works* is possibly an even larger issue. As long as we remain in limbo about how we name things, with our odd nonoverlapping regional dialects (the worst being the terms "computer music" and "electronic music" in the U.S., vs. "electroacoustic music" most everywhere else), we will not move forward in terms of solving this problem. There are all sorts of ramifications of this. Access and accessibility issues will not be addressed as long as we have difficulty in terms of works' placement. It might be imagined that what is being suggested here is that we pigeonhole every work of sound-based music. To strive for this would be nonsense. The late twentieth century and early twenty-first century are thriving on "in-between category" works. Nevertheless, such works need to be placed within one or more frameworks which make them accessible to people, whether specialist or novice.

Let us look at the classification of works from another point of view. There exist a reasonable number of archives to be found around the globe for this repertoire. One of the most urgent initiatives in the field is the preservation of analog tape works and early live electronic compositions (see Teruggi 2004 and Battier 2004). Magnetic tapes are aging and many are slowly but surely turning into vinegar. These works need to be digitized. Software programs have been replaced; some old electronic instruments are (almost) beyond repair. How do we preserve these? Clearly, this work can be done on an ad hoc basis, but such an initiative is ideally undertaken internationally with clear descriptors. In short, these days, archives and preservation go hand in hand, at last in this field. For example, Daniel Teruggi is leading an international team (Teruggi 2004) that intends to deal with this very issue. Besides the team's goal of creating an archive of digital recordings, members are investigating a number of types of information that also need to be archived in an accessible form such as prescriptive scores, diagrams (e.g., patches, diffusion information), program notes, software, hardware electroacoustic instruments and devices or any other equipment relevant to performance, and any other data, including performance rights information, relevant to facilitating performance. They also plan to develop a host of types of information that can be used to make these works accessible to nonspecialists. Some of this information may exist already; some might need to be prepared especially for the archive.

The challenge is obviously more easily described than solved. Without a coherent classification system for the repertoire, any preservation project is already destined to offer lower quality information than one might desire or expect. This example has been chosen to identify the urgency of further work. Such classification systems are completely fundamental to any high-level research. It is astonishing how, for example, so much analysis has been undertaken without a generally accepted foundational vocabulary.

Let's look briefly at a rather tricky example. *Brain Opera* is a work by Tod Machover (see, e.g., brainop.media.mit.edu). This work has been revised since its original performance in 1996 and has been installed in its "definitive" version in Vienna since 2000. It is an interactive work in which audience and online participation is sought. In many ways *Brain Opera* is a multimedia interdisciplinary collaborative arts work; it is also an opera (a somewhat similar example can be found in Bonardi and Rousseaux 2004). Ultimately, this work might never be classified under one header in any classification system we devise and may always lack a designator that best describes it other than the rather vague term new media art.

This subsection had to appear first in our list of areas of focus within sound-based music studies. It is clearly of vital importance and foundational. It is also evident how much work is still needed that has not been undertaken during the last five to six decades. To provide further food for thought, let us think of our students. When learning about the art of organized sounds, what might be the equivalent of the fundamentals of music theory? Does tomorrow's sonic artist need to be taught a diminished seventh chord or be able to differentiate granular from FM textures? In a sense educators have to improvise, many of us having been brought up on a healthy diet of traditional musical skills (e.g., harmony, counterpoint), a large percentage of which seem far away from our daily tasks involving the organization of sonic materials. What is the name of the field of horizontal and vertical architectures in sound-based works? Without the needed terminology and related classification systems, such theories can only be developed in isolation. We will return to this interesting issue of fundamentals in the final section of this chapter.

(2)   The Listening Experience
The study of the listening experience of sound-based music is for us a stepping stone toward the areas of discourse and analysis, as it is a fundamental aspect of aesthesic analysis. The study of the listening experience forms part of the world of critical musicology (i.e., the discussion concerning authoriality or to whom a work belongs after it has been completed), but it is more specifically the fact that Schaeffer took such a strong stance on the primacy of the ear early on in the developing years of sound-based music, positioning himself as an opponent to the formalist attitudes of the German school, that has catalyzed the increase in importance of this subject area.

Investigations concerning the listening experience are by nature interdisciplinary. One cannot discuss this subject without acknowledging the areas of, say, perception, psychoacoustics, cognition, music psychology, and semiotics. Emotion and meaning evolve through the listening experience. This is true of all music. Nevertheless, one wonders to what extent new theories related to the listening experience are needed when one takes into account, for example, the difference between an abstract work for string quartet and a soundscape composition.

The listening experience is also our means of better gaining knowledge concerning the reception of sound-based music. The Intention/Reception project is a case in point.

The terms on the EARS site under this index entry find their roots in a great deal of the theory introduced in the last chapter, in particular the work of Schaeffer *cum suis*,[7] Schafer, Norman, Smalley, and Wishart. Here are the key terms from this list:

Acousmatic

Causal Listening

Clairaudience

Composed Space

Contextual Listening

Gesture[8]

Intention and Reception

Listening Strategy

Modes of Listening

Morphology

Quatre Écoutes

Reduced Listening

Referential Listening

Semantic Listening

Sound Image

Source Recognition

Source Bonding

Surrogacy

Technological Listening

Texture

Timbre

Utterance

This EARS list of terms does not yet do justice to the interdisciplinary nature of the listening experience. The related disciplines have not offered many terms that are focused specifically on sonic works. Nevertheless, important publications have appeared that are of use to the art of sound organization, not least the study of auditory scene analysis, a process in which the auditory system takes the mixture of sound that it derives from a complex natural environment and sorts it into packages of acoustic evidence in which each package probably has arisen from a single source of sound. This grouping helps pattern recognition not to mix information from different sources (and involves both physical renditions of sound and listening data).[9] Furthermore, the work in cognition and psychoacoustics by Stephen McAdams (see, e.g., McAdams and Bigend 1993), Perry Cook (2001), and others like them can also be of significant relevance to this subject area.

The listening experience is the first step toward gaining an understanding relevant to reception and analysis. Part of the critical musicology movement was concerned with a break from the study of the score toward a study of the listening experience. Phenomenological approaches to the musical experience focus on listening issues. Writers have dealt with the subject in isolation, but for those interested in aesthesis in the following section, integrating listening experience information into analytical methodologies might prove valuable. Like our first subject, the classification from the level of sound to that of work, this subject is foundational and essential. The more we work with our partners in the sister disciplines, focusing on the art of sound organization as something more than a *Fremdkörper* within the greater world of music, the more we will be able to comprehend our reception and appreciation of this diverse repertoire. When at least some of our cognition and psychoacoustics colleagues spend less time on pitch and rhythmic aspects of music and more on sonic relationships,[10] our foundation will become much stronger and these disciplines will also find a much more important place within the world of sound-based music analysis.

(3) Modes of Discourse, Analysis, and Representation

A large part of the theory introduced in the previous chapter was intended in one way or another to contribute to analytical methodologies. It may therefore seem strange to note that many analyses of sound-based works appear to be elementary in comparison with those in other forms of music, fine art, and so on. This is most likely because people tend to lean too heavily on certain technological aids, or work at those high levels, some *ex nihilo*, in isolation, on particular aspects of works without much of a foundation having been worked out. Regardless, one of the keys to musical knowledge is through a greater understanding of its content and its architecture. This third subsection takes us to the heart of the MEM area within the EARS site, as the study of musical works is of primary importance.

The EARS site has six main terms under analysis: aesthesis and poiesis, audio analysis (including spectral analysis), aural analysis, *faktura* (to be discussed in section 5 below), parametric analysis (which covers most traditional approaches) and structural analysis. Discourse is treated separately on the site and representation appears in several places.

Our discussion below will obviously focus on these main terms; it will also be approached primarily from two of three of Molino's (see Nattiez 1990) approaches to analysis, namely poiesis (construction) and aesthesis (reception). The neutral level, where neither poiesis nor aesthesis can be called upon—for example, the use of representation systems generated through the physical analysis of sound such as a spectral analysis of a recording—will also play a role, albeit a supportive one.[11] Furthermore, in line with the rest of this book, information about intentions forms part of the potential materials for analysis. Where relevant, EARS index terms will be introduced briefly. A number of special cases of sound-based music analysis, in particular holistic approaches, will also be briefly presented.

In general, any discussion of *discourse* cannot be disassociated from analysis and the listening experience. Discoveries concerning discourse should be integral to any analysis. A relatively strong context for this term has been established in the previous chapter's investigation of sound-based works. In particular, Simon Emmerson's language grid was one of the first empirical methods defined that allowed listeners to make classifications across a wide diversity of works based on choice of material and structural behavior. Some of the writings of François Bayle, R. Murray Schafer, Denis Smalley, and Simon Waters are also pertinent here. These influential authors' concepts are reflected in the EARS site's current list of the more important terms associated with discourse, which includes:

Abstract Syntax and Abstracted Syntax

Aural and Mimetic Discourse

Aural Landscape

Mimesis

Motion

Musical Landscape

Narrative

Representation

Sampling

Sound Image

Sound Symbol

Transcontextuality

This list contains several often-used terms as well as a few more specific cases; there are hundreds of others that can also be of assistance when discussing this subject. Terms such as motion and narrative are in a sense difficult, as they are flexible terms that can be used in several senses. Regardless, they are both cited regularly in discussions involving discourse.

Sampling is a term that, like others, also appears elsewhere on the EARS site. Its inclusion here has to do with the fact that soundscape and anecdotal works (see, e.g., Ferrari 1996), cut-and-paste works such as plunderphonic compositions, and so on are driven by identifiable recordings which are placed within a more musical or narrative (though not in the literal sense) discourse.

Let us take a step back and think about just what we want from a *sound-based musical analysis*. To answer this, a good starting point is an article by Marcel Frémiot in which he asks: "In electroacoustic music, which arguments do we possess to convince our students that their works are successful or not?" Granted, valorizing works—to use a more current term—and critical analysis do not always work hand in hand. Still, Frémiot makes a legitimate claim for forms of consensus and the development of tools to support that consensus: "Given the wide diversity of musical languages in contemporary music, from the minimal to the most sophisticated, what type of analysis might one propose which is not simply based at the formalism level?" (Frémiot 2001, 228)

Other authors have raised foundational issues that are worthy of mention here. For example, Michael Norris is not totally satisfied with some of the more traditional tools of analysis. "[A]nalysis 'quantises,' 'segments' and 'classifies' the continuum of pitch, duration and timbre to extract meaning, and it does so by operating on a written, idealised representation—the score." Clearly he is less than happy about this and proposes an interest in "[t]he meanings listeners construct from music [that] draw on huge reservoirs of personal and communal 'narratives,' 'contexts' or 'codes,' especially when the music incorporates source recordings from the environments, (our 'sound contexts') . . . I call them 'socio-cultural sound narratives'" (Norris 1999, 64). This remark illustrates the holistic connection between intention, discourse, and analysis and supports the growing interest in meaning in music.

Denis Smalley and Lelio Camilleri contributed several important remarks in the introductory article to a themed issue on *The Analysis of Electroacoustic Music* in the *Journal of New Music Research* (27[1–2], 1998). We were introduced to their view concerning "a more comprehensive understanding of music and listening as cultural practices" (ibid., 4) in the last chapter. They are interested not solely in listening strategies, but also in how listeners construct their listening and, consequently, their construction of meaning. They are firm believers in the discovery of "salient sonic features (pertinences)" (ibid., 5) within and across electroacoustic works whether in terms of sonic characteristics or structural development. One should note that pertinences can "refer to sonic phenomena outside the immediate musical context of the work . . . [i.e.,] in the outside world. . . . [F]eatures might be seized by the listener and invested with pertinence because they refer to the outside world" (ibid., 6). They summarize their view: "An important goal of analytical exploration is, therefore, to attempt to reconcile and relate the internal world of the work with the outside world of sonic and non-sonic experience" (ibid., 7). The internal world has to do with the sonic relationships in a given work and therefore is best investigated by including, although not necessarily limiting oneself to, a reduced listening strategy, according to the authors.

Agostino di Scipio is one of many who are very interested in poiesis. He supports a search for what he calls the "téchne of electroacoustic music" (di Scipio 1995). He suggests that what is missing is "a methodology capable of characterising the technical processes and the designing of tools that make up the compositional environment, models, representations, and knowledge-level strategies, which is understood as traces of cognitive and aesthetic paradigms specific to the medium. It is also shown that an analysis of such kind—drawing on the téchne of the making of music—is indispensable in order to shed light on the renewed relation of sound materials to musical form in electroacoustic music" (di Scipio 1995, 369). Similar in a sense to the Intention/Reception project, di Scipio seeks "the dialectic between the conceptual and the perceptual in the musical experience" (ibid., 370–371); however, in this case, the author is more interested in process and construction information than in the dramaturgy of works in the first instance. Camilleri and Smalley seem to look at things from a complementary point of view.

How do we reconcile these two very different approaches to analysis? To what extent does sound-based music analysis need to rely upon the "primacy of the ear"? This question is simply a microcosm of what is taking place in musicology in general and in many similar fields. Critical theory moved the debate from the maker's point of view to the receiver's. There can also be reason to rely on both, as was the case in the I/R project in chapter 1, although this project employs very particular information provided by the composers. Of the writers above, only di Scipio makes this suggestion, and yet, what he suggests seems ambitious. He also assumes that those involved with analysis fully understand the tools used in making works. This is fine as long as we accept the experience expected of both analysts and their readership.

As this book has been conceived to delineate the area of sound-based music studies, it would therefore be counterproductive to choose one methodology over another. In fact the analysis questions raised are useful as they assist in directing analysts toward their chosen methodology. As Norris states in the above-mentioned article, "Electroacoustic music analysis should be more of a research programme, one that reinstates individual acts of interpretation rather than a systematised self-perpetuating model, while retaining non-subjective data as an evidential foundation. . . . This would mean that no analytic investigation is ever complete. There may be a sense of comprehensiveness, but never a sense of completion" (Norris 1999, 66). With this in mind, we can now look at analysis in terms of aesthesis, poiesis, and anything in between.

Aural analysis on the EARS site is not solely the discovery of salient details of a piece through listening. It is an interdisciplinary area ranging from the psychoacoustic notion of an acoustic model[12] to more semantics-based processes that occur during semantic listening. It is equally the home of Pierre Schaeffer's and Denis Smalley's analytical concepts as well as more general ones involving streams and/or layers of sound. Visual representations may be produced to aid within certain aural analytical methodologies.

Our proponents for aural analysis thus far have included the likes of Schaeffer, Bayle and Delalande (and colleagues) at the GRM, Smalley and those associated with his spectromorphological explorations, Emmerson and Wishart, and Schafer, McCartney, and others working in the soundscape and related areas. A brief glance at the EARS bibliography will demonstrate a relatively substantial amount of work in aural and related analytical areas. What is rare, however, are complete analyses of works based on methodologies that have been fully introduced and, as it were, defended beforehand. To support their work a few authors specializing in aural analysis also use neutral spectral analysis information; they may also use other, perhaps more subjective forms of visual representation for support.

A major figure not yet presented who is deeply involved with the area of aural analysis of sound-based music is Stéphane Roy. Roy is a realist in that he is aware of the multitudes of possible approaches to sound-based music analysis. His book (Roy 2003b), based on his Ph.D., a major analytical study under the supervision of Nattiez, demonstrates this by comparing quite a number of analytical approaches and then applying some of these one by one and in combination with regard to a single work by Francis Dhomont (see also Roy 1996, 1998).[13] He is clearly a product of his composition teacher (Dhomont, very much a member of the GRM school of acousmatic composition) and his supervisor, Nattiez, leaning heavily on reduced listening strategies and a variety of Nattiez's concepts. Roy succeeds in incorporating Schaefferian and post-Schaefferian concepts while finding means to treat sound-based music beyond the sonic or musical object level, discovering pertinence in his treatments at both morphological and structural levels. He is one of the most aware and capable analysts today. There is one major limitation here, however. Curiously, given the fact that Roy has been working in Montreal, it is regrettable that the Canadian soundscape movement has not seemed to have influenced him at all. The external world is not one of his key concerns; instead, he is much more interested in the French school's approach to the acousmatic.

Roy's approach is based primarily on the advancement of an assemblage of his own and others' existent methodologies. Another project, the "Signed music project" taking place at IRCAM, seems more original. Although still in its early stages, there are some very intriguing ideas behind its "Écoutes signées" (see Stiegler 2003, 15; Donin 2004). It should be stated immediately that this is a project that sees no boundary between vocal/instrumental and sound-based works. It is an approach that, according to the team involved, is potentially of equal relevance to analysts and to composers. Its relevancy here is its particular slant on the listening experience. Nicolas Donin writes: "A 'signed listening' is a hypermedia product which aims at making a personal and original way of listening transmissible (i.e., the listener assumes credit for his or her individual listening, hence 'signs' the listening), by suggesting types of graphic and acoustic representations and manipulations of music based on a pre-existing listening practice" (Donin 2004, 99). The team accepts the fact that individuals' listening approaches can vary, but the idea here is to capture a particular listening and to make the resulting information available to others. In a sense this approach insists on a wide diversity of responses to the same piece of music. What is also of great interest, is that it is image-led with accompanying words as opposed to word-led with accompanying images, common to many approaches taken by of the authors mentioned above. The signed listening project forms a close link to our next category, spectral analysis.

The next stop on our journey through the worlds of analysis is *spectral analysis*, which appears under Audio Analysis on the EARS site. The question that might be raised immediately is: is spectral analysis synonymous with Nattiez's neutral level? The answer is: it can be, but in some cases it is part of either poiesis (drawn up by a composer or someone involved with a work's creation, not independently) or aesthesis (involving an interpretation of an investigator's aural perception of a work). A spectrogram or sonogram and the like are clearly neutral-level tools. An image generated by the GRM's acousmographe is more evocative and although generated originally as a physical audio representation, the user of the program molds the output of this program in terms of its salient qualities to aid in a work's reading.

It was Robert Cogan who was the key propagandist for what he called "spectrum photos" (Cogan 1984). He found these to be of relevance to both vocal/instrumental music and sound-based music. Not only did these photos play a major role in Cogan's analytical framework, he also used a set of thirteen "oppositions" as further tools to describe musical behavior. Since this time, the sonogram seems to have increased in importance. Martha Brech's dissertation (Brech 1994), Mara Helmuth (Helmuth 1996), and Mary Simoni et al. (1999) carry on the Cogan tradition by making significant use of sonograms, placing these images in the context of their individual formal methodologies. Such images seem to play a rather central role in most sound-based music analyses found in the books edited by Thomas Licata, *Electroacoustic Music: Analytical Perspectives* (2002) and Simoni, *Analytical Methods of Electroacoustic Music* (2006). Simon Waters and Tamas Ungvary also see many opportunities for sonogram application, in particular concerning musical structure (Waters and Ungvary 1990).

Sonograms are undoubtedly very useful images when used in analysis, particularly when dealing with complex spectra found in some sound-based compositions. The issue to be raised here is: can we hear everything that we see in these images? Of the information we cannot perceive, how relevant is it in the end? Conversely, there are often sonic details we can hear that we cannot retrieve in a sonogram (e.g., separate elements of a complex sound). If this is the case, how heavily can we lean on this image when it does not offer all that we can perceive? Regardless, sonograms seem to be an excellent tool in terms of verifying hypotheses about a work. I do, however, have some reservations about using the sonogram as a point of departure, given the questions raised above.

In an ideal world, this image should reflect not only physical reality, but also psychoacoustic reality, that is, it should be a hybrid of what exists and what is heard. Equally, some composers might support the use of images to reflect what they consider important in their compositions, similar to the concepts of foreground and background, *Hauptstimme* and *Nebenstimme*.

This brings us to the notion of evocative transcriptions—that is, graphic scores that illustrate particular characteristics of a sound-based work in a legible manner—taking into account either the listening experience or the composer's intention or both. These images, however, are not neutral. Diffusion scores exemplify this well. There have also been at least two examples of attempts to visualize MIDI behavior, although this need not be applied in electroacoustic works as such (Berenguer 1997; Graves, Hand, and Hugill 1999).

Any composer or analyst who has created graphic scores to assist in diffusion, analysis, or any other goal, tends to keep spectral information in mind. The more "hand-made" they are, the less detailed they tend to be. Researchers at the GRM have developed transcription tools, in particular the acousmographe (e.g., Geslin and Lefevre 2004), for several applications, pedagogy being one of them. Excellent examples of the usage of evocative acousmographe images can be found in the Ina/GRM's unique *Portraits Polychromes* series, a series of composer portraits, each including interviews, work discussions and analyses combining published booklets with online information using a wide variety of media.[14] Here highly user-friendly images are provided taking into account information that has been captured in the form of sonograms and made more manageable, attractive if you prefer, reduced if you are a purist, by those who decide how to translate the sonogram information into an acousmographe image. For listeners who like to see what they hear and obviously for younger listeners, this is an invaluable access tool.

The acousmographe is increasingly being used as part of multimedia (or hypermedia) presentations of electroacoustic music (see, e.g., Couprie 2004a, 2004b). The GRM, in collaboration with multimedia designers Hyptique, published *La musique électroacoustique* in 2000, a CD-ROM applying acousmographe images liberally in a wonderfully presented portrait of analysis, sound manipulation, and history.[15] IRCAM's answer to this, *Dix jeux d'écoute* (ten listening games), made with Hyptique equally demonstrates great effort in terms of finding relevant graphic symbols for their pedagogical CD-ROM.[16]

In fact, Pierre Couprie, one of the key figures associated with the EARS project, is an important developer/musicologist in this area. He has published widely using evocative transcriptions. His first English language publication on the subject is the article, "Three Analysis Models for *L'oiseau moqueur*, one of the *Trois rêves d'oiseau* by François Bayle" (Couprie 1999), in which a Schaefferian, a semiotic, and a graphic approach are all applied to a single work by François Bayle. It is nice to see a variety of successful applications of postscriptive notation used to further our analytical understanding of the works in a normally nonnotated form of music.

The subject of *structural analysis* in terms of sound-based music is a curious one. This approach to analysis often concerns the (re)discovery of constructional approaches of the composers in question. Alternatively, it can, as in the case of traditional studies of music, involve more general structural approaches devised by theorists. One might consider potential sound-based approaches analogous to, for example, Schenkerian analysis that was created for application with certain varieties of tonal works. This reflects the subhead "Grammar" on the EARS site. Other than the formalist construction principles introduced in the previous chapter, such theoretical analytical approaches to sound-based music are currently few and far between. The other EARS subhead, "Visual Representation," often refers to graphic scores—including diffusion scores—that are used to reflect or identify structure in sound-based works.

Our digital age has offered new means of investigating structural analysis. For example, visual representation can also refer to other forms of documentation such as printouts of computer programs used to create a work. Christopher Burns (2002) has written about using software synthesis code as documentary evidence of a work, evidence that can be applied in analytical contexts. In some cases, this will bring the analyst closer to "the work" than would a traditional composer's score. However, unless one intends to analyze a composer's programming or coding style, this is but a new means toward a traditional goal.

As suggested, currently there seem to be two main types of structural analysis. The first, a more prominent means, is to attempt to gain awareness of a composer's methods (this is perhaps easier when the analyst is the composer). In the early years of sound-based music, when the top-down structuring choice was usually either related to neoserialism or more sophisticated mathematical approaches, learning the formalist tendencies of Stockhausen *cum suis* (see, for example, Giomi and Ligabue 1998, but there are dozens of other published treatments, particularly of early works) and Xenakis provided an adequate foundation. Of course as time went on and several composers and developers became increasingly interested in the opportunities offered by mapping information from a given domain onto the musical plain, formalist approaches expanded. This not only reflected an increasingly technological age, it also reflected the individualist spirit that was so prominent during a great deal of the previous century.

The second type tends to lean more heavily on graphic information and is more common among analysts dealing with works by composers who are not highly affiliated with or who even shun formalism. In almost all such cases structural analysis is not (primarily) poietic and is focused on either aural analysis, spectral analysis, or both. Such publications have already been treated under those separate headers above.

Agostino di Scipio is one of few researchers to combine a personal approach to structural analysis with an investigation of the composer's attitude. In one of the many articles he has written on Xenakis (di Scipio 1998), he claims that he wants to understand the material of a given work, the methods used to create and/or treat the material and how these help to bring forth the perceived musical structure, a case of poiesis and aesthesis combined. Although I was trained in poietic analysis, I must admit that I fully subscribe to di Scipio's approach, at least when formalism is of relevance, to combine an investigation of how a piece was made with what is received; otherwise the analytical work seems more theoretical, showing less interest in the practical results of that theory regardless of the fact that they exist. Di Scipio's method can be applied to determine to what extent theoretical concepts are audible and, if valorization is involved, to what extent they aid in a work's appreciation.

Structural analysis of sound-based works is a huge subject area, reflecting the breadth and depth of activities in formalism and architectural devices used within the repertoire. As the majority of poietic studies remain based on composers' information, and it is difficult to imagine this changing soon given the relative lack of tested analyst-driven systems, an ideal, ambitious approach currently might involve the understanding of process, product, and sounding result within the same study to determine whether all of that theory in fact contributes to the finished work. This assumes some sort of evaluation system, an area where too little work has been undertaken thus far.

Prior to leaving the subject of analysis, there are a few *special cases* worthy of introduction in this context. All five fall outside the EARS site's current three main analysis headers owing to their specificity; the site does offer index entries related to the specific areas of focus. Although only a few examples are presented here, there are certainly other approaches that could be added that involve the analysis of a focused topic related to sound-based music.

The first example has to do with analytical work that focuses on a specific element within electroacoustic music. For example, there are a number of publications concerning the presence of the human voice (real, manipulated, or synthesized) in electroacoustic works, for example Bosma 2003 and Bossis 2004. This type of approach can easily slot into each of our three categories, aural, spectral, and structural, yet is concentrated on a single aspect in several works as opposed to the works in their entirety. The insights gained from this type of research can often be applicable to other foci or even general analytical methodologies. In the case of Bosma's writing, her findings are of great relevance to gender studies and sound-based music, a subject that has not been mentioned thus far.[17] In the case of Bossis, questions are raised in terms of the study of synthetically created vocal sounds from various points of view including how they resemble real voices, how they are used in musical contexts, how they are generated, and so on. The more such publications appear, the more categories EARS will add in the analysis section of the site.

The second example was raised in the previous chapter and is similar in that it transcends single works; here the search is for national (or regional) characteristics in sound-based music (see, e.g., Norris and Young 2001;[18] Fujii 2004). Studies like these form a particular type of

analytical studies that provide greater insights in terms of genre classification. Granted, many composers over the last sixty years have avoided
being classified into schools as if it were an illness; many, too, would not
like to be stereotyped as being "typically Norwegian" or of any other
nationality, yet these characteristics do exist and deserve to be celebrated
where relevant. A related subject of interest is that of the conscious use
of elements from one's own or other cultures in sound-based composition. There are many issues that arise concerning the appropriation of
such practices; however, the use of culturally based aspects of music also
allows works to be about something (see, e.g., Emmerson 2000c and
issue 10/1 of *Organised Sound*).[19]

On occasion a composer's discussion of a work goes beyond providing very basic technical or contextual information. Other than discussions of specific formalisms used in the construction of works composers
here also present a work's dramaturgy. An excellent example of this
approach is Trevor Wishart's booklet presentation of his analog work,
Red Bird (Wishart 1978). Although Wishart does not take the final step
toward listeners' experiences concerning the reception of his piece, he is
offering the two sides of poiesis—construction and concept—the latter
of which is often trivialized in composers' writings. Barry Truax and his
students' CD-ROM composition presentation/analyses mentioned in the
previous chapter form another example of this type.

Continuing the discussion of analysis-transcending single works, our
ongoing genre issues might be considered a topic worthy of analysis.
What are the binding characteristics of works belonging to a particular
genre? How does this relate to our sources, construction, listening experience dimensions? Furthermore, how might valorization fit in within
genre analysis? These are all questions that deserve further investigation
and debate.

Finally, a new kind of analysis is slowly but surely coming to the fore.
An example of this is Michael Clarke's recent treatment of Jonathan
Harvey's *Mortuos Plango, Vivos Voco* (Clarke 2006). In this analysis,
Clark is primarily interested in poiesis. Instead of restricting himself to
the description of the work, he provides software where interested parties
can try out Harvey's procedures with the bell and vocal textures in a
manner that are identical (or at least very similar) to Harvey's specific

techniques when he made this work at IRCAM. Interactive analysis will play a larger role in the future, whether it is about specific sound construction, phrasing, or any other relevant factor of analysis, as it is a hands-on means of gaining practical musical knowledge and thus leads to a greater understanding of a composer's circumstances when he or she is realizing such a work.

(4)   Organizing Sound from Micro- to Macro-level

In the previous discussion it was noted that in terms of poietic analysis, a significant number of analysts favor formalist composers. Similarly, in discussing sound organization other than specific sound synthesis and manipulation techniques, it is again the formalists who have articulated their ideas more often and more clearly than others. What differentiates sound-based music from other forms of music is the ability to formalize at the microsound level to the largest levels, for example, one covering entire series of works.

These approaches fall under the "Structure, Musical" (Str) section of the EARS site. This section includes disparate loose high-level terms including: Architecture (which is another word for structural organization); Collage (perhaps one of the least formalized paths toward structural development); Layering (today's form of counterpoint found in a very large percentage of sound-based works ranging from the pure acousmatic reduced listening work to techno); Sequencing and Editing (two specific forms of creating sequential order using new technologies); and Spectromorphology (an odd member of this list as it is normally associated with more micro-level Structure aspects of acousmatic composition and the related listening experience, but Smalley's theory can also be applied to larger scale aspects of works).

More important for our purposes, the key terms in the Str section of the EARS site are: Formalism, Micro-level Structure, and Macro-level Structure. The former term has already been introduced. It can, of course, be used at both micro- and macro-levels and everything in between and is an umbrella term that includes, for example, algorithmic composition. With this in mind, this subsection has been divided into three parts: micro-level structure, from micro- to macro-level, and macro-level structure.

The first things that come to mind at the *micro-level* are forms of microsound: grains of sound (and the related terminology introduced in Roads 2001) and glitches;[20] similarly, at a slightly higher level (that is, longer duration), there are more candidates including the musical object, the plunderphone, perhaps even the short musical gesture. To state the obvious, it is much easier to find writings on how one generates grains than it is to find writings on how to structure them. This is similar to what might be called the fallacy of Schaefferian theory that focuses only at the local level, unable to express itself in terms of creating structure in composition. As we have discovered, Smalley's theory fortunately evolves Schaefferian thought in the right direction.

There are relatively few discussions related to formalization at the micro-level. Nick Fells' presentation of applying algorithmic concepts at micro-level (1999) and di Scipio's (1997) article concerning Xenakis' combining grains to timbral/structural level represent two of the relatively few that go beyond pure description of sound generation. There is great scope here to combine constructional principles with analytical ones, taking sound generation and manipulation as well as relevant modes of representation into account. For example, how does one best represent microsound composition visually? Is this simply a mapping of microsound techniques?

There is a shared interest at microsound level for listeners to possess the ability "to enter into textures," owing to the their complexity, which can be found throughout most of Truax's publications and in an interview with Paul Lansky (Cody 1996). Unlike many dealing with microsound, Truax and Lansky often do not mask their sources; so while there is indeed complexity, there is also a clear sense of source, simultaneously allowing for both reduced and source-based listening strategies.

Greater knowledge of potential timbral and structural principles of organization starting at the micro-level will be essential if we are to appreciate the diverse repertoire of sonic artworks. This can take place by way of practical experience. It can also occur analytically, yet the analytical side remains underdeveloped at present. For those practitioners who have achieved great insights while creating their composition procedures, sharing some of these discoveries would be welcome in this key section of sound-based music studies. If we take the documentation strategy presented in the Wishart *Red Bird* discussion as an example, how many users of microsound have shared their approach, organizing principles, and criteria for choice with others to establish examples of practice when it comes to this fairly new manner of sound organization?

The study of sound organization ranging *from micro- to macro-level* is also relatively rare. Those writers, including di Scipio, who relate material to structure, are of central importance here. Laurie Spiegel has fantasized about the creation of "nonhierarchical music," music in which micro- and macro-links are predefined or generated (Spiegel 1999). Giovanni de Poli has written that "synthesis and control models need to converge" (de Poli 1996, 39), which theoretically could take the micro-level concepts into more macro-level development. Certainly there are composers investigating such protocols; however, too little of that knowledge has been shared thus far in an area that demonstrates great potential both in creative and analytical circumstances. The subject investigating the creation of structure, ranging from the gesture to say, the section of a work, is in need of more theoretical discussion and composition-based descriptions.

Macro-level sound organization is one of the key areas of innovation throughout all of contemporary music, not only sound-based varieties. This treasure chest of structuring devices ranging from indeterminacy to anything algorithmic is relatively well documented, although such documents rarely discuss elements of greatest interest to sound-based composers, namely, how a sound's content is related to the structuring procedures and what aspects of the listening experience are related to them as well. It is almost as if the French antiformalist and the German formalist polemic were still alive and well today. Thank goodness things have started to converge in recent years, so that structural formalism and timbral interest are more combined. We need more literature concerning, for example, generative algorithms that investigates the choice of sounds and why such mappings are considered "musical." Although Lejaren Hiller once successfully composed a work entitled *Electronic Sonata* (and explained this challenge in his notes), the form was not created for the sound-based repertoire and, in general, is not appropriate for that repertoire. Nonchalance in terms of relating structure to material is not helpful given the wide range of experimentation at the macro-level. Are those who create such structures interested mainly in structure for structure's sake? If not, the sounds involved might be related to the algorithm applied. Furthermore, as discovered in the previous chapter, the audibility of fundamental aspects of the structuring principles should also be monitored more carefully.

As with the next two subsections below, which focus on the Performance Practice and Presentation (PPP) and Sound Production and Manipulation (SPM) headers on the EARS site, the majority of writing on structure that is currently available has been written from the composer's (or at least construction's) point of view. Obviously such writings are relevant; however, if composers and analysts continue to prefer discussions of an algorithm over discussions of the listening experience, our co-hear-ence problems are likely to continue. Furthermore, if traditional musicologists continue to avoid this musical corpus, the "how to" bias from the composer's point of view will also continue. In short, all three areas of the site, PPP, SPM, and Str, are ripe for exploration, particularly when applying holistic approaches.

(5)   New Virtuosity

With the development of sound-based music throughout recent decades, a wide variety of new forms of virtuosity have come into being. Some are developments of previous practices, such as the ability to "perform" a controller or an interface with the same type of virtuosity as one plays an instrument. There are entirely new forms as well, such as the person who demonstrates great ability in a voltage-controlled analog studio or with a software program such as MAX/MSP. This section focuses on some of these forms of virtuosity and is closely connected with the following section concerning new means of presentation. EARS terms such as "live electronics" and "real time" are clearly pertinent here.

This tale will start in the studio. Marc Battier has borrowed a term from the Russian Constructivists, *faktura*, and applied it to the study of works of sound organization. He writes: "In the Constructivists' sense, *faktura* may help analyse certain electronic music and audio art pieces, as it focuses on the nature of how the artist, who, in this case, is the composer or the performer/composer, transforms and adapts the technology" (Battier 2003, 251). It "deals with any type of relationship between the building of a work and its technological environment" (ibid., 253). Battier sees *faktura* as a tool for analysis. I actually see this concept in a slightly wider sense, at least as far as this section is concerned, for it allows one to investigate the application of a particular technology or set of technologies by the user. Anecdotally, it has been said that people at the GRM could tell whether a composition was made in a certain studio of theirs as that studio had, in their terms, a particular "sound," an excellent example of listening to technology. It is, in fact, the facility of achieving this "sound" or, alternatively, in achieving expertise with a given software program that in principle has no particular "sound," that is of interest here. The analyst, however, is normally interested in the sonic result. Battier, on the other hand, is more interested in poiesis than aesthesis, and part of his approach to poiesis is the investigation of efficient and effective use of technology, a subject most writers have carefully avoided. This may be a very difficult area to develop, but many highly respected composers are, in fact, demonstrating their virtuosity in their studios or with their PCs. Why this rarely plays a role in analysis is a bit puzzling. There is, in fact, little difference between this discussion and a statement regarding, say, Gustav Mahler's abilities in orchestration. *Faktura* can be applied to the following EARS terms (among many others): Recording, Synthesis and Resynthesis Techniques, Mixing, Sampling, and Sound Shaping, as well as the use of Space (see next section), that is, most of the areas under the Sound Production and Manipulation header.[21]

The next port of call concerning virtuosity involves the live performance of sound-based music. Virtuosity in mixed pieces will normally be similar to virtuosity in acoustic works with the possible addition of a given interface or the delicate challenges of a click track or aural synchronization. Moving on from traditional instruments, important sections of the EARS site are devoted to electroacoustic music instruments and controllers. In both cases virtuosity can be of great importance.

The late Hugh Davies' name is synonymous with his encyclopedic knowledge of sound-based music history. He was also one of the pioneers of live electronic music. His article "Instruments électroniques: classification et mécanismes" (1990) is one of many in which he attempted to classify electroacoustic instruments, as he had been curator for museum collections and was well versed in some of the more obscure varieties. Others actively involved in the organology of sound-based music and the preservation of electroacoustic instruments are Joel Chadabe and Marc Battier, another member of the field with encyclopedic knowledge. Instrumentalists often aim to achieve a certain level of virtuosity. However, in the world of music technology this is not always so straightforward. A frequently uttered complaint, particularly in the years when the synthesizer was widely used, was that instruments were changing constantly. How can it be that a violinist needs almost an entire career to master a Stradavarius, and a musician needs the same to master the Indian vina, and yet we need to learn how to program our presets differently every other year? The study of the potential of these electroacoustic instruments is integral to our work, and so are the means by which they are performed.

Controllers and interfaces are at least as diverse as the experiments with new instruments.[22] Most articles are concerned with what led to these controllers and how they work. Few articles discuss how they have been used and whether they have been used effectively. There have not been many attempts to find means of classification for musical devices, Birnbaum et al. 2003 being an exemplary exception. This echoes remarks on instruments and non-real-time environments and is another one of the major "holes in the market" in the field of sound-based music studies and *faktura*.

Some of these instruments, controllers, and the like are used in interactive ways. Again, writings (some of which were introduced in chapter 2) tend to favor the subject of what the interactivity involves more than how it was used and, in particular, how effectively. Valorization is an underresearched topic in terms of interactivity as it is elsewhere.[23]

One aspect concerning the use of new controllers was brought to my attention by Garth Paine who pointed out to me that in some cases, including certain of his own projects, the means of preparing and employing a controller in performance was fully interwoven with his approach in terms of content. He speaks of "integrated music software environments." In such cases there is a direct link between software development, instrument building, and musical strategy. In a sense, traditional instruments have dictated compositional options in the past; now compositional ideals are becoming interrelated with instrument and synthesis/sound manipulation design. In this way *faktura* and musical architecture are intertwined. Paine spoke of the blurring of roles between composer, performer, and instrument builder when discussing integrated environments and live sound-based music performance practices. Tim Ingold in his book *The Perception of the Environment: Essays in Livelihood, Dwelling, and Skill* (2000) coins the term *wayfinding*, which seems apropos in such cases. This is a concept that stands in contrast to the art of map reading typical of traditional scores.

Continuing the discussion of the notion of *faktura* in performance, another distinction should be mentioned, a traditional one this time, namely that between fixed (e.g., fully notated) pieces and improvised ones. John Bowers, a writer introduced in the previous chapter, is one of only a few who specifically discuss the challenges of improvisation within a sound-based context. This is particularly odd, given the enormous amount of improvisation taking place in laptop music and the like these days.

The subject of Internet music and other forms of local networked music is also most intriguing in terms of our current subject. Internet music, of course, can be undertaken in solo form or collaboratively. Dante Tanzi is one of very few writers who have asked questions about the classification, the societal role, and value of the music being made on the Internet, especially its collaborative forms (e.g., Tanzi 2001). Most authors tend to celebrate their systems. As this field is one of the most rapidly growing, much more study is needed to comprehend its place, its creative and musical potential, and its cultural functions.

One of the most interesting issues related to collaborative Internet music making is how much is imposed by the site's author(s) and how much can be determined by the users. It is here where our brief discussion on *collaboration* and *devising* in sound-based music begins.

A great deal of the music discussed thus far in this book has been single authored. Much of this music is performed at the push of a button. Some works involve performers. In many cases, these performers have been given some sort of score to play following Western art music tradition. This section is not about those sorts of works, unless the performers in question have somehow actively collaborated with the composer (co-composed it) in the process that led to the completion of a work's score.

Because the majority of music made around the globe is collaborative, the field of sound-based music studies must also investigate different forms of collaboration and how this influences sonic artworks' production, participation issues, and reception. I would like to make a distinction between collaboration in a general sense and "devising" in a more specific one (see Landy and Jamieson 2000). A devised work is a collaborative work made collectively by a project's participants, as is the case in a good deal of folk and popular musics around the globe. Collaboration in general is led or at least assigns ownership or responsibility to particular participants. In the case of devising, the group is credited with the making of a work.

The question concerning imposition and Internet sound-based music protocols is an excellent case in point. Do people come to make music on particular Internet sites because they prefer the choices prepared by the site's creator(s), or do they come to these sites because they can more or less be as creative as they like? In other words, to what extent does imposition (or the lack thereof) work as a magnet for some Internet users, and which types of users prefer to retain responsibility for their own musical approaches? In all cases musical communities are being formed. As is so often the case, the situation here is by no means black and white. People often discover such sites out of curiosity and, like trying out a new game, participate in what is on offer. What I am considering here is more along the lines of the ideal Internet music site(s) for individuals. In imposed contexts, the site's rules, sounds, and structures dictate results. In an ideal context, participants are much more in control of what they do. Those who are attracted to the former might already adhere to the style the site represents or shun freedom in terms of creativity, perhaps because of their lack of experience and confidence.

This may seem like a lengthy contextualization, but as suggested, some of tomorrow's folk music, both sound and note-based, may indeed be found on the Internet. With this in mind, we need further study regarding the desires of potential participants and the potential participation of online sound organization.

The Internet is of course not the only collaborative venue in sound-based music. In my studies for the preparation of this book I found very few reports on collaborative efforts; the flutist Elizabeth McNutt's (2003) report on working with electroacoustic composers and Diane Thome's (1995) article concerning her collaborations with people working in other art forms were two of the modest number of welcome publications in this field. Similarly, there are far too few writers who have written about the devising experience. Discussions of the Edison Studio's (Cipriani et al. 2004) work in the area of real-time performance with silent films and of the interdisciplinary approach of Tomie Hahn and Curtis Bahn's (2002) work in the areas of sound, image, and movement represent two well-formulated examples of work on sound-based music and devising practices.

People of all ages can find artistic areas, including quite possibly that of sound organization, in which they feel fully at ease when working collectively in such a context. This is because feedback mechanisms often form part of the collective artistic endeavor. In consequence, discussions concerning new collaborative practices will play a pioneering role in terms of learning more about novel approaches to sound organization.

The conclusion of this subsection on virtuosity is that too much research thus far has been concerned with formalism, technological development, and, to a lesser extent, analysis, and too little has been involved with *faktura*, appreciation, and innovative forms of collaborative if not collective music making. The study of the physical process of creating sound-based artworks should perhaps be brought into balance with the study of concepts behind art making, the ideas that feed into a work's construction and its reception.

Take, as an example, the case of turntablist teams, a product of hip-hop culture. Part of their virtuosity can be found in their various turntable and mixing techniques. Creating sound-based music that is experimental, innovative, and rooted in popular culture at the same time, these teams devise work and allow a small margin for improvisation once a piece has reached performance level.[24] So here one has an excellent example of a virtuosic art of sound organization that is relatively under-documented and, for once, rather popular. Its performers are clearly stimulated by the experimental part of the preparation of their performances and at the same time are creating challenging and entertaining work. Shouldn't we be demonstrating more curiosity in terms of gaining insights into such initiatives?

Faktura is one of the main elements at the basis of the study of creative sound organization. It is one of the least developed concepts within sound-based music studies, despite the fact that many sonic musicians aim to achieve it—an odd situation, to say the least.

(6)   New Means of Presentation

This penultimate subsection overlaps a bit with the previous one, for it is clear that the use of real-time live electronic performances using specially made instruments and controllers plays a key role in terms of new means of presentation. However, this subsection is also about where works of sound organization are presented and how these spaces are taken into account (or not) in performance. It also acknowledges the large amount of cross-arts work, including audiovisual varieties, being undertaken that involves sound-based music.

Faktura is one way of looking at how our new instruments and controllers are being used; the role of these devices within musical presentation is another. For example, it goes without saying that today's laptop can be a versatile controller or even performance instrument for today's music, but what is it like for the audience to be watching the performers sitting at tables hunched over these machines? Clearly, one notices that something is taking place in real time. Are the results of their physical gestures always audible? To what extent is human presence integral to the performance? When a performance is not improvised, would it work just as well on a fixed medium, and why (or why not)?

Speaking of works on a fixed medium, the controversy concerning the notion of the "tape concert," that is, a concert in which prerecorded works are performed, is as old as the tape concert itself. Today, after some sixty years, as we have already concluded, many people still find the idea of attending a concert in which little to nothing happens visually extremely odd. There is, of course, a community of interested parties who meet to share the appreciation of these works; but how much has this public grown in recent years? Has the tape concert been the undoing of sound-based music? This question cannot be answered satisfactorily, but it does lead to another question: why do more people tend to attend tape concert events in galleries and the like than in concert halls? Are gallery visitors perhaps more open minded than concert audiences?

Issues surrounding today's image culture cannot be disregarded. Live visuals seem to form an important aspect of the Zeitgeist of today's performance. This does not mean that MTV versions of old acousmatic pieces need to be made and that *cinéma pour l'oreille* should simply become *cinéma*. There is little risk of tape or fixed medium concerts becoming a thing of the past. Still, in recent years there seems to be an increase of live performed work, particularly in the areas of electronica. There are also festivals, such as the NewMix event introduced in the previous chapter, where the programming is of tape works combined with live performance works, combined with audiovisual ones. Not only is there a pleasantly diverse aesthetic present during these events, but the tedium of "looking at nothing" is restricted to selected works, thus giving those works their own particular context.

The other option with such works is that its composers accept, for the time being at least, that their listeners listen to such works on their stereo or more sophisticated (e.g., Dolby 5.1) systems at home or wherever they happen to be. Most composers acknowledge that their works can be heard in two versions, similar to any piece of staged music. They must also acknowledge that the compromised version of their works will be the one most often listened to. The reliance on home listening does take the collective aspect out of the listening experience in most cases.

Leaving this awkward point aside, there is a lot more to be said about developments in terms of presentation. The twentieth century included several revolutions in music. Spatial awareness is one of the major ones. As sound diffusion developers are all working toward the ultimate spatialized sound experience, an interim art form has been created, that of sound diffusion whether mixed in real-time or programmed on multitrack recordings. One would expect the first sound diffusion textbook to have been published in the 1970s; but, other than the occasional article, it has yet to be written. Fortunately, most specialists have been willing to contribute some writing about the subject (see, e.g., Dhomont 1988; Duchenne 1991; Smalley 1991; Stockhausen 1996; Harrison 1998; Menezes 1998; and Moore et al. 2004).

In recent years, various forms of surround sound have been added to the diffusion systems many have employed thus far. Virtually all publications have described how these systems work and what the advantages are between one and another from an acoustics point of view. As in the case of publications on controllers, very little consideration has been given thus far to the musical and, more specifically, sound-based musical advantages of these spatialization systems. Furthermore, many of these discussions pay little attention to the diversity of spaces and the quirks thereof where these sound systems are being installed. It is surprising, for example, to discover how small the "sweet spot" is on most multi-channel diffusion systems. The composer or the person at the mixing desk and the mixing desk itself tend to take up a large portion of this special position. The further away one is from this center position, on virtually all systems, the more skewed the diffusion is. This cannot be right.

One response has been the creation of purpose-built spaces and loudspeaker placement for sound-based music. The early twenty-first century will see statistics increase rapidly in this area as our knowledge increases. This will aid the sweet spot problem sketched above. The goal is to work in three dimensions, yet most diffusion systems still seem to cover only two. If we are interested in sending sounds around spaces like an airplane's loop-the-loop, we need to control the third dimension as well.

Assuming the ultimate architecture for a sound-based musical space is not too far away, will it still be considered the concert hall? Simon Emmerson's "Sound House" concept, mentioned in the previous chapter, is just a start on the long path to optimize experiences in concert halls including ones specialized in sound-based music, with experiences in clubs, galleries, alternative venues including site-specific locations, the Internet, and the home. I look forward to the further evolution of such ideas. More discussion is urgently needed, particularly from the points of view of access and community forming.

Before the Sound House becomes a common venue for our art form, we still have all of those alternative, non-concert venues many of which seem to draw larger publics than the music venues themselves. Curiosity seems to be greater in a museum than at a concert hall; and similarly, curiosity is greater for installations and public art than for more formal events.[25]

In the same way that we should be conscious of the venues we use, we should also be aware of how much access is facilitated in audiovisual contexts than in audio-only ones. This is clearly one of the reasons for the renaissance of live electroacoustic performance. For artists who enjoy working in cross-arts contexts, the impact of sound-based music has enormous potential. Yet here, again, there are reports of what people have achieved (such as the Edison Group, Cipriani et al. 2004), but few concerning the potential and processes involved in working in such contexts including multimedia digital arts.[26] Those who call their work sound art are better documented, at least, than electroacoustic artists who work in audiovisual contexts. This discrepancy is a reflection of the awkward terminology still in place and traditional customs related to venues. As the visual plays an increasingly important role in various forms of sound-based music, our means of describing this work and evaluating it, for example investigating audiovisual relationships, deserve to be developed further.

Naturally, multimedia objects such as the GRM's *La musique électroacoustique* are particularly successful, as they introduce acousmatic music with evocative images that don't go beyond representations of the music itself. Of course many works on a fixed medium are quite strong as they were originally conceived, but it is not surprising that some seem to work better, at least in my experience, when they have been visualized, for example by being choreographed. Clearly for this to happen the audiovisual relationship needs to be successful, but when it is, the audio lifts the visual and vice versa.

Thus far in this subsection we have been focusing on real spaces and human presence. Telepresence is a rapidly developing area, and the audio and audiovisual implications of this are still unclear. The potential of immersive environments, though common in computer games, is only just emerging in terms of audiovisual artistic potential. New audio opportunities will become part of our experience of mobile phones and computers in no time.

The move from radio and television to the Internet and whatever follows it forms another very urgent subject. The Internet is also a key venue for tomorrow's broadcasting, reaching a much wider variety of publics and tastes than the radio has ever been able to offer (see Pope 1999). This could be just what has been missing in terms of audience and participant development. How this is best achieved is one of the most relevant subjects to the greater appreciation of sonic artworks imaginable.

Internet music has been making its *acte du présence* quite often in these chapters. The implications in terms of means of presentation are potentially enormous, not least because here, as with many public installations, one does visit not only to hear and see, but also to participate. The traditional choice between make or "take" (listen to) music is being broadened. This is yet another radical change in musical behavior that has been born of recent developments involving music and technology (although here not limited to sound-based varieties). The notion of linking new collaborative musical practices to particular social situations is a product of this broadening; in consequence, potential access is increased.

(7)   Achieving Interdisciplinarity and Holism

Although still focusing on the musicology of sound-based music, the time has come to return to the EARS rubric, Disciplines of Study (DoS). Some of these disciplines have been mentioned in the sections above, but others have hardly been called upon, in particular anything dealing with the sociocultural aspects of sonic artworks.

On several occasions it has been pointed out that the interdisciplinary nature of this music is to a large extent one involving technology and the sciences. Links with the likes of philosophy, semiotics, and anthropology should also receive their due attention. Let's take a brief walk through some of these areas again and attempt to identify where research needs appear to be most acute.

The *sociocultural* areas are the most impoverished. What I called ethno-electroacoustic musicology in 1999—the sociocultural study of sound-based music sounds better to me today—has limited itself to a large extent to the field of cultural studies. There is nothing particularly objectionable about this; however, many cultural studies treatments of sound-based music belong to the upper floors of a building for which the ground floor has hardly been started. Such treatments need to coexist with foundational studies of which too few are currently available.

We have already discovered that Georgina Born's controversial 1995 portrait of IRCAM is one of the few studies with a specific subject. The writing of Douglas Kahn (e.g., Kahn and Whitehead 1992) has been important in terms of relating product, history, and cultural positioning at the same time. Some of his writing (e.g., Kahn 1999), nevertheless, comes across as much more philosophical than pragmatic. We need more methodologically strong evidence-based research for the missing rooms and suites of the ground and lower floors of the building representing sound-based music studies. Studies of impact and appreciation—the likes of the I/R project—need to be undertaken in this broad area.

Other authors worthy of mention here are Sean Cubitt (1997 focusing on the politics of digital aesthetics; 1998), Jonathan Sterne (2003, for a historical view concerning sound reproduction), Timothy Taylor (2001, *Strange Sounds: Music, Technology, and Culture*, which is unusual owing to its strong political views) and Paul Théberge (1997, *Any Sound You Can Imagine: Making Music/Consuming Technology*). These last two come closest to what I believe we need more of in the field. If only such authors (if they have not tried this already) would go to the musicians and the public to pick up more grassroots information as an ethnomusicologist would while using appropriate fieldwork methodologies. What is laudable in most such researchers' writings is their lack of need to focus on either the *E* or *U* side of the traditional musical fence. This open-minded view toward music that involves technology is as welcome as it is unusual. As convergence continues, one hopes that this will become increasingly commonplace.

Another area that has increasingly received attention in research involves gender, although serious gender imbalances unfortunately continue in this field. There are also many specialists who have written about the economic reality of the more marginal forms of sound-based music from the points of view of financial support and public response (e.g., Pennycook 1992).

It could be said that the sociocultural study of the impact of ubiquitous music technology on today's society in conjunction with how small and large communities have dealt with the new opportunities offered by sound-based music is a field ripe for harvest. As a good deal of this music relates to our daily experiences in a number of ways, not least of which is the presence of real-world sounds, why does so much of the music remain so remote from society? It is in this area of interdisciplinarity where certain essential questions concerning access and accessibility can be investigated. One wonders whether the techniques of acoustic communication with those of, say, social anthropology or sociology, should not be combined to assist in the work that has yet to be done here.

Ever since the early writings of Schaeffer, many have called on *philosophy*, in his case phenomenology, to support the raison d'être of their approach to sound-based music. The subject of *textuality* appears fairly regularly as part of philosophical discussions. Palombini (1998), Fields (1999), and Richard (2000) are three of several who have investigated developments in others' works from a philosophical point of view. It seems evident why one might look into the philosophical foundations of sound-based music.

Furthermore, the first major essay on *semiotics* in electroacoustic music was Jean-Jacques Nattiez's contribution to a book on Bernard Parmegiani's *De natura sonorum* (Mion, Nattiez, and Thomas 1982). This piece was much more involved with texture than source identification, reflecting the GRM heritage of the work. The text therefore did not focus on what one might expect from a semiotics treatment of a sound-based work, namely the relationship between real-world sonic references, semiotic signifiers, and the signified. Twenty years later, I wonder whether the field of semiotics is equipped to deal with sound-based music in this manner. Perhaps some of today's semiotics experts might indeed work with cognition and psychology specialists to gain important insights concerning how we listen, what we listen for, and how we react to music in terms of narrative, in terms of content, in terms of emotion, and so on.

The areas of *cognition*, *perception*, and *psychoacoustics* are completely fundamental to work on sound-based music, as are *acoustics* and various other fields of *science* and *technology*. It is here where this volume's bibliography will seem to fall short, for a great deal of research thus far in cognition and its associated fields hardly touches upon sound-based music. What seems to take place most often is that people in sound-based music borrow from these associated fields for a specific purpose during this waiting period, until specialists in these fields finally decide to move from the lattice-based parameters of traditional music to those of texture and of sound organization. As far as the technology areas are concerned, finding this information is relatively easy in general; however, as we have discovered, exemplars of research in technology involving the "why" of the research are much less common. Regardless, cross-field research is inevitable. Sound-based music composers and authors appear to have been able to apply many concepts already in their artistic work as well as their writings. Still, a foundation of relevant interdisciplinary studies involving science and/or technology as well as the musical dimension deserves further attention.

Fortunately there are indications that a growing number of people from science and arts backgrounds are thinking in interdisciplinary ways, sometimes using a workshop approach to develop ideas. An excellent example of the science-arts approach can be found in David Worrall's (1996) discussion of his course in design structures. Not only does he cross the audiovisual border with ease, he combines influences from mathematics, philosophy, history, and cultural studies, and calls upon technological and scientific paradigms. Similarly, Xavier Serra (2003), in a lecture given for the U.K.'s Digital Music Research Network, makes a strong plea for science, technology, and arts specialists to work together (or, alternatively, for these specialists to specialize in more than one area). In his case, he speaks of music, psychology, computer science, engineering, and physics. He places sound-based music studies ("musical understanding") within the subject area of music. It is individuals like Serra who will aid in the path of bringing together the skills needed from these areas to cast new light upon the world of sound-based music in terms of its content, potential, and impact.

A few subjects have gone unmentioned thus far, yet they are far from unimportant. The *history* of sound-based music is one of the few areas that is relatively well documented, readily accessible and often written at levels that those with relatively little background can understand. As suggested above, it is promising that some recent authors recognize the cross-fertilization, particularly in recent years between the *E* and *U* sides of the traditional fence. This tendency supports the view that a new paradigm for sound-based music as defined above is worthy of investigation. It is to be hoped that future historical studies will investigate technological, theoretical, cultural, and, above all, musical aspects of this corpus of work in a holistic manner.

Other areas not often mentioned by name, but certainly referred to throughout the last two chapters, are *criticism* and *aesthetics*. Our dynamic world is becoming increasingly technologically savvy. To provide just one example, although one cannot assume that criticism will often focus on software programs, synthesizers, and the like, it seems unlikely that these elements can be ignored as listeners will probably be more interested in both musical and technological applications as time goes on. In other words, criticism may need take *faktura* into account. The potential relevance of aesthetics, presented here in the form of valorization scholarship, has been demonstrated elsewhere in this book.

All of these areas contribute to the conclusion for this section of the chapter. If sound-based music studies are to flourish, not only will these subjects need to be worked on as separate subfields of study, their combinations will also need to be investigated wherever relevant. Sound-based music is an interdiscipline and its study will therefore often be an interdisciplinary one. The more we approach this exciting body of work in the search for synergies, the closer we will come to creating a architecture that links the ground floor, much of which I am still searching for, with existent and new upper-floor rooms and suites that are so desperately needed.

(C) Looking Forward

This book has been quite difficult to put together. The ideals behind it are easy to express; but the challenge encountered just in choosing a provisional term to cover the body of art represented here is a symbol of the problems that continue to exist as we approach the sixtieth birthday of sound-based music. I am by no means against some tension in terminology, but the current state of play between, for example, "computer music," "electronic music," "electroacoustic music," "sonic art," "sound art," and "audio art" is simply ridiculous. The implications in terms of categorization are worrying.

International working groups comprising parties from the many constituencies that form the main communities in which we work should be represented in this debate and should be given the task to attempt to break through this impasse. We currently seem to operate in a manner similar to that of Wikipedia, where if someone is dissatisfied with a definition, he or she attempts simply to overwrite it with another one. In short, we seem to be a self-defeating community to the extent that our terminology remains in such a messy state.

We must face the facts; the music of technology represents the majority of music heard today. Although sound-based music is not that large a chunk of this music, the sounds of this music permeate through a very large number of nonspecialist genres and are not about to diminish. Therefore, sound-based music holds an important stake in terms of today's and tomorrow's music making.

This being the case, the odd state of affairs related to appreciation also deserves to be investigated internationally. It is exciting to see that organizations such as Unesco, by way of its DigiArts scheme, are introducing the means to create digital art, including digital music, in developing countries. This organization is also investigating exciting new opportunities for Internet music collaboration. As this book is being written, people of all ages from all continents are making pieces using water, for example, and associated sounds as part of their thematic series of approaches to sound organization. The program leaders believe in linking art with life, which is a very clever way to increase access and accessibility. The fact that Unesco is also subscribing to more sophisticated reference tools such as EARS, means that for those who are curious to learn more, the answer may be just a click away regardless of where they are.

If Unesco is able to share such potential through its networks, why are we unable, in the developed world, to insist that our tools and our music be placed prominently in our national curricula? As appreciation is gained, the desire and curiosity to create will increase and, consequently, the need for greater knowledge related to this music and its potential will grow. These are the most urgent tasks ahead.

A sound-based music paradigm   In the future scenario that is being proposed by way of this paradigm, one key task will be to classify the works belonging within the wider realm of sound organization. Although I would never suggest that my expectation is that many people will feel at home with the entire spectrum this music spans, I do believe that some people are unaware of a good deal of the work that might interest them given their specific background or circle of influence. That is, some people who are interested in experimentation in music related to popular music genres might find a good deal of other work of potential interest and vice versa. Many individuals are potentially fairly eclectic beings and, therefore, might enjoy a reasonably large repertoire of sound-based works. Instead of personal identity being equated with a "niche," artists can perhaps achieve a unique identity within a broader context, and thereby address themselves to those potential communities; in this way genres may give birth to subgenres, and so on. New eclectic concerts and festivals are offering the opportunity to hear a diversity of approaches and place these works into a coherent world of sonic artworks. I subscribe to François Delalande's notion of an electroacoustic (or, in our case, sound-based) paradigm, but I would prefer it to extend to all sound-based works rather than just works recorded on a fixed medium, which is Delalande's restriction, for with today's very fast digital processing, live improvised performance can easily be fit into the same type(s) of classification.

If more people were to accept this notion of a new paradigm that is not reliant on traditional E and U differences, and taking into account the results gained thus far in the Intention/Reception project, the stated goal of seeking new curricula from our education ministries and obtaining greater recognition from the broadcasting media are within our grasp. As far as distribution is concerned, inexpensive media and the Internet or its successor will help to facilitate access in new and efficient ways.

The field of sound-based music studies must stop being reactive and realize it is unnecessary to work with a fairly substantial delay time. It cannot work on the basis of the traditional notion of "one must wait several years before defining the historical value of a musical composition" (or development). Given that tomorrow's digital music making will be able to happen anywhere—owing to the increasing affordability and availability of relevant tools—people involved in sound-based music studies must help prepare the next stages of the important revolution foreshadowed by the futurists and the Dadaists that has begun to be realized in the postwar mid-century years.

If those working in the field were to become more proactive in terms of some of the issues raised in this book, the current lack of artistic (not to mention scholarly) coherence would be vastly reduced. Through better communication channels, mutual support would lead toward greater appreciation and therefore greater participation.

Many people working in sound-based music studies are also sound-based musicians. If these people demonstrate flexibility, following the results of their own forms of I/R research, we may inevitably discover new feedback mechanisms that facilitate access, appreciation, and our understanding of musical communication simultaneously.

I do accept the point of view put forward by Rosemary Mountain (2004) that sound-based music need not become too separated from music in general, for there exist commonalities in taste that have evolved between the two. This is part of the eclecticism referred to above. Still, there is something that draws many individuals of all backgrounds to sounds, whether those related to real life or the more abstract varieties. This being the case, we should feel short-changed that after so many years so few people are aware of the work we do, and yet so many are fascinated once introduced.

We also need to attempt to define the basis or bases of musicianship relevant to sound-based artworks, as this is part of the foundation for the field. We should beware, however, that as with musics from around the globe, there are very few true universals. Tuning systems are different in various parts of the world. Water to one is a fight for survival while for another it is omnipresent mud.

This being the case, the inevitable question follows: will there ever be a foundational musicianship course (or, in Schaeffer's terms, solfège) of sound-based music? I do think so, but not necessarily in the singular. Terms such as layering, transforming, and masking will be part of this study. But I do not envision an aural exam in which different types of "fire" need to be identified, nor do I hope exams will be offered where one guesses settings on a comb filter. And, as mentioned anecdotally above, exactly where something like a diminished seventh chord fits into this scheme is hard to tell. Some people will want to be able to identify one, others another type of sound or something that does not even exist yet. Still, there are means of producing, manipulating, combining, and layering sounds that are fairly common. We need to categorize these so that they can become part of such a program.[27]

The speed with which music that involves sound and technology continues to evolve will not diminish. We can, for example, expect an increase of creative work involving real-world sounds that are linked to our lived experience. People interested in related fields of study should become more proactive in terms of forging paths by which to acquire greater knowledge of music and its (potential) function in society. The resulting developments could then very well lead to the increased relevance of these forms of creative endeavor.

Appendix

The Keyword Index from the ElectroAcoustic Resource Site (EARS)

Disciplines of Study (DoS)

Acoustic Communication
  Electroacoustic Communication and
    Audio Media
  Listening
  Noise Pollution
    Audiology and Hearing Loss
    Background Music
    Clairaudience
    Ear Cleaning
    Effects of Noise
    Hi-Fi and Lo-Fi
  Soundmaking
    Language and Soundmaking
  Soundscape Studies
    Acoustic Ecology
    Clairaudience
    Community Soundscapes
    Disappearing Sound
    Ear Cleaning
    Earwitness
    Hi-Fi and Lo-Fi
    Keynote Sound
    Morphology
    Sacred Noise
    Schizophonia
    Sound Event
    Sound Phobia
    Sound Romance
    Soundmark
    Soundscape Design
    Sound Signal

    Soundwalk
Acoustics
  Acoustic Space
  ADSR
  Ambience
  Amplitude
  Beating
  Diffusion
  Distortion
  Doppler Effect
  Dynamic Range
  Envelope
  Feedback
  Formant
  Frequency
  Fundamental
  Harmonic
  Inharmonic
  Intrinsic Morphology and Imposed
    Morphology
  Modulation
  Noise
  Oscillation
  Phase
  Overtone
  Parameters of Sound
  Partial
  Pulse
  Pulse-train
  Resonance
  Reverberation
  Spectrum
    Spectral Space

Acoustics (cont.)
  Transient
  Tuning Systems
  Waveform
Audiovisual Theory
  Added Value
  Empathetic Sound and
      Anempathetic Sound
  Internal Logic and External Logic
  Internal Sound
  Magnetization
  Rendering
  Synchresis
Cognitive Science
  Complex Systems
    Chaos Theory
    Fractal Theory
  Computing
    AI
    Graphic Interface
    Object-oriented
  Critical Theory
  Cultural Theory
    Gender Theory
  Cybernetics
  Interactivity
  Interdisciplinary Studies
    Connectionism
    Sonification
  Linguistics
    Phonetics
  Media Theory
    New Media Theory
  Music Cognition
  Music Education
  Music Perception
  Music Psychology
    Gestalt
  Philosophy
    Phenomenology
    Philosophy of Art
    Philosophy of Music
  Probability Theory
    Stochastic Music
  Psychoacoustics
    Auditory Illusion

Auditory Scene Analysis
  Combination Tones
  Masking
  Source Recognition
  Spectral Fusion
  Spectral Space
  Stream
  Texture
  Timbre
Semiotics
Signal Processing
  DSP
Virtual Reality
  Immersive Environment

Genres and Categories (G&C)

Acousmatic
Adaptive Music
Algorithmic Music
Ambient Music
Analog Electroacoustic Music
Anecdotal Composition
Audiovisual Works
Avant-Rock
Background Music
Bruitisme
Cinéma pour l'oreille (Cinema for the
    Ears)
Clicks and Cuts
Collage
Computer Music
Concept Art
Cut-up
Diapositive Sonore (Sound Slide)
Digital Art
Digital Music
DJ Culture
Drum 'n' Bass
Electro
Electroacoustic Music
Electronic Music
Electronica
Elektronische Musik
Experimental Music

Field Recording
Free Music
Fusion
Glitch
Hip-Hop
Hörspiel
House
IDM (Intelligent Dance Music)
Immersive Environment
Improvisation
Industrial (Music)
Interactivity
Interdisciplinary Artistic Work
Installation Art
Internet Art
Internet Music
Japanese Noise Music
Krautrock
Laptop Music
Live Electronics
Lowercase Sound
Minimalism
Mixed Work
Multimedia
Musique Concrète
New Media Art
Noise Music
Organised Sound
Phonography
Plunderphonics
Post-Digital (Music)
Process Music
Public Art
Radiophonics
Remixing
Rock Concrète
Serialism
Site Specific
Sonic Art
Sound Art
Sound Design
Sound Installation
Sound Sculpture
Soundscape Composition
Spectralisme
Stochastic Music

Tape Music
Techno
Text-sound Composition
Timbral Composition
Turntablism
Video Art
Visual Music
VJ Culture

Musicology of Electroacoustic Music (MEM)

Aesthetics
  Digital Aesthetics
    Creative Abuse
    Circuit Bending
    Hybrid Thinking
    Intervention
    Recycling
Analysis
  Aesthesis and Poiesis
  Audio Analysis
  Auditory Scene Analysis
  Data Reduction
  Masking
  Spectral Analysis
    Acousmographe
    FFT
    Sonogram
    Waveform
    Wavelet
  Archiving
  Aural Analysis
  Acoustic Model
  Spectromorphology
    Continuum
    Gesture
    Indicative Fields and Networks
    Stream
    Typo-morphologie
      (Typo-morphology)
  Visual Representation
    Diffusion Score
  Faktura
  Parametric Analysis

Utterance
Paralanguage
Schaefferian Theory
  Abstrait et Concret (Abstract and
    Concrete)
  Acoulogie
  Acousmatic
  Anamorphose (Anamorphosis)
  Caractèrologie (Characterology)
  Écoutes Banales et Practiciennes
    (Ordinary and Practical
    Listening)
  Écoutes Naturelles et Culturelles
    (Natural and Cultural
    Listening)
  Époché
  Morphologie (Morphology)
  Musique Concrète
  PROGREMU
  Quatre Écoutes
  Reduced Listening
  Solfège
  Sound Object
  Synthèse (Synthesis)
  Typologie (Typology)
  Typo-morphologie
    (Typo-morphology)
Philosophy of Music
Sociocultural Aspects of
    Electroacoustic Music
  Access (to Electroacoustic Music)
  Dramaturgy of Electroacoustic
    Music
    Something to Hold on to Factor
  Acoustic Communication
  Acoustic Ecology
  Cultural Theory
  Culture-jamming
  Ethnomusicology
  Communities
  Electroacoustic Communities
  National and Regional Practices
    and Styles
  Free Music
  Gender Studies

Impact of Electroacoustic Music
Music Sociology

Performance Practice and Presentation (PPP)

Access (to Electroacoustic Music)
Cinéma pour l'oreille
Collaboration
  Devising
Composed Space
  Architectonic
  Faktura
  Immersive Environment
Improvisation
Interactivity
  Emergence
  Gestural Interface
  Interactive Instruments
  Internet Music
  Free Music
  Live Electronics
Performance Space(s)
Public Art
Real Time
MIDI
  Pitch-to-MIDI
Real-time Transformation
Site Specific
Spatialisation
  Ambisonic
  Architectonic
  Automated Spatialisation Systems
  Binaural
  Diffusion
  Fader Gesture
  Immersive Environment
  Loudspeaker Orchestra
  Motion
  Octophony
  Panoramics
  Quadraphonic
  Site Specific
  Sound Projection

Spatialisation (cont.)
  Stereophonic
  Surround Sound
Turntablism
Visual Representation
  Diffusion Score
  Graphic Score

Sound Production and Manipulation (SPM)

Abstract Shaping
Amplification
Breakbeat
Composed Space
  Architectonic
  Aural Perspective
  Immersive Environment
  Panoramics
Distortion
DSP
Effect
Electroacoustic Devices
  Controller
  Data Tracking
    Gesture Capture
    Movement Detection
    Pitch-tracking
      Pitch-to-MIDI
    Sensor
  Historical Electroacoustic
    Devices
  Interface
    Gestural Interface
  MIDI
    Pitch-to-MIDI
  Strong Action
  Triggering
Electroacoustic Instruments
  E- and I-instruments
  Historical Electroacoustic
    Instruments
  Interactive Instruments
    Games
  Live Electronics

MIDI
  Pitch-to-MIDI
Synthesizer
Faktura
Mixing
  Crossfade
  Xenochrony
Oscillator
Recording
  Ambisonic
  Binaural
  Close-mic Recording
  Field Recording
Remixing
Sampling
Scratching
Sequencing
Sound Shaping
  ADSR
  Brassage
  Chorusing
  Compression
  Constructed Continuation
  Constructive Distortion
  Convolution
  Delay
  Echo
  Editing
    Splicing
  Envelope
  Envelope Following
  Envelope Generation
  Equalisation
  Expansion
  Fader Gesture
  Feedback
  Filter
  Flanging
  Freezing
  Gating and Ducking
  Harmonising
  Limiting
  Loop
  Modulation
  Morphing
  Morphology

Intrinsic Morphology and Imposed
 Morphology
Phase-shifting
Phasing
Pitch-shifting
Plug-in
Reverberation
Reverse
Sample and Hold
Scrubbing
Sound Transformation
 Intermodulation
 Process Focused Transformation
 Real-time Transformation
Spectral Shaping
Spectral Thickening
Strong Action
Temporal Shaping
Time-compression
Time-scaling
Time-stretching
Transposition
Varispeed
Vocoding
Sound Source
 Environmental Sound
 Found Sound
 Grain
 Phonemic Object
 Utterance
Synthesis and Resynthesis Techniques
 Additive Synthesis
 Cross-synthesis
 Diphone Synthesis
 FOF
 Frequency Modulation Synthesis
 Granular Synthesis and Resynthesis
 Graphic Synthesis
 Hybrid Synthesis
 Klanglomeration
 Linear Predictive Coding
 Phase Vocoder
 Physical Modeling
  Karplus Strong Algorithm
 Pulse-train
 Real-time

Schwellenreiten
Speech Synthesis
Subtractive Synthesis
Synthrumentation
Visual Representation
 Synthesis Score
Waveset
Waveset Distortion
Waveshaping
Wavetable
Voltage Control

Structure, Musical (Str)

Architectonic
Architecture
Collage
Continuum
Dynamo
Editing
 Splicing
 Time-compression
Formalism
 Acoustic Model
 Adaptive Music
 AI
 Aleatory
 Algorithm
 Automated Composition
 Cellular Automata
 Chaos Theory
 Constraint-based Composition
 Entropy
 Generative Music
 Genetic Art
 Grammar
 Indeterminacy
 Mapping
 Neural Nets
 Object-oriented
 Serialism
 Stochastic Music
  Spektastik
 Tuning Systems
Layering

Macro-level Structure
  Klanglomeration
  Open Form
  Phase Patterns
  Sequencing
  Sound Flow
  Texture
  Xenochrony
Micro-level Structure
  Gesture
    Causality
  Grain
  Microsound
  Transzeitlichkeit
Momentform
Morphology
Spectromorphology

Notes

Preface

1. The word *access* and words associated with it, *accessible* and *accessibility*, will appear often throughout this book, in particular in chapter 1. The former term might be found to relate to people's ability to find out about music, whereas the latter refers to an appreciation or understanding of music. In the U.K., "access" is used in both senses. It is hoped that the context of usage makes clear which (or both) of these issues is being addressed.

2. EARS is currently coordinated by Simon Atkinson and myself at De Montfort University in the U.K., and forms part of the work of the Music, Technology, and Innovation Research Centre (MTI). During the period 2004–2007 Pierre Couprie and Rob Weale have been postdoctoral Research Fellows attached to the project. It has received funding from the Arts and Humanities Research Council and forms part of Unesco's DigiArts scheme. The DigiArts homepage at the time of this book's completion can be found at: http://portal.unesco.org/digiarts. The EARS project's current coordinating consortium members are Marc Battier (France), Joel Chadabe (U.S.), Ricardo Dal Farra (Argentina), Rosemary Mountain (Canada), Kenneth Fields (China), and Martin Supper (Germany).

3. The EARS site originally did not include acoustic sound-based music despite the fact that it forms a part of the work discussed in the current volume. The site's content has subsequently been widened to cover the entire breadth of this book.

4. At the time of completing this book, the EARS glossary and index were being translated into French and Spanish. The addition of other languages and the construction of a multilingual thesaurus of terms were also under investigation. Furthermore, there were plans for abstracts of bibliographic resources to be published in English as well as the publications' original language.

5. This is so regardless of the fact that the site's name does not correspond to the book's preferred terminology—see the terminology discussion in the introduction below.

Introduction

1. Here I am separating the "high arts" from the "popular arts" and the "folk arts," a simplistic although useful distinction I have borrowed from ethnomusicologists. We will return to the perceived divide between the first two frequently throughout the following chapters, after its introduction in chapter 1.

2. Dante Tanzi blames this gulf to a large extent on what he calls "self-referentiality as a value" (Tanzi 2004, 26). This has to do with an artist's greater interest in musical construction than in communication.

3. Matthew Adkins takes Windsor's approach to affordances a step further by introducing his concept of "acoustic chains" (Adkins 1999, 56). Acoustic chains offer the possibility of linking certain sound-based works. Adkins suggests that the listener, "when presented with a sounding object, perceives its affordance in relation to previous works before considering what the sounding object affords within the internal structure of the work" (ibid.). This concept is based on Lacan's notion of "signifying chains."

4. The Schaefferian notion of sound object will be introduced in chapter 2, section A1, where his theories will play a significant role.

5. See, e.g., Varèse 1940. Sources often claim that he first coined the term in 1924, but I have unfortunately been unable to track down specifically where he launched the concept.

6. Joseph Hyde (2003) has offered a peculiar variant on this definition in which he excludes electronica (in its popular music-related sense—see below) from sonic art, thus suggesting that certain forms of experimental popular music be kept separate from art music varieties. As this volume aims toward inclusion, this definition is only mentioned here in a note and not further pursued.

7. There are those who make a clear distinction between sound art and, say, electroacoustic or electronic music. In fact I have met more than one individual who believes that sound artists do not possess the necessary skills and insight to gain the musical denomination. This is a view that is not synonymous with the Varèse vs. Cage discussion but leads to the same separation that, as stated, I do not support.

8. At the International Computer Music Association's (ICMA) annual International Computer Music Conferences (ICMC), research in computer music is also considered to include any issue related to music technological research, e.g., cognition research in which the computer can be used, computational analysis of sounds and works, and so on.

9. Jose Manuel Berenguer words this similarly: "Beyond any other type of classification to which it may belong, an artistic product that satisfies a prescribed body of aesthetic needs and that appropriates sound as its principal medium, can be called 'electroacoustic music' insofar as an electronic operation is indispensable to its realisation" (Berenguer 1996, 30). Richard Orton once stepped from electronic music to electroacoustic music "since it does indicate the electronic mediation of acoustic principles" (Orton 1992, 320).

10. There is also the difference between electroacoustic, electromechanical, and electronic instruments. The late Hugh Davies defines these differences as follows: "*electroacoustic*—instruments whose sound sources are derived from vibrating objects, equivalent to acoustic instruments, but influencing an electrical circuit by means of special transducers (microphones) and often (deliberately) producing a minimum of acoustic sound; *electromechanical*—instruments whose sounds result from a rotating mechanism (that produces no acoustic sound) influencing an electrical circuit; *electronic*—instruments whose sounds are created by an electrical circuit that consists of electronic components and has no moving parts" (Davies 1992, 502).

11. The non-Cageian reader can opt for the term "sound-based art works" where relevant.

12. The EARS site's name was chosen because the use of electroacoustic music fits well within British scholarly efforts. Recently the Electroacoustic Music Studies Network (EMS Network, www.ems-network.org) has also been created and is being coordinated by Marc Battier of the MINT/OMF group at the Sorbonne, Daniel Teruggi of the Groupe de Recherches Musicales (INA/GRM), and myself. Time will tell which choice of umbrella term is most appropriate.

Chapter 1   From Intention to Reception to Appreciation

1. Blacking has written: "The function of music is to enhance in some way the quality of individual experience and human relationships . . . the value of a piece of music is inseparable from its value as an expression of human experience" (Blacking and Byron 1995, 31). This mirrors one of the points raised in this book's introduction. Blacking clearly found most contemporary music separable from his notions of human experience. Supporting this, Bruce Pennycook once noted: "to an untrained ear, [i.e., to the general public] the consistently dissonant harmonies and jerky rhythms of Free Jazz and contemporary composition sound uniformly grey and generally unappealing" (Pennycook 1992, 559). He warns that through this estrangement future subsidies to various forms of contemporary art music may be in peril, as funding organizations might consider lowering their support given lack of public interest.

2. Suffice to say that there exist works of fusion that cross the *E-/U-Musik* boundary; there are also works of "serious" or experimental rock that are not necessarily that popular or focused on entertainment in the first instance. More recent excursions including selected forms of electronica and ambient music do not fit easily on either side. The issue of the relationship between sound-based music and the *E/U* demarcation is discussed in some detail in chapter 2.

3. Another poignant example of making works more accessible through audio-visual application comes from Terre Thaemlitz. While discussing a public he finds quite conservative in a region where he once lived, he notes that these same people are listening to works of progressive electronica on advertisements (Thaemlitz 2001, 182) in what he calls an "electronica-free community." His

point is clear: progressive music seems to work when presented by stealth in "acceptable" contexts, e.g., audiovisual ones in general as alluded to above, and commercial ones in particular.

4. A musical equivalent comes to mind. Mladen Milicivic has suggested, with a hint of irony: "Now, when I see an electronic music composer who, in making a piece of music is primarily focused on its internal structure with its use of fractals, Fibonacci numbers, solar systems, palindromes, permutations, interpolations, pitch-sets, algorithms, timbral manipulations, etc. etc. and less concentrated on how the cultural environment reacts to it, I get worried about the future of such music" (Milicivic 1998, 30). Naturally, any of these can be used to achieve an excellent musical result, but the result is not necessarily due to the tool. Milicivic is simply making a plea for the composer to take the listening experience into account.

5. Jeff Pressing, reflecting a statement by Dante Tanzi that appeared in the introduction (note 1), has put this even more poignantly: "Like other progressive art musics, electroacoustic music suffers a distinct lack of attention from the general public and is sometimes beset by a ghetto or excessively self-referential mentality within its professional community" (Pressing 1994, 27). His solutions include the increase of "human mediation" in the production of creative works and the E-culture's acceptance of a beat and even dance-like works, bringing the notion of corporeality to sound-based artwork, in particular electroacoustic works. This is an interesting view as it is a plea for conservation of traditional musical elements, although, I believe, not as a *sine qua non* for accessible sound-based music, as will be demonstrated later on. More radically, he would like to see an investigation take place to determine whether the division between high and low (*E* and *U*) art is still valid, a question I return to in the final section of chapter 2. Ben Neill (2002, 3) supports this view when he suggests that the key difference between art and popular electronic music is rhythm. One wonders to what extent that is still true. Barry Truax has dealt with these issues more diplomatically: "One of the dilemmas facing the contemporary music composer today, particularly a younger one, is whether and to what degree one should follow the largely European-based pursuit of abstraction as the goal and direction of art music" (Truax 1996a, 13).

6. This subsection relies heavily on ideas launched in "The Something to Hold on to Factor in Timbral Composition" (Landy 1994a).

7. Anecdotal composition involves works in which source recognition is fundamental.

8. The term *acousmatic* will be introduced in chapter 2, section A1. For the moment, it concerns sounds heard without the source of the sounds being seen.

9. Another form of homogeneity occurs in the case where people perceive the technology being used, a specialist mode of listening introduced in this subsection's final example. People who listen to the technology tend to have less need for access tools than inexperienced listeners.

10. In a 1994 article, I wrote: "Denis Smalley best exemplifies user-friendliness without necessarily being overly friendly to the user" (1994, 55); that is, his works are very sophisticated yet he offers a clear means to access to his works as will be illustrated in the section concerning intention and reception.

11. The term *plunderphonic* will be introduced in chapter 2, section A3.

12. The 1994 article also suggests that the presence of a narrator in an acousmatic tale can often become the center of attention, taking the listener's focus away from the sonic narrative. This supports the claim about the magnetism of vocal sounds.

13. On a similar subject, Jon Appleton, known for his connection to the once revolutionary Synclavier music computer, has complained that almost everywhere he travels people come to see the technology (Appleton 1999). He recounts an anecdote in which he was pleasantly surprised during a performance in Moscow where the audience was primarily interested in the music, showing curiosity about the technology only later. Appleton's worry is that today's obsession with technology can get in the way of appreciation of artistic quality.

14. Besides the addition of dramaturgy (see under section B), Rob Weale (2005) has added greater detail to this list as part of his Ph.D. study concerning the Intention/Reception project introduced below. His list (chapter 4.1.3) reads as follows:

(A) Real-world sounds: (i) Source/cause, (ii) Voice, (iii) Location
(B) Parameters of sound: (i) Timbral quality, (ii) Spatiality, (iii) Dynamics, (iv) Movement, (v) Morphology, (vi) Pitch, (vii) Rhythm
(C) Structure: (i) Narrative (real-world), (ii) Narrative (acoustic), (iii) Layers of sound, (iv) Juxtaposition of sound (real-world), (v) Juxtaposition of sound (acoustic)
(D) Transformation: (i) Static transformation, (ii) Dynamic transformation
(E) Homogeneity of sounds: (i) Real-world sounds, (ii) Parameters of sounds
(F) Extrinsic information: (i) Title, (ii) Dramaturgy

The research into the "something to hold on to" factor continues.

15. One must be very careful not to construct a picture here that is too black and white. The suggestion that people build works from materials does not suggest that they are uninterested in structure or that structures inevitably arrive only very late in the compositional process. Similarly, not all top-down composers are necessarily as rigorous as their theoretical writings sometimes suggest. This implies that aural choices may occur in what is presented as, for example, a formalized work.

16. Another, more recent project is worthy of mention in this context, this time concerning contemporary dance (see Grove, Stevens, and McKechnie 2005). Two of the work group's three key questions demonstrate this well: "What elements encourage audiences to respond to [contemporary] dance work with insight, pleasure and understanding? How do previous knowledge, experience and education affect audience responses?" (ibid., 6). It also includes a focus on how

appreciation can be increased (ibid., 9). This e-book contains a chapter by Renee Glass focusing specifically on observers' cognitive reactions and affective responses to contemporary dance (ibid., chapter 8). In so doing, Glass attempts to identify aspects of reception in terms of contemporary dance that are similar to the "something to hold on to" factor introduced in this chapter.

17. This proves to be a slightly awkward restriction when one takes into account Bridger's conclusions, one of which concerns listeners' enthusiasm for spatial manipulation.

18. As this duration was too long for three full listening phases, after discussion with the composer it was decided to play the first roughly six minutes, a complete section of the work in which the key structuring principles are all exposed, during the first two listening phases.

19. *Valley Flow* appears on the CD *Impacts intérieurs*, Empreintes DIGITALes IMED-9209-CD (Smalley 1992b); *Prochaine Station* on *Électro Clips: 25 electroacoustic snapshots*, Empreintes DIGITALes IMED-9604 (Calon and Schryer 1990).

20. Smalley's spectromorphological theory will be introduced in chapter 2, section A1. For the time being, spectromorphology can be taken as the study of sonic spectra being shaped in time.

21. Dante Tanzi discusses the I/R project in Tanzi 2004. In this article he suggests that the project be expanded to involve collective sonic composition including new forms of collaborative music making on the Internet. This is one of a host of logical next steps for the I/R project, given that communication, or at least common understanding, is a *sine qua non* of collective performance.

22. A book by Hans Schneider, *Lose Anweisungen für klare Klangkonstallationen* (2000), represents a more recent publication in which music technology is specifically called upon (for example the use of sampling and DJ-ing in improvisation), as a potential didactic tool that offers valuable skills to younger people.

23. This is also reflected in some of the developmental work on instruments and devices for children of all ages such as those developed at Bourges. (U.S. examples are described in Weinberg 2002a.) Furthermore, the Groupe de Recherches Musicales published the CD-ROM, *La musique électroacoustique*, which introduces younger people to sound and means of manipulating it while encouraging their interest in sound-based music and opportunities. This publication was supported by the French Ministry of Education.

24. The Bourges Festival, its Académie, and a few of its developments will appear from time to time throughout the book, at times discussed from a critical perspective (such as in the current section). Bourges is by no means a unique example, although it is one of the better-known festivals globally, at least as far as electroacoustic art music is concerned. It will be treated as a case in point more than either an example of good or bad practice. I would also suggest that in recent years most festivals have become more conscious of the social issues that will be raised, a product of how funding organizations are changing with the times.

25. Bruce Pennycook, when discussing individual artists, has spoken of a "sonic signature" (Pennycook 1986, 121), suggesting that such signatures often involve ideas, technologies, or sounds relevant to the time of their creation.

26. Examples include Margaret Anne Schedel, who has suggested that sound-based artists consider performing their works in art venues such as galleries and museums as she believes that these publics (communities) are perhaps more open to such new experiences than some concert publics (Schedel 2004). Along these lines Warren Burt has taken the trouble to make a diary of his experiences concerning performances of his music across a variety of venues, in the style of: "if Mohamed can't come to the mountain, then the mountain can come to Mohamed" (Burt 2001).

27. Soundwalks are introduced in chapter 2, section A2.

28. Throughout much of the rest of this section I shall be recycling a number of thoughts that were launched in Landy 1996 and 1998a.

29. There is rare early work such as Wolfgang Martin Stroh's 1975 book on the sociology of electronic music, but this looks at elite electronic art works, a few possessing some form of political message, in the first instance. The social aspect is therefore seen primarily in terms of the existent *E-Kultur*. What Waters is looking for is much more than this. There are some in the field of cultural studies who are trying to make up for lost time. We will return to this issue in the final chapter.

Chapter 2   From Concept to Production to Presentation to Theory

1. The term in the title, "co-hear-ence," was created in Landy 2000, not to be trendy, but instead to emphasize that sonic artworks deserve to be brought into some form of *audible* coherence, a reaction against the last century's drive toward individual voices, languages, and so on, which led to a map of music that is filled with small isolated islands, (works and/or composers), an occasional cluster of islands, and then some fairly substantial land masses, mainly representing the popular music worlds.

2. Microsound does have its own discussion group, and genres have emerged using microsound as the key means of source material creation. Nevertheless, microsound itself is not a proper genre.

3. This chapter is directly linked to the "Genres and Categories" section of the EARS site. The theoretical discussions are linked primarily to the "Musicology of Electroacoustic Music" section.

4. I called layers "textures" in my 1994 article. This original term is in fact problematic as two or more layers can create a single texture at any given moment.

5. Bob Ostertag (1996) wrote earlier in a similar manner of most computer music focusing on extended timbral exploration or algorithmic composition. Ingeborg Okkels and Anders Conrad make a distinction between what they call "bricoleur and engineer composers," the former relating to Waters' spectralists.

As far as the latter is concerned, "[the] engineer composer works with sounds as an abstract physical entity rather than a cultural artefact" (Okkels and Conrad 2000, 10).

6. Early 2006, at the time of the completion of this chapter.

7. Entries followed by an asterisk (*) indicate that the entry goes beyond sound-based music, e.g., through its application in vocal-instrumental music or another art form.

8. Although it might be assumed that most readers are acquainted with this and similar terms, definitions are being provided for those who are uncertain or who have not yet been introduced to sound-based music terminology.

Acousmatic: A Pythagorean term reintroduced in 1955 by Jérôme Peignot which considers the "distance which separates sounds from their origin," i.e., an audio-only presentation of sound common to electroacoustic music. For some, the term is very precise and refers specifically to this listening situation. However, the term has gained wider usage, in describing a genre, which, to a large extent derives from the musique concrète tradition and is founded upon this listening situation. (EARS site)

9. To add to this confusion, Bayle also considers acousmatic music as *l'art des sons projetés* (the art of projected sounds) in the sense that the listening experience is based on vibrations created from a number of loudspeakers.

10. This term has been translated by Carlos Palombini (one of the key authors on Schaeffer whose work has appeared in English and Portuguese) as "sonic objects" and by Brian Kane as "sonorous objects."

11. This was the name in use before they became the Groupe de Recherches Musicales.

12. Dhomont's powerful view is not universally accepted, however. Rosemary Mountain (2001) has offered a word of caution concerning this claim to having no past in her article, "Caveats from a Dyed-in-the-Wool Futurist," in which she suggests that new technology-driven forms of music should not deny the past, but instead integrate it among all the new possibilities that new technologies are offering.

13. Other key Schaeffer sources are Schaeffer 1952, Schaeffer 1967, Pierret 1969, Brunet and Schaeffer 1970, Schaeffer 1970, Schaeffer 1972, and Brunet 1977. Obviously there are several books and articles treating and celebrating his work as well.

14. I would like to point out that I found it unnecessary to translate Chion's work, as John Dack and Christine North had already done an impeccable job of this. They sent me their as yet unpublished translation which is the one used throughout this discussion. I am grateful to them both for permitting me to share their excellent work. I equally want to thank Michel Chion for his permission to quote him rather liberally in this discussion. Unless otherwise stated, all other translations in this book are mine; I therefore take full responsibility for their accuracy.

15. In this book, Cox and Warner, in celebrating this approach to music, have written the following concerning Schaeffer's influence: "Schaeffer prefigured today's music producer, who manipulates sound with inexpensive hardware and software on his or her home computer, he also prefigured the age of the remix. For recorded sound obscures the difference between the original and the copy, and is available for endless improvisatory manipulations and transformations" (Cox and Warner 2004, xxiv).

16. Throughout the rest of this discussion, numbers in square brackets, such as [15] refer to the relevant entry in Chion's *Guide*. There are one hundred entries in this volume.

17. Schaeffer often added the clarification that "concrete" does not mean specific, recognizable sounds.

18. Words here within single quotation marks are directly from Schaeffer's *TOM*—Chion usually includes page references for these citations in this *Guide*.

19. After Pythagoras.

20. Sound artist Francisco López uses the terms *blind* or *profound listening* as synonyms (López 2004, 82). Electroacoustic music for which no source or cause is identifiable has also been called *pure music* (Delalande 2002).

21. *Balanced* is a term that is introduced later in the current discussion.

22. François Bayle compares ideas about modes of listening of Barthes, Peirce, Husserl, and Schaeffer (Misch and von Blumröder 2003, 78–83); Denis Smalley reduces Schaeffer's four to three (Smalley 1992; for further detail see below), but equally identifies the notion of "listening to technology," our *5ième écoute*, listening to how sounds have been produced and/or transformed. In other texts: Katharine Norman introduces the notions of referential, contextual, and reflective (similar to reduced) listening (Norman 1996)—they will be presented under subsection 2 below; Michel Chion adds two of his own: causal and semantic listening (Chion 2002, 238). Finally, François Delalande coined the term *conduits d'écoutes* (listening mode behavior) as a means of dealing with the listening experience as an analytical tool (see, e.g., Delalande 1986, 56).

23. Schaeffer uses the word *identify* to describe this.

24. Schaeffer often uses the term *naming*.

25. He rejected the term musique concrète as both ambiguous and dated; electroacoustic music meant to him the sum of acousmatic and electronic music (that is, at the time; he later found this word, too, to be dated). He also occasionally uses an even more all-embracing term, *musique technologique* (introduced in Bayle 1998), which might one day become a reasonable candidate to replace some less popular terms. I, for one, know very few people—Marc Battier being one—who use this rather sensible term frequently. In any event, to him the era of musique concrète belongs to the past; he feels that "acousmatic" was a better description of music made during the period of his writings.

26. Bayle tends to place this term alongside its associate, *cohérences* (something evolving through a "system of related qualities").

27. *Salience*: property of sounds whose role are local, immediate; *pregnance*: property of sounds that are "translocal."

28. In fact, Bayle likes to use descriptive verbs to portray his metaphors, analogous to Stockhausen's use of descriptive adjectives used in the score to assist in the notation of the moments (sections) of his work, *Mikrophonie 1* (1964).

29. This is accompanied by five levels of acousmatic audition: acoustical/physical, sonorous/physiological, auditive/psychological, musical/symbolic, and "imaginal"/figurative (Bayle 1993, 82 note).

30. "[E]ach sound, heard from a loudspeaker, is an image: thus an *i-son*" (Bayle, speaking in Misch and Blumröder 2003, 124). "Sound diffusion is the projection and the spreading of sound in an acoustic space for a group of users—as opposed to listening in a personal space" (Denis Smalley, in Austin 2000, 10). Smalley also refers to the "dramatization of the space [and] . . . of gestures" (ibid., 13).

31. Bayle uses the term *paysage sonore* ("sonic landscape" or "soundscape") to exemplify the *im-son*, and refers to works pertaining to this term.

32. For true adventurers, Jean-Christophe Thomas (2003) has written an article discussing fifty-three terms he associates with Bayle.

33. Chion does allow himself to be slightly critical of Schaeffer at times, for example in *Le Son*, chapter 11, section 5: "The 'errors' in the solfège of the sound object"; Chion criticizes Schaeffer for suggesting that a sound object cannot be defined without taking its context (Chion uses the word "space") into account.

34. Rodolfo Caesar presents an unusual translation, or perhaps alternative term for *tournage sonore*, namely "mike-shaping," which better describes the act (Caesar 1992, glossary).

35. At the time of writing, an up-to-date bibliography of his writings can be found at: http://www.ina.fr/grm/outils_dev/theorique/articles_chrono.fr.html.

36. Delalande, like Chion, is not always uncritical of Schaeffer. In his book *Le son des musiques* he notes three different definitions of sound object from Schaeffer, two appearing in TOM (Delalande 2001b, 227 note). In the article "En l'absence de partition: le cas singulier de l'analyse de la musique électroacoustique," he criticizes Schaeffer for studying only sound objects, not pieces (Delalande 1986: 55).

37. Elsewhere Delalande has commented on what he believes specialists in perception expect from those in the electroacoustic field: first, a better understanding of electroacoustic musical material (from the perception, not physical point of view); second, a better understanding of the perception of full works (reception: hearing and appreciation); and third, to invent in the future the equivalent of a solfège (for reception and production application) (Delalande 1985, 199–200).

38. Granted, a reasonably similar approach to the analysis of the Bernard Parmegiani work "Aquatisme" is presented in Delalande 2002, but we are still limited to two examples with a restricted subject group in each case.

39. These two terms were originally written with a hyphen before *morphology.* I am spelling these terms as Smalley does today.

40. Smalley describes his view as follows: "Real and imagined provenances of the sound are ignored as a result of repeated listening to the same sound, and as a result of the need to direct aural attention to spectromorphological detail" (Smalley 1999, 183). This holds true for the composer, the analyst, and ideally, the general listener. Still, things are not so black and white; he later suggests that pertinences in a given work can create (imagined) relationships with the real world in response to the musical context (ibid., 188).

41. Smalley 1986 was originally presented at a conference organized by the Elektronmusikstudion in Stockholm in 1981 and later revised. Smalley 1997 originally appeared in French in Smalley 1995, later in Italian in Smalley 1996, and in German in Smalley 2004. I would like to personally thank him for allowing me to cite his works as extensively as I have.

42. Smalley has suggested that spectromorphology is a practical means of applying a reduced listening strategy, especially when there is repeated listening (Smalley 1999, 183).

43. Smalley avoids the word *timbre* as he finds it to be too often associated with pitch and prefers to use terms like *texture* to describe spectromorphological aspects.

44. In Smalley 1991, he adds the notions of superimposed space, "a nesting of the composed spaces within a listening space," and musical space, which he subdivides into pitch space and temporal space.

45. In Smalley 1994, he relates such models to his notion of behavior in discussing nonreferential sounds that demonstrate aspects of real-world behavior.

46. Elsewhere Emmerson uses Smalley's terminology (and some new terms of his own) to discuss dislocation in live electroacoustic performance in particular concerning unrecognizable or ambiguous causal relationships (see, e.g., Emmerson 1994a, 2000a). Emmerson's ideas will be presented in greater detail in subsection 8 below.

47. Natasha Barrett (2002) introduces a few terms of her own involving space, e.g., *spatial illusion, allusion,* and *implied spatial occupation,* in an article that is rooted in Smalley's theory.

48. In the sense used by Smalley.

49. Ambrose Field has provided an interesting example of collective memory. In discussing Katharine Norman's *London,* he notes that early in the piece, one hears urban sounds that seem fairly generic. As one gets closer to the work, it becomes clear that the sounds have been recorded in London itself (Field 2000: 30). Listeners can share the experience at their own level whether they have been in London or not. Such experiences can involve any identified sound, emotional memory, or otherwise, whether at a more generic or more specific level.

50. There are, of course, researchers who use ecology as a basis for the creation of models for application in sonic artworks. For example, see Keller and Cappaso

2000, Barrett 2000, and Burtner 2005 (ecoacoustic concept). Damián Keller writes (Keller 2000, 59): "Ecologically based composition makes use of everyday sound models that are constrained to perceptually meaningful parameter ranges. Complementarily, it provides references to the social context in which the music is created. The characteristics of the source material inform the development of techniques for re-synthesis and transformation of environmental sounds."

51. Combining the notions of lo-fi and moozak, Truax notes that people wearing walkman headphones in open spaces are embedding one environment—whatever the walkman is playing—within another, that is, the one in which the person is located.

52. Truax points out elsewhere (Truax 1996b, 19) that he considers Smalley's spectromorphological approach typical of what he calls the European urge toward abstraction, as transformed sounds tend to be abstracted from their original context and/or source recognition.

53. A *soundmark* is "derived from landmark to refer to a community sound which is unique or possesses qualities which make it specially regarded or noticed by the people in that community" (Schafer 1994, 276). This term is associated with *keynote sounds*, which are "those which are heard by a particular society continuously or frequently enough to form a background against which other sounds are perceived" (ibid., 272), e.g., the sea at the seaside, or engine sounds in the city. A third term completes Schafer's trilogy, namely *sound signal*: "any sound to which the attention is particularly directed" (ibid., 275). These are all known as *archetypal sounds* (ibid., 9).

54. A worthy article investigating Truax from philosophical, artistic, and technological development points of view can be found in Voorvelt 1997.

55. Readers interested in following current debates in the areas of soundscape and acoustic ecology are referred to the journal *Soundscape: The Journal of Acoustic Ecology* (the voice of the World Forum for Acoustic Ecology), and national journals such as *Earshot: Journal of the UK and Ireland Soundscape Community*.

56. Katharine Norman's two key publications relevant to this and other sections of this chapter are Norman 1996 and 2000. The 1996 article formed part of a thematic issue of *Contemporary Music Review* entitled *A Poetry of Reality* that she edited. Many of the other articles in this issue have also been cited in this book.

57. Many authors interested in appropriation seem to gain credibility by citing Igor Stravinsky, who was known to have said: "the best composers are simply the best thieves." Strange how a remark concerning neo-classical thinking can be rediscovered under such an entirely different guise!

58. Those in the know will already be aware that Oswald's plundering of sounds was not what got him into trouble. It was, instead, the cover image of Michael Jackson's face projected onto a naked female body that led to his being forced to destroy any remaining copies of the CD once he had been "caught."

Fortunately many of us did not join him in the destruction ceremony and he has subsequently found highly legal means to continue his craft. There are several CDs of his that are currently commercially available.

59. His opponents may consider this broad spectrum of source material a form of musical tourism.

60. And then there are those artists who believe in "copyleft" (i.e., not requesting copyright), not to mention those people whose sense of appropriation goes beyond sounds to involve tools and more, such as today's hackers (see, e.g., Polansky's insightful 1998 article concerning "hacking together"). National authors' rights organizations are in a constant battle with these radical figures who advocate appropriation and sharing.

61. See, e.g., the discussion of Martijn Voorvelt's (1998) dissertation under subsection 7 below for other approaches to experimental pop music.

62. James Harley also mentions Iannis Xenakis in this context, as he was an early innovator "embracing of technology and high-density/high-amplitude sound set off by disorienting, hallucinatory light-shows" (Harley 2002, 33) and therefore was an obvious figure to include in such performance contexts.

63. In Montreal, there was some tension for a number of years between the primarily acousmatic "Rien à voir" (nothing to see) festival and the Mutek festival which featured new approaches to *électro*, the local name for anything electroacoustic. It seemed for a while as if there was a generational split in audience. Now "Rien à voir" has unfortunately ended; ironically, the newer festivals have become more eclectic, demonstrating the strengths of the more traditional tape or mixed music concert with the new protocols of recent live digital music performance.

64. Jean-Claude Risset recently suggested that development work in analysis-synthesis might bring people from the worlds of the electronic as well as the concrète together, as the former are interested in synthesis and the latter in processing (Risset 2002: xv).

65. This example ironically brings us back to the terminology debate. Cort Lippe (1994) has written that granular synthesis is an evolution rooted in the electronic music tradition, whereas granulation of samples is a product of the musique concrète tradition. Many musicians using granulation are looking for spectralist-related texture regardless of the tradition from which the method of sound creation and/or manipulation evolved.

66. Phil Thomson (2004) sites three others as highly influential in terms of early developments of microsound, namely Karlheinz Stockhausen through his concept of *Punkte* (points), Gottfried Michael Koenig through the development of his SSP software, and Herbert Brün with his Sawdust software, the last two both working at sample level (e.g., 1/20,000 of a second).

67. Truax seems to find the description of paradigm shifts a relatively easy task; a third shift, overlapping with this first one, was presented under subsection 2 above.

68. Curtis Roads says the same thing in a different way in his discussion of the difference between waves and particles (Roads 2001, 44); waves can be broken up into constituent elements, particles cannot. At the level of the sound object, Roads uses the terms *homogeneous* (able to be reduced into its parametric components) and *heterogeneous* (containing time-varying or morphological properties) (ibid., 18).

69. Michel Chion coined the term *micro-editing* for the creation of microsound in tape music (Roads 2001, 82).

70. See also Stuart 2003a on "damaged sound," Ashline 2003 on "pariahs of sound," and Sherburne 2001 on microsound beyond the academy.

71. The subject has been investigated from a philosophical dimension (Back 2003), sociocultural and political dimensions (Monroe 2003), the issue of appropriate venues for laptop music (Turner 2003—none is found to be ideal; see also Cascone 2003 who also discusses reception issues), key techniques to laptop performance (Nick Collins 2003; he mentions presets—preprogrammed patches, previewing—listening to sounds by way of headphones like a DJ before mixing them into a performance, autopilot—algorithm-driven, and live coding—real-time programming during performance), and the blurring of production, performance, and distribution (Reddell 2003; here he coins the term *laptopia,* which he defines as follows: "Laptopia is a collective media-scape of increasingly mobile computer networks, electronic and digital audio performances, distributed studio productions, synchronized live video mixes and streaming internet content" [ibid., 11]).

72. Alex McLean came up with one interesting solution to this issue by projecting his computer screen onto the wall in the performance space so that people who were present could see what he was viewing and how he was performing his patches (in Nick Collins 2003, 69).

73. The alternative CD label name, Mille Plateaux, associated with this music is borrowed from a title taken from contemporary French philosophers, Gilles Deleuze and Félix Guattari, a rather rare acknowledgment to academic thought from the independent music world.

74. This phrase is in fact a paraphrase of Trevor Wishart's view that "there is no such thing as an unmusical sound-object" (Wishart 1985, 6). Wishart will play the leading role in this subsection.

75. This list includes, for example, the former "Rien à voir" series in Montreal and the annual Electroacoustic Music Festival in Brazil, as well as events hosted by national or regional organizations focusing on electroacoustic music such as the U.K.'s Sonic Arts Network, Canada's CEC, France's JIM, and others.

76. Equipment-based "sounds" exist, too; for example, there is normally an audible difference between an analog and a digital work.

77. Interesting discussions concerning Colombia specifically (Cuellar Camargo 2000) and Latin America in general (Aharonián 2000) can be found in the "Southern Crosses" issue of *Leonardo Music Journal.*

78. A couple of examples of such personal contributions include Alain Savouret's "phonoculture" (culture of sound) and "musique inscrite" (inscribed music, i.e., on a fixed medium such as tape or a harddisk—Savouret 2002); Kodwo Eshun's bouquet of unusual terms (Eshun 1998, 4), some of his own making, some of others, the meanings of which are left to the reader, such as "scratchadelia" (Sonz of a Loop da Loop Era's term); "turntablization" (DJ Krush) and "mixadelics" (George Clinton); and Frank Zappa's term "xenochrony" (or "re-synchronization," the procedure involved in taking a track off a master and combining it with something entirely different—Watson 1996, 132). Clarence Barlow also comes to mind; his contributions are primarily related to formalism and are introduced below. Finally, Rodolfo Caesar (1992) takes a number of existent terms and investigates them critically as well as proposing a modest number of his own for general use in his Ph.D. dissertation. He also has been one of the main people deciding which terms to employ in Portuguese.

79. Simon Emmerson edited and was involved with the republication of *On Sonic Art*. This later version, published in 1996, is clearer than the original. One of Wishart's focuses, particularly in his first book, is the potential of the human voice to create virtually any sound. This unique aspect of his work will not be treated in the current discussion, but other key concepts will be presented. An outsider's view on his writings can be found in, e.g., Brattico and Sassanelli 2000.

80. Please note Wishart's preference for the word *landscape* as opposed to *soundscape* used by many others. As Wishart's work tends to be relatively more abstract than soundscape compositions, this key term of his is a logical choice. It is, however, awkward in terms of our subject's terminology, as I have seen the two terms conflated and misused by writers.

81. There is the occasional individual who maps one form of musical information to another. See, e.g., McLaughlin 2000, where African and Indonesian rhythmic patterns are used as mapping data, and Arfib et al. 2002 in which the subject of mapping is applied to musical gestures in terms of synthesis model parameters.

82. Two interesting views concerning why one may turn to biological models and genetic algorithms can be found in the same issue of *Contemporary Music Review* (Berry and Dahlstedt 2003 and Gartland-Jones and Copley 2003). Although not entirely convincing, it is nice to see artists and developers explaining why they turn to such extramusical worlds in the first place; the latter notes the limited amount of work undertaken thus far in terms of the evaluation of the output of genetic algorithms.

83. And the use of such clever terms is not limited to musicians. Frank Popper in discussing connectionist art that uses new technologies speaks of the *Gesamt-datenwerk* (data replacing art, in *Gesamtkunstwerk*, Popper 1993, 125).

84. It is interesting that in such cases, Curtis Roads sees the computer as a musical *idiot savant* (Roads 1992, 400).

85. In a recent thematic issue of the journal *Organised Sound* on complex systems, there were several contributions involving formalization including

articles on self-organization ("swarm music," Blackwell and Young 2004), modeling storms in sound (Polli 2004), and "spontaneous organisation, pattern models, and music" (Visell 2004). QED.

86. He also raises an interesting point in the same article that one cannot necessarily hear differences in timbral sophistication between high-end and commonplace systems today, which may be a positive thing, whereas in contemporary animation the quality of system and the amount of labor are both (still) perceptible.

87. Another discovery of his, less pertinent to the current discussion, is how often experimentalism in popular music coincides with what he calls musicians' abuse of existent technology. This view is supported by Robert M. Poss who speaks of "archaic technology" and "vintage gear" in his 1998 article on distortion.

88. See http://en.wikipedia.org/wiki/Trance_music#The_sound_of_modern_.28 progressive.29_trance/.

89. The EARS site restricts itself in the first instance to areas of music making in which the sound plays the lead role or, at least, is essential to the genre or category in question. It cannot be exhaustive in terms of areas in which electroacoustic techniques are applied but are not necessarily a focus.

90. Some of her initial ideas can also be found in Smith 2000.

91. It is worth noting that some consideration has been given to body gesture in terms of diffusion of fixed medium works; see Garcia 2000.

92. Joel Chadabe coined the term *interactive composing* in 1981 "to describe a performance process wherein a performer shares control of the music by interacting with an instrument that itself generates new material" (Chadabe 1999, 29). Tod Winkler defines interactive music as "a music composition or improvisation where software interprets a live performance to affect music generated or modified by computers" (Winkler 1999, 4). Morton Subotnick (1999) has also proposed a rudimentary list of modes of usage of computers in live performance.

93. Marco Stroppa has noted that when performers follow or are conducted by pre-recorded materials, interpretation can often be seen to be too "stiff, ascetic and often mechanical" (Stroppa 1999, 73–74 note).

94. See, e.g., Emmerson 1994a, but also Harvey 1986, 178; Schloss 2003; and Norman 2004, 156–157, in this last case referring to laptop performance.

95. For a discussion of image (art) to sound (music) mappings, see, e.g., Giannakis and Smith 2000.

96. Horacio Vaggione (2001) believes that this type of convergence involves the combination of interactive composition processes with sound design.

97. Stefan Fricke (1999), quoting Folkmar Hein, has observed a great surge of interest on the part of visual artists at the studio of the Technical University in Berlin in recent years, leading to a broadening of aesthetic scope. Alain Thibault is of the view that not too many people are interested in studying electroacoustic

music (read *E* music on a fixed medium) in music departments, but that "everyone studying visual arts wants to make electronic music and minimalist sound art. These approaches are perceived to be key to the contemporary scene and are more and more attractive to a young public. These artists tend to fuse an intellectual experimental culture with one that is accessible to a large public" (Thibault 2002, 53).

98. It is interesting that the term *Schallspiel* (sound play) was added to the more common *Hörspiel* (literally, play to be listened to; a synonym for radio play) in the 1960s (Glandien 2000, 170), implying that a type of sound art for the radio had been born that was distinct both in terms of the radio play and pertinent musical developments, including musique concrète, that evolved from the radio play.

99. Müller uses the word *flowing* or *fließend*, which does not come across as clearly in English.

100. Similarly, Rosemary Mountain has written of her desire that more musicians take their (potential) performance spaces into account, citing a lovely example of a stage surrounded by water providing inspiration for the work performed there (Mountain 2001, 99).

101. This is not particularly relevant here as it refers to physical presence.

102. In 2005 the *Neue Zeitschrift für Musik, Organised Sound*, and *Contemporary Music Review* all published thematic issues concerning Internet music.

Chapter 3   Toward a Framework for the Study of Sound-based Artworks

1. And then, of course, there are subareas that belong to these fields, such as acoustic ecology belonging to acoustic communication, gender studies to cultural studies, or specific items such as auditory scene analysis pertaining to psychoacoustics.

2. The book by Martin Supper, *Elektroakustische Musik und Computer Musik*, provides a welcome example of the combination of the first and last area. Despite the book's relatively short length, he does try to relate musical and technological developments as well as theoretical concepts diachronically. The study of the music in a cultural context is missing, as is so often the case.

3. In the same issue of *Contemporary Music Review*, Deta Davis published a rare bibliography focusing on an area that she called "Aesthetics of Computer Music" (Davis 1996). It is interesting that aesthetics seems to be used in some quarters as a word that covers anything ranging from sociopolitical viewpoints, to critical theoretical treatises, to new theoretical concepts. Regardless, the majority of the citations in Davis's bibliography are pertinent to the wider subject area of sound-based music studies. Moreover, while on the subject of aesthetics: Marc Battier edited one of the very few themed issues on aesthetics and

electroacoustic music issues in the same journal, *Contemporary Music Review* 18(3), specifically focusing on live electronics (Battier 1999).

4. Evan K. Chambers cites F. Richard Moore, who stated in his *Elements of Computer Music* that there exists a division between "two kinds of knowledge and science, the -ology model, which is limited to forms of knowing that can be expressed in words, and the -onomy model, which is an inclusive sum of the entire field of knowledge in a given area" (Chambers 1994, 19). Although no direct comparisons are made, fortunately, the example of astrology/astronomy is presented alongside musicology/musiconomy, where the latter is able to employ mathematical representations of music. Although the term "musiconomy" is not used on the EARS site and will not be used further in this chapter, the distinction is useful given the amount of mathematical approaches to sound organization that exist today both creatively as well as in terms of theoretical study (e.g., grammars of music).

5. Physical modeling includes any means of synthesizing sound "from scratch" or "first principles" through a mathematical acoustical model, generally of an existing musical instrument. Normally physical modeling offers models of the manner in which a resonator responds to some form of excitation (i.e., energy input) (see EARS).

6. Convolution here has to do with one acoustic signal's influencing another, such as "spectral and rhythmic hybriding, . . . excitation/resonance modelling" (EARS).

7. Part of the *cum suis* mentioned above are François Bayle, Michel Chion, François Delalande, Denis Smalley, and Jean-Christophe Thomas, most likely the most prolific writers on this subject.

8. The authors Silvio Ferraz and Leonardo Aldrovandi suggest in an article (Ferraz and Aldrovandi 2000) that it would be useful to find a means of gestural information to be linked to modes of listening and suggest new modes, textural, figural, and symbolic, to support their idea.

9. This is a paraphrase from http://www.psych.mcgill.ca/labs/auditory/introASA .html/. See also EARS, Bregman 1993, 1994.

10. Stephen Malloch (2000) and Lee Tsang (2002) have investigated timbral analysis from a cognition/psychoacoustics point of view, a step in the right direction. If there were only more specialists willing to concentrate on timbre and sound, more holistic research relevant to sound-based music might be on the horizon.

11. The idea behind the three forms of analysis is that together they should describe the total musical fact, the goal of analysis. This tripartite approach in terms of sound-based music is certainly worthy of exploration, but it has not been adopted by analysts.

12. An acoustic model is a representation of a sound based on the understanding of the behavior of sound (EARS).

13. Dhomont's work is also approached from a very specific point of view by the author Anna Rubin (2000). In her case, her quest is toward the investigation/representation of the unconscious. She is seeking streams of association in narrative electroacoustic works.

14. At the time of writing this book, English translations of the *Portraits* were in preparation.

15. In fact, the *Portraits Polychromes* are the successor to this publication.

16. Another multimedia analysis project worthy of mention is Momilani Ramstrum's analysis of Philippe Manoury's *K...* (Ramstrum 2004a, 2004b). Although spectral analysis is not featured here, Ramstrum combines information contextualizing of the work in terms of its musical content with analytical and technological information. It also includes more general components focused particularly on the process leading toward production. One specifically useful aspect is that of offering Manoury's MAX patches for users of this DVD-ROM to try them out on their own. In fact, Ramstrum's publication appeared shortly after IRCAM published a CD-ROM on Manoury's electroacoustic works (see Battier et al. 2003). In this multimedia publication, some of his Max patches are included as part of the works' presentations.

17. *Organised Sound* 8(1) (2003) is an example of a volume that discusses gender and sexual preference issues in sound-based music.

18. There were also other regional or national portraits in *Organised Sound* 6(1), in which this article appeared.

19. On a personal note, I must admit that this form of celebration is not always the case. An emotional debate among ethnomusicologists and world music performers took place based over a composition of mine that celebrated both African and Bulgarian music within a mixed music context. Some understood what I was aiming for; others felt that such music (whether quoted or appropriated stylistically) should not be removed from its original function. A very interesting statement in a reversed situation comes from Ricardo Arias (1998), who speaks of people from developing nations, in his case Colombia, being at the "margins of the periphery" owing to their dependency on equipment that is created in the industrialized world.

20. Furthermore, Horacio Vaggione has introduced the notion of spectral modeling in micro-time (in Vaggione 1994, 1996).

21. Martin Laliberté (2004) has made an interesting suggestion that may have some bearing here. He suggests that throughout the twentieth century, three types of virtuosity developed simultaneously: virtuosity of interpretation (the number of specialist performers rises, and the difficulty of some scores does, too), virtuosity of composition (the word complexity comes to mind), and sonic virtuosity (think of extended instrumental techniques). His interest is not only in performance, but also in the studio. Interpretation in terms of the studio is, according to Laliberté, linked to composition on a fixed medium or through automated processes; composition is linked to computer-aided compositional means; and

sonic virtuosity is linked primarily to sound synthesis (but could equally be generalized to *faktura* as presented here).

22. See, e.g., Dannenberg 1996 and Goebbel 1996 on control models; Wanderley and Battier 2000 for their large-scale edited CD-ROM on gesture control; Mulder 2000 for a typology and Essl 2003 for a remarkable treatment on controls and gender; and Manning 1999 on graphic control interfaces.

23. Admittedly, defining either aesthetic or *faktura* criteria is no easy thing. After all, a particular violin interpretation can be a delight to one person and irritating to another.

24. Some historic information concerning the turntable as instrument can be found in Manning 2003 and Nicolas Collins 2003, the latter discussing the move from medium to instrument. Smith's writings on the subject have already been cited.

25. The entire issue of *Organised Sound* 10(2) published in 2004 is about sound-based public art.

26. Jean Piché has been an important spokesperson here; see, e.g., Piché 2003, supporting audiovisual sonic artists or collaborations.

27. I look forward to seeing the first textbook that attempts to write a modern-day introductory guide to these types of procedures, presenting sound examples that are acoustic and electroacoustic alike to demonstrate that many of these techniques are not necessarily new. Consequently, people will be able to enjoy working on their art in the knowledge that others are working on the same or similar challenges.

References

Adkins, Matthew. 1999. Acoustic Chains in Acousmatic Music. *Proceedings of the 1999 Australasian Computer Music Conference, Victoria University of Wellington*, 56–62.

Aharonián, Coriún. 2000. An Approach to Compositional Trends in Latin America. *Leonardo Music Journal* 10: 47–52. (Originally published in *World New Music Magazine* 4: 47–52, 1994.)

Appleton, Jon. 1999. Reflections on a Former Performer of Electroacoustic Music. *Contemporary Music Review* 18(3): 15–19.

Arfib, D., J. M. Couturier, L. Kessous, and V. Verfaille. 2002. Strategies of Mapping between Gesture Data and Synthesis Mode Parameters Using Perceptual Spaces. *Organised Sound* 7(2): 127–144.

Arias, Ricardo. 1998. From the Margins of the Periphery: Music and Technology at the Outskirts of the West. *Leonardo Music Journal* 8: 49–54.

Ashline, William L. 2003. The Pariahs of Sound: On the Post-Duchampian Aesthetics of Electro-acoustic Improv. *Contemporary Music Review* 22(4): 23–33.

Attali, Jacques. 1985. *Noise: The Political Economy of Music.* Minneapolis: University of Minnesota Press. (Originally published as *Bruits: essau sur l'économiepolitique de la musique.* Paris: Presse Universitaires de France, 1977.)

Austin, Kevin. 2001. Electroacoustic definition. Extract from cecdiscuss list 7 September 2001: alcor.Concordia.ca/~kaustin/cecdiscuss/2001/3023.html.

Austin, Larry. 2000. Sound Diffusion in Composition and Performance: An Interview with Denis Smalley. *Computer Music Journal* 24(2): 10–21.

Austin, Larry, and Rodney Waschka II. 1996. Computer Music for Compact Disc: Composition, Production, Audience. *Computer Music Journal* 20(2): 17–27.

Back, Glenn. 2003. The Extra-Digital Axis Mundi: Myth, Magic, and Metaphor in Laptop Music. *Contemporary Music Review* 22(4): 3–9.

Bahn, Curtis, Tomie Hahn, and Dan Trueman. 2000. Physicality and Feedback: A Focus on the Body in the Performance of Electronic Music. In *International Computer Music Conference 2000 Havana Proceedings*, 44–51.

Barbanti, Roberto, Enrique Lynch, Carmen Pardo, and Makis Solomos, eds. 2004. *Musiques arts technologies: Pour une approche critique.* Paris: L'Harmattan.

Barbosa, Alvaro. 2003. Displaced Soundscapes: A Survey of Network Systems for Music and Sonic Art Collaboration. *Leonardo Music Journal* 13: 53–59.

Barenboim, Daniel. 2006. Reith Lectures—3rd in the Series. Broadcast on BBC Radio 4, 21 April 2006.

Barlow, Klarenz. 1999. Methoden algorithmischer Klangerzeugung anhand eigener Arbeiten: Von Klanglomeration und Schallwellenreiten zu Synthrumentation und Spektastik. In Jörg Stelkens and Hans G. Tillman, eds., *Klang-Forschung '98*, 67–82 Saarbrücken: Pfau.

Barrett, Natasha. 2000. A Compositional Methodology Based on Data Extracted from Natural Phenomena. In *International Computer Music Conference 2000 Havana Proceedings*, 20–24.

Barrett, Natasha. 2002. Spatio-musical Composition Strategies. *Organised Sound* 7(3): 313–323.

Barrière, Jean-Baptiste. 1989. Computer Music as Cognitive Approach: Simulation, Timbre, and Formal Processes. *Contemporary Music Review* 4: 117–130.

Barrière, Jean-Baptiste. 1992. Le sensible et le connaissable. *Les Cahiers de l'IRCAM: Recherches et Musique* 1: 77–86.

Barthelmes, Barbara. 1999. Klangkunst—eine neue Gattung oder ein interdisziplinäres Feld? in Jörg Stelkens and Hans G. Tillman, eds., *KlangForschung '98*, 117–126 Saarbrücken: Pfau.

Battier, Marc. 1995. Une nouvelle géométrie du son: Le paradoxe de la lutherie électronique. *Les Cahiers de l'IRCAM: Recherches et Musique* 7: 43–56.

Battier, Marc, ed. 1999. *Contemporary Music Review* 18(3): "Live Electronic Music."

Battier, Marc. 2001. De la machine à l'oreille: le paradoxe de la musique concrète. In Sylvie Dallet and Anne Veitl, eds., *Du sonore au musical: Cinquante années de recherches concrètes (1948–1998)*. Paris: L'Harmattan.

Battier, Marc. 2003. A Constructivist Approach to the Analysis of Electronic Music and Audio Art—Between Instruments and Faktura. *Organised Sound* 8(3): 249–255.

Battier, Marc. 2004. Electronic Music Studies and the Danger of Loss. *Organised Sound* 9(1): 47–53.

Battier, Marc, Bertrand Cheret, Serge Lemouton, and Philippe Manoury. 2003. *PMA LIB: Les musiques électroniques de/The Electronic Music of Philippe Manoury*. CD-ROM. Paris-IRCAM/Centre Pompidou.

Bayle, François. 1989. Image-of Sound, or I-Sound: Metaphor/Metaform. *Contemporary Music Review* 4: 165–170.

Bayle, François, ed. 1990. *Pierre Schaeffer—l'œuvre musicale*. Paris: INA/ Librarie Séguier.

Bayle, François. 1993. *musique acoumatique: propositions . . . positions*. Paris: INA-GRM/Buchet/Chastel.

Bayle, François. 1998. L'espace des sons et ses "défauts." In Marc Chouvel and Makis Solomos, eds., *L'Espace: Musique/Philosophie*, 365–371. Paris: L'Harmattan.

Berenguer, Jose Manuel. 1996. On the Necessity of Defining Electroacoustic Music. *Académie Bourges I: Aesthetics and Electroacoustic Music, 1995*. Paris: Actéon-Mnémosyne.

Berenguer, Jose Manuel. 1997. Analytical Reveries I. *Académie Bourges II: Analysis in Electroacoustic Music, 1996*, 216–221. Paris: Mnémosyne.

Berry, Rodney, and Palle Dahlstedt. 2003. Artificial Life: Why Should Musicians Bother? *Contemporary Music Review* 22(3): 57–67.

Birnbaum, D., R. Fiebrink, J. Malloch, and M. M. Wanderley. 2003. Towards a Dimension Space for Musical Devices. In *Proceedings of the 2005 International Conference on New Interfaces for Musical Expression (NIME05), Vancouver, B.C., Canada*, 192–195.

Blacking, John, and Reginald Byron. 1991. *Music, Culture, and Experience: Selected Papers of John Blacking*. Chicago: University of Chicago Press.

Blackwell, Tom, and Michael Young. 2004. Self-organised Music. *Organised Sound* 9(2): 123–136.

Bodin, Lars-Gunnar. 1997. Aesthetic Profile Mapping—An Outline of a Practical Aesthetic Analysis. *Académie Bourges II—Analysis in Electroacoustic Music*, 222–226. Paris: Mnémosyne. 1996.

Bogdanov, Vladimir, Chris Woodstra, Stephen Thomas Erlewine, and John Bush, eds. 2001. *All Music Guide to Electronica: The Definitive Guide to Electronic Music*. San Francisco: All Media Guide/Breakbeat Books.

Bonardi, Alain, and Francies Rousseaux. 2004. Un exemple de mediation numérique opératique: L'opéra interactif sur CD-ROM Virtualis. In Robert Barbanti, Enrique Lynch, Carmen Pardo, Makis Solomos, eds. *Musiques Arts Technlogies: Pour une approche critique*, 123–140. Paris: L'Harmattan.

Born, Georgina. 1995. *Rationalizing Culture: IRCAM, Boulez, and the Institutionalization of the Musical Avant-garde*. Berkeley: University of California Press.

Bosma, Hannah. 2003. Bodies of Evidence, Singing Cyborgs, and Other Gender Issues in Electrovocal Music. *Organised Sound* 8(1): 5–17.

Bossis, Bruno. 2004. Reflections on the Analysis of Artificial Vocality: Representations, Tools, and Prospective. *Organised Sound* 9(1): 91–98.

Bouhalassa, Ned. 2002. Electroniquoi? Chronique de la naissance d'une nouvelle constellation sonore. *Circuits* 13(1): 27–34.

Boulez, Pierre. 1958. "At the ends of fruitful land. . . ." *Die Reihe* 1: 19w–21. (Original German version published in 1955.)

Bowers, John. 2003. Improvising Machines: Ethnographically Informed Design for Improvised Electro-acoustic Music. *ARiADA* 4: www.ariada.uea.ac.uk.

Brattico, Elvira, and Fiorella Sassanelli. 2000. Perception and Musical Preferences in Wishart's Work. *Journal of New Music Research* 29(2): 107–119.

Brech, Martha. 1994. *Analyse elektroakustischer Musik mit Hilfe von Sonagrammen.* Frankfurt: Peter Lang.

Bregman, Alexander. 1993. Auditory Scene Analysis: Hearing in Complex Environments. In Stephen McAdams and Emmanuel Bigend, eds., *Thinking in Sound: The Cognitive Psychology of Human Audition.* Oxford: Clarendon Press.

Bregman, Alexander. 1994. *Auditory Scene Analysis.* Cambridge, Mass.: MIT Press.

Bridger, Michael. 1989. An Approach to the Analysis of Electro-acoustic Music Derived from Empirical Investigation and Critical Methodologies of Other Disciplines. *Contemporary Music Review* 3(1): 155–160.

Bridger, Michael. 2002. Narrativisation in Electroacoustic and Computer Music—Reflections on Empirical Research into Listeners' Response. Available at www.mbridger.pwp.blueyonder.co.uk.

Brunet, Sophie. 1977. *Pierre Schaeffer: De la musique concrète à la musique même. Revue Musicale 303–305.* Paris: Ed. Richard-Masse.

Brunet, Sophie, and Pierre Schaeffer. 1970. *Pierre Schaeffer par Sophie Brunet suivi de Réflexions de Pierre Schaeffer.* Paris: Ed. Richard-Masse. (This book includes the section entitled "Recherches de Pierre Schaeffer.")

Burns, Christopher. 2002. Tracing Compositional Process: Software Synthesis Code as Documentary Evidence. *International Computer Music Conference 2002/Göteborg Proceedings,* 568–571.

Burt, Warren. 2001. Expanding Contexts for Computer Music: One Composer's Experience. *Organised Sound* 6(1): 29–37.

Burtner, Matthew. 2005. Ecoacoustic and Shamanic Technologies for Multimedia Composition and Performance. *Organised Sound* 10(1): 3–19.

Cadoz, Claude, and Marcelo Wanderley. 2000. Gesture—Music. In Marcelo Wanderley and Marc Battier, eds., *Trends in Gestural Conrol in Music.* CD-ROM, 28–65. Paris: Ircam.

Caesar, Rodolfo. 1992. The Composition of Electroacoustic Music. Ph.D. Thesis, University of East Anglia (Norwich, UK).

Cage, John. 2003. *Conversations with John Cage,* 2nd edition Ed. Richard Kostelanetz. New York: Routledge. (First edition, 1987.)

Calon, Christian, and Claude Schryer. 1990. Prochaine Station. On *Électro Clips: 25 electroacoustic snapshots.* Montreal: Empreintes DIGITALes 9604.

Camilerri, Lelio, and Denis Smalley. 1998. The Analysis of Electroacoustic Music: Introduction. *Journal of New Music Research* 27(1–2): 3–12.

Camurri, Antonio, Riccardo Trocca, and Gualtiero Volpe. 2002. Real-time Analysis of Expressive Cues in Human Movement. In *International Computer Music Conference 2002/Göteborg Proceedings,* 423–428.

Cascone, Kim. 2000. The Aesthetics of Failure: "Post-Digital" Tendencies in Contemporary Computer Music. *Computer Music Journal* 24(4): 12–18.

Cascone, Kim. 2003. Grain, Sequence, System: Three Levels of Reception in the Performance of Laptop Music. *Contemporary Music Review* 22(4): 101–104.

Casey, Michael A. 2001. General Sound Classification and Similarity in MPEG-7. *Organised Sound* 6(2): 153–164.

Casey, Michael A. 2005. Acoustic Lexemes for Organizing Internet Audio. *Contemporary Music Review* 24(6): 489–508.

Chadabe, Joel. 1997. *Electric Sound: The Past and Promise of Electronic Music.* Upper Saddle River, N.J.: Prentice-Hall.

Chadabe, Joel. 1999. The Performer Is Us. *Contemporary Music Review* 18(3): 25–30.

Chadabe, Joel. 2000. Remarks on Computer Music Culture. *Computer Music Journal* 24(4): 9–11.

Chadabe, Joel. 2004. Look Around and Get Engaged. *Organised Sound* 9(3): 315–316.

Chambers, Evan K. 1994. The Computer Music World View: Sketch of an Ethnomusicological and Aesthetic Approach. In *International Computer Music Conference 1994/Århus Proceedings*, 19–22.

Chion, Michel. 1982. *La musique électroacoustique.* Paris: Presses Universitaires de France.

Chion, Michel. 1985. *Le son au cinema.* Paris: Cahiers de Cinéma, collection "Essais."

Chion, Michel. 1990. *Audio-vision: Sound on Screen.* New York: Columbia University Press. (Published in French by Nathan, Paris—2nd edition, 2000.)

Chion, Michel. 1991. *L'art des sons fixés ou la musique concrètement.* Fontaine: Eds. Metamkine/Nota Bene/Sono-Concept.

Chion, Michel. 1994. *Musiques, Médias, Technologie.* Paris; Flammarion.

Chion, Michel. 1995. *Guide des objets sonores: Pierre Schaeffer et la recherche musicale.* Paris: INA/Buchet/Chastel. (Originally published in 1983; an unpublished translation by John Dack and Christine North has been cited.)

Chion, Michel. 2002. *Le son.* Paris: Nathan. (Originally published in 1998.)

Chouvel, Jean-Marc, and Makis Solomos, eds. 1998. *L'Espace: Musique/ Philosophie.* Paris: L'Harmattan.

Cipriani, Alessandro, Fabrio Cifariello Ciardo, Luigi Ceccarelli, and Mauro Cardo. 2004. Collective Compotition: The Case of Edison Studio. *Organised Sound* 9(3): 261–270.

Clarke, Michael. 2006. Jonathan Harvey's Mortuos Plango, Vivos Voco. In Mary Simoni, ed., *Analytical Methods of Electroacoustic Music*, 111–143. New York: Routledge.

Clozier, Christian. 1996. The Aesthetic Situation and Outlook of Electroacoustic Music, Related Question: A Definition of Electroacoustic Music. In *Académie Bourges I—Aesthetics and Electroacoustic Music 1995*, 31–42. Paris: Mnémosyne.

Cody, Joshua. 1996. An Interview with Paul Lansky. *Computer Music Journal* 20(1): 19–25.

Cogan, Robert. 1984. *New Images of Musical Sound*. Cambridge, Mass.: Harvard University Press.

Cole, Bruce. 1996. MIDI and Communality. *Organised Sound* 1(1): 51–54.

Collins, Nick. 2003. Generative Music and Laptop Performance. *Contemporary Music Review* 22(4): 67–79.

Collins, Nicolas. 2003. Introduction to Groove, Pit, and Wave: Recording, Transmission and Music. *Leonardo Music Journal* 13: 1–3.

Cook, Perry, ed. 2001. *Music, Cognition and Computerized Sound: An Introduction to Psychoacoustics*. Cambridge, Mass.: MIT Press.

Copeland, Darren. 2003. Survival Strategies for Electroacoustic Music. *Circuit* 13(3): 59–65.

Couprie, Pierre. 1999. Three Analysis Models for L'oiseau moqueur, One of the Trois rêves d'oiseau by François Bayle. *Organised Sound* 4(1): 3–14.

Couprie, Pierre. 2001. Le vocabulaire de l'objet sonore. In Sylvie Dallet and Anne Veitl, eds., *Du sonore au musical: Cinquante années de recherches concrètes (1948–1998)*, 203–225. Paris: L'Harmattan.

Couprie, Pierre. 2004a. La place de l'informatique et du multimedia dans l'analyse des musiques électroacoustiques. In Robert Barbanti, Enrique Lynch, Carmen Pardo, and Makis Solomos, eds., *Musiques Arts Technlogies: Pour une approche critique*, 361–374. Paris: L'Harmattan.

Couprie, Pierre. 2004b. Graphical Representation: An Analytical and Publication Tool for Electroacoustic Music. *Organised Sound* 9(1): 109–113.

Cox, Christoph, and Daniel Warner, eds. 2004. *Audio Culture: Readings in Modern Music*. New York: Continuum.

Cubitt, Sean. 1997. Online Sound and Virtual Architecture (Contribution to the Geography of Cultural Translation). *Leonardo Music Journal* 7: 43–49.

Cubitt, Sean. 1998. *Digital Aesthetics*. London: Sage.

Cuellar Camargo, Lucio Edilberto. 2000. The Development of Electroacoustic Music in Columbia, 1965–1999: An Introduction. *Leonardo Music Journal* 10: 7–12.

Cutler, Chris. 2000. Plunderphonics. In Simon Emmerson, ed., *Music, Electronic Media, and Culture*, 87–114. Aldershot: Ashgate.

Cutler, Chris. 2004. Plunderphonia. In Christoph Cox and Daniel Warner, eds., *Audio Culture: Readings in Modern Music*, 38–156. New York: Continuum. (This is an amended version of a text originally published in *Musicworks* 60 [fall 1994].)

Dack, John. 1998. Strategies in the Analysis of Karlheinz Stockhausen's *Kontakte für elektronische Klänge, Klavier und Schlagzeug. Journal of New Music Research* 27(1–2): 84–119.

Dack, John. 1999. Systematising the Unsystematic. In George E. Lasker and James Rhodes, eds., *Systems Research in Arts*, vol. I: *Musicology. Proceedings of the Symposium for Systems Research in the Arts, Baden-Baden*, 53–58. Windsor, Ontario: The International Institute for Advanced Studies in Systems Research and Cybernetics.

Dack, John. 2002. Histories and Ideologies of Synthesis. In *MAXIS 2002: Proceedings*, 35–40. Sheffield: Sheffield Hallam University.

Dallet, Sylvie, and Anne Veitl, eds. 2001. *Du sonore au musical: Cinquante années des recherches concrètes*. Paris: L'Harmattan.

Dannenberg, Roger B. 1996. A Perspective on Computer Music. *Computer Music Journal* 20(1): 52–56.

Daoust, Yves. 2002. Entrevue avec Jean-François Denis, directeur d'Empreintes DIGITALes. *Circuit* 13(1): 57–62.

Dart, William, John Elmsly, and Ian Whalley. 2001. A View of Computer Music from New Zealand: Auckland, Waikato, and the Asia/Pacific Connection. *Organised Sound* 6(1): 11–20.

Davies, Hugh. 1990. Instruments électroniques: classification et mécanismes. *Contrechamps* 11: 53–69.

Davies, Hugh. 1992. New Musical Instruments in the Computer Age: Amplified Performance Systems and Related Examples of Low-level Technology. In John Paynter, Tim Howell, Richard Orton, and Peter Seymour, eds. *Companion to Contemporary Musical Thought*, vol. 1 (2 volumes), 500–513. London: Routledge.

Davis, Deta. 1996. Aesthetics in Computer Music: A Bibliography. *Contemporary Music Review* 13(1): 147–157.

Day, Gary. 2004. There's No Greater Way to Win the Respect of Your Peers Than to Write Gobbledegook: The Less They Understand the More Clever They Think You Are. *Times Higher Education Supplement*, 27 February 2004: 15.

Decroupet, Pascal. 1994. Timbre Diversification in Serial Tape Music and Its Consequence on Form. *Contemporary Music Review* 10(2): 13–23.

Delalande, François. 1985. Perception des sons et perception des oeuvres (questions et méthode). In Tod Machover, ed., *Quoi? Quand? Comment? La recherché musicale*, 197–209. Paris: Christian Bourgeois/IRCAM.

Delalande, François. 1986. En l'absence de partition: le cas singulier de l'analyse de la musique électroacoustique. *Analyse Musicale*, 2e trimestre 1986: 54–58.

Delalande, François. 1989a. La terrasse des audiences du claur de lune de Debussy: essai d'analyse esthésique. *Analyse Musicale* 16(3): 75–84.

Delalande, François. 1989b. Éléments d'analyse de la stratégie de composition. In *Actes du colloque:. Structures musicales et assistance informatique*, 51–65.

Laboratoire Musique et Informatique (MIM) de Marseille.

Delalande, François. 1998a. Music Analysis and Reception Behaviours: Someil by Pierre Henry. *Journal of New Music Research* 27(1–2): 13–66.

Delalande, François. 1998b. Écoute interactive, imagerie musicale. *Dossiers de l'audivisuel* 81: 42–44.

Delalande, François. 2001a. Le GRM et l'Histoire de l'Éveil Musical en France. In Sylvie Dallet and Anne Veitl, eds., *Du sonore au musical: Cinquante années des recherches concrètes*, 89–100. Paris: L'Harmattan.

Delalande, François. 2001b. *Le Son des Musiques: Entre technologie et esthé-tique*. Paris: INA/GRM Buchet/Chastel.

Delalande, François. 2002. Eine Musik ohne Noten: Einführung in das Hören und Analysieren elektroakustischer Musik. In *Konzert-Klangkunst-Computer, Wandel der musikalischen Wirklichkeit*. Mainz: Schott (Institut für Neue Musik und Musikerziehung Darmstadt).

Delalande, François, and Dominique Besson. 1992. Problèmes théoriques et pra-tiques de la transcription des musiques électroacoustiques. In *Actes du second congrès européen d'analyse musicale*, University of Trento, Italy. (This can also be found as part of the "Portraits Polychromes"—Bernard Parmegiani: http://www.ina.fr/grm/acousmaline/polychromes/parmegiani/aquatisme/aqua_in tro.html/.)

Desantos, Sandra. 1997. Acoustic Morphology: An Interview with François Bayle. *Computer Music Journal* 21(3): 11–19.

d'Escriván, Julio. 1989. Reflections on the Poetics of Time in Electroacoustic Music. *Contemporary Music Review* 3(1): 197–201.

Dhomont, Francis. 1988. Parlez moi d'espace. In Francis Dhomont, ed. *L'espace du son?* (1) Ohain, Belgium: Eds. Musiques et Recherches, 37–39. (This publi-cation belongs to the series "Liens: Revue de l'aesthétique musicale.")

Donin, Nicolas. 2004. Towards Organised Listening: Some Aspects of the "Signed Listening" Project, IRCAM. *Organised Sound* 9(1): 99–108.

Drever, John Levack. 2002. Soundscape Composition: The Convergence of Ethnography and Acousmatic Music. *Organised Sound* 7(1): 21–27.

Duchenne, Jean-Marc. 1991. Habiter l'espace acousmatique. In Francis Dhomont, ed. *L'espace du son?* (2), 82–84. Ohain, Belgium: Eds. Musiques et Recherches. (This publication belongs to the series "Liens: Revue de l'aesthétique musicale.")

Duckworth, William. 1999. Making Music on the Web. *Leonardo Music Journal* 9: 13–18.

Dufour, Denis, and Jean-Christophe Thomas, eds. 1999. *Ouïr, entendre, écouter, comprendre après Schaeffer*. INA/Buchet/Chastel.

Duteutre, Benoît. 1995. *Requiem pour une avant-garde*. Paris: Éditions Robert Laffont.

Dutilleux, Henri. 2001. Allocution de vienvenue. In Sylvie Dallet and Anne Veitl, eds., *Du sonore au musical: Cinquante années des recherches concrètes*, 7–12. Paris: L'Harmattan.

EARS site. The ElectroAcoustic Resource Site (EARS), http://www.ears.dmu. ac.uk/.

Eimert, Herbert. 1958. Werner Meyer-Eppler. *Die Reihe* 8: 5–6. (Original German edition published in 1962.)

Emmerson, Simon. 1982. Analysis and the Composition of Electroacoustic Music. Ph.D. dissertation, London: City University.

Emmerson, Simon. 1986. The Relation of Language to Materials. In Simon Emmerson, ed. *The Language of Electroacoustic Music*, 17–39. Basingstoke: Macmillan.

Emmerson, Simon. 1989. Composing Strategies and Pedagogies. *Contemporary Music Review* 3: 133–144.

Emmerson, Simon. 1991. Computers and Live Electronic Music: Some Solutions, Many Problems. In *International Computer Music Conference 1991/Montreal Proceedings*, 135–138.

Emmerson, Simon. 1994a. Live versus "Real-time." *Contemporary Music Review* 10(2): 95–101.

Emmerson, Simon. 1994b. "Local/Field": Towards a Typology of Live Electroacoustic Music. In *International Computer Music Conference 1994/Århus Proceedings*, 31–34.

Emmerson, Simon. 1996a. Analysis of Live Electronic Music. In *Académie Bourges I—Aesthetics and Electroacoustic Music, 1995*, 48–50. Paris: Actéon—Mnémosyne.

Emmerson, Simon. 1996b. Electroacoustic Music: Aesthetic Situation and Perspectives. In *Académie Bourges I—Aesthetics and Electroacoustic Music, 1995*, 51–55. Paris: Actéon—Mnémosyne.

Emmerson, Simon. 1998a. Acoustic/Electroacoustic: The Relationship with Instruments. *Journal of New Music Research* 27(1): 146–164.

Emmerson, Simon. 1998b. Aural Landscape: Musical Space. *Organised Sound* 3(2): 135–140.

Emmerson, Simon. 2000a. "Losing Touch?": The Human Performer and Electronics. In Simon Emmerson, ed., *Music, Electronic Media, and Culture*, 194–216. Aldershot: Ashgate.

Emmerson, Simon. 2000b. Introduction. In Simon Emmerson, ed., *Music, Electronic Media and Culture*, 1–4. Aldershot: Ashgate.

Emmerson, Simon. 2000c. Crossing Cultural Boundaries through Technology? In Simon Emmerson, ed., *Music, Electronic Media and Culture*, 115–137. Aldershot: Ashgate.

Emmerson, Simon. 2001a. From Dance! to "Dance": Distance and Digits. *Computer Music Journal* 25(1): 13–20.

Emmerson, Simon. 2001b. New Spaces/New Places: A Sound House for the Performance of Electroacoustic Music and Sonic Art. *Organised Sound* 6(2): 103–105.

Emmerson, Simon, and Denis Smalley. 2001. Electroacoustic Music. In Stanley Sadie, ed., *The New Grove Dictionary of Music and Musicians*, 2nd ed. London: Macmillan.

Eno, Brian. 2004a. Ambient Music. In Christoph Cox and Daniel Warner, eds., *Audio Culture: Readings in Modern Music*, 94–97. New York: Continuum. (Originally published in Brian Eno, *A Year with Swollen Appendices*. London: Faber and Faber, 1996.)

Eno, Brian. 2004b. The Studio as Compositional Tool. In Christoph Cox and Daniel Warner, eds., *Audio Culture: Readings in Modern Music*, 127–130. New York: Continuum. (Originally published in Howard Mandel, ed., *Down Beat* 50[7, 8], July and August 1983.)

Eshun, Kodwo. 1998. *More Brilliant Than the Sun: Adventures in Sonic Fiction*. London: Quartet Books.

Essl, Georg. 2003. On Gender in New Music Interface Technology. *Organised Sound* 8(3): 19–30.

Fells, Nick. 1999. Kendhang, Or, and Vug: Three Works for Performer and Live Computer System. *Organised Sound* 4(2): 79–85.

Ferrari, Luc. 1996. I Was Running in So Many Different Directions. *Contemporary Music Review* 15(1): 95–102.

Ferraz, Silvio, and Leonardo Aldrovandi. 2000. Loop-Interpolation-Random and Gesture: Déjà Vu in Computer-aided Composition. *Organised Sound* 5(2): 81–84.

Field, Ambrose. 2000. Simulation and Reality: The New Sonic Objects. In Simon Emmerson, ed., *Music, Electronic Media, and Culture*, 36–55. Aldershot: Ashgate.

Fields, Kenneth. 1999. Post-Formalism. In *International Computer Music Conference 1999/Beijing Proceedings*, 531–534.

Fischman, Rajmil. 1994. Music for the Masses. *Journal of New Music Research*. 23(3): 245–264.

Fischman, Rajmil. 1997. Analysis of *Crosstalk*, A Work by Michael Vaughan. *Organised Sound* 2(3): 225–251.

Frémiot, Marcel. 2001. De l'objet sonore à "l'unité temporelle de sens." In Sylvie Dallet and Anne Veitl, eds., *Du sonore au musical: Cinquante années des recherches concrètes*. Paris: L'Harmattan.

Fricke, Stefan. 1999. Klang im unentdeckten Raum: Einige Aspekte zur elektroakustischen Musik heute. In Jörg Stelkens and Hans G. Tillman, eds., *Klang-Forschung '98*, 29–35. Saarbrücken: Pfau.

Friedl, Reinhold. 2002. Some Sadomasochistic Aspects of Musical Pleasure. *Leonardo Music Review* 12: 29–30.

Fujii, Koichi. 2004. Chronology of Early Electroacoustic Music in Japan: What Types of Source Material Are Available? *Organised Sound* 9(1): 63–77.

Gallet, Bastien. 2002. *Le boucher du prince Wen-houei: Enquêtes sur les musiques électroniques.* Paris: Musica Falsa.

Garcia, Denise. 2000. Body Representations in the Electroacoustic Music. In *International Computer Music Conference 2000/Berlin Proceedings,* 16–19.

Garnett, Guy E. 2001. The Aesthetics of Interactive Computer Music. *Computer Music Journal* 25(1): 21–33.

Gartland-Jones, Andrew, and Peter Copley. 2003. The Suitability of Genetic Algorithms for Musical Composition. *Contemporary Music Review* 22(3): 43–55.

Geslin, Yann, and Adrien Lefevre. 2004. Sound and Musical Representation: The Acousmographe Software. In *International Computer Music Conference 2004/Miami Proceedings,* 285–289.

Geslin, Yann, Pascal Mullon, and Max Jacob. 2002. Ecrins: An Audio-content Description Environment for Sound Samples. In *International Computer Music Conference 2002/Göteborg Proceedings,* 581–590.

Giannakis, Kostas, and Matt Smith. 2000. Auditory-Visual Associations for Music Compositional Processes: A Survey. In *International Computer Music Conference 2000/Berlin Proceedings,* 12–15.

Giomi, Francesco, and Marco Ligabue. 1998. Evangelisti's Composition Incontri di Fasce Sonore at WDR: Aesthetic-Cognitive Analysis in Theory and Practice. *Journal of New Music Research* 27(1–2): 120–145.

Glandien, Kersten. 2000. Art on Air: A Profile of New Radio Art. In Simon Emmerson, ed., *Music, Electronic Media and Culture,* 167–193. Aldershot: Ashgate.

Goebbel, Johannes. 1996. Freedom and Precision of Control. *Computer Music Journal* 20(1): 46–48.

Graves, Alan, Chris Hand, and Andrew Hugill. 1999. MidiVisualiser: Interactive Music Visualisation Using VRML. *Organised Sound* 4(1): 15–23.

Gresham-Lancaster, Scot. 1998. The Aesthetics and History of the Hub: The Effects of Changing Technology on Network Computer Music. *Leonardo Music Journal* 8: 39–44.

Grove, Robin, Catherine Stevens, and Shirley McKechnie, eds. 2005. *Thinking in Four Dimensions: Creativity and Cognition in Contemporary Dance.* Melbourne: Melbourne University Press (e-book).

Hahn, David. 2002. Creating the Soundscape for "Zagreb Everywhere." *Organised Sound* 7(1): 57–63.

Hahn, Tomie, and Curtis Bahn. 2002. Pikapika—The Collaborative Composition of an Interactive Sonic Character. *Organised Sound* 7(3): 229–238.

Harley, James. 2002. The Electroacoustic Music of Iannis Xenakis. *Computer Music Journal* 26(1): 33–57.

Harrison, Jonty. 1998. Sound, Space, Sculpture: Some Thoughts on the "What," "How," and "Why" of Sound Diffusion. *Organised Sound* 3(2): 117–127.

Harvey, Jonathan. 1986. The Mirror of Ambiguity. In Simon Emmerson, ed., *The Language of Electroacoustic Music*, 175–190. Basingstoke: Macmillan.

Hegarty, Paul. 2001. Noise Threshold: Merzbow and the End of the Natural Sound. *Organised Sound* 6(3): 193–200.

Heiniger, Wolfgang. 1999. Der Unsichtbare Interpret. In Jörg Stelkens and Hans G. Tillman, eds., *KlangForschung '98: Symposium zur elektronischen Musik*, 191–198. Saarbrücken: Pfau.

Helmuth, Mara. 1996. Multidimensional Representation of Electroacoustic Music. *Journal of New Music Research*. 25(1): 77–103.

Hirst, David. 2003. Developing Analysis Criteria Based on Denis Smalley's Timbre Theories. In *International Computer Music Conference 20003/Singapore Proceedings*, 427–434.

Holm-Hudson, Kevin. 1997. Quotation and Context: Sampling and John Oswald's Plunderphonics. *Leonardo Music Journal* 7: 17–25.

Hoopen, Christiane ten. 1994. Issues in Timbre and Perception. *Contemporary Music Review* 10(2): 61–71.

Hoopen, Christiane ten. 1997. Perceptions of Sound: Source, Cause, and Human Presence in Electroacoustic Music. Ph.D. dissertation, Amsterdam: University of Amsterdam.

Hyde, Joseph. 2003. Off the Map?—Sonic Art in the New Media Landscape. *Circuit* 13/3: 33–40.

Igma, Norman. 1986. Recipes for Plunderphonics: an interview with John Oswald, Part I. *Musicworks* 34: 5–8.

Ina/GRM-CDMC. var. Portraits Polychromes. Paris: INA/GRM-CDMC. Http://www.ina.fr/grm/acousmaline/polychromes/index.fr.html/.

Ina/GRM-Hyptique. 2000. La musique électroacoustique. *Collection Musiques Tangibles* 1. CD-ROM. Éditions hyptique.net.

Ingold, Tim. 2000. *The Perception of the Environment: Essays in Livelihood, Dwelling, and Skill*. London: Routledge.

IRCAM-Hyptique. 2000. Dix jeux d'écoute. *Collection Musiques Tangibles* 2. CD-ROM. Éditions hyptique.net.

Jaeger, Timothy. 2003. The (Anti-)Laptop Aesthetic. *Contemporary Music Review* 22(4): 53–57.

Jordà, Sergi. 1999. Faust Music Online: An Approach to Real-time Collective Composition on the Internet. *Leonardo Music Journal* 9: 5–12.

Kagel, Mauricio. 1965. Translation-Rotation. *Die Reihe* 7: 32–60. (Original German edition published in 1960.)

Kahn, Douglas. 1999. *Noise Water Meat: A History of Sound in the Arts*. Cambridge, Mass.: MIT Press.

Kahn, Douglas, and Gregory Whitehead, eds. 1992. *Wireless Imagination: Sound, Radio, and the Avant-garde.* Cambridge, Mass.: MIT Press.

Keller, Damián. 2000. Compositional Processes from an Ecological Perspective. *Leonardo Music Journal* 10: 55–60.

Keller, Damián, and Ariadna Capasso. 2000. Social and Perceptual Processes in the Installation *The Trade. Organised Sound* 5(2): 85–94.

Koenig, Gottfried Michael. 1961. Studium im Studio. *Die Reihe* 5: 30–39. (Original German edition published in 1959.)

Laliberté, Martin. 2004. Aux origins des "nouvelles technologies musicales": Virtuosités et archetypes. In Robert Barbanti, Enrique Lynch, Carmen Pardo, and Makis Solomos, eds., *Musiques Arts Technlogies: Pour une approche critique,* 347–360. Paris: L'Harmattan.

La Motte-Haber, Helga de, ed. 1999. *Klangkunst: Tönende Objekte und klingende Räume.* Laaber: Laaber-Verlag.

Landy, Leigh. 1987. Comp(exp. $\int$) = f$_t\Sigma'$parameters'($\sim$). *Avant Garde.* 0 "Presentation": 27–39.

Landy, Leigh. 1991. *What's the Matter with Today's Experimental Music? Organized Sound Too Rarely Heard.* Chur: Harwood Academic Publishers.

Landy, Leigh. 1994a. The "Something to Hold on to Factor" in Timbral Composition. *Contemporary Music Review* 10(2): 49–60.

Landy, Leigh. 1994b. *Experimental Music Notebooks.* Chur: Harwood Academic Publishers.

Landy, Leigh. 1996. Quality and Quantity (If We're Lucky), or Marcuse's Problem Ain't Been Solved Yet. *Contemporary Music Review* 15: 63–70.

Landy, Leigh. 1998a. Digital Music Technology Can Aid in Bringing Music Back as a Part of Life. In Bernd Enders and Niels Knolle, eds., *Klang Art—Kongreß 1995,* 175–183. Musik und Neue Technologie 1. Osnabrück: Universitätsverlag Rasch.

Landy, Leigh. 1998b. L'espace divisé vs l'espace unifié (la séparation est-elle en train de disparaître?). In Jean-Marc Chouvel and Makis Solomos, eds., *L'espace: Musique/Philosophie,* 319–329. Paris: L'Harmattan.

Landy, Leigh. 1999. Reviewing the Musicology of Electroacoustic Music. *Organised Sound: An International Journal of Music Technology* 4(1): 61–70.

Landy, Leigh. 2000. Co-hear-ence and Electroacoustic Music. In *SBC2000 Anais do XX Congresso.* Curitiba, Brazil: Proceedings on CD-ROM. Nacional da Sociedade Brasileira de Computação.

Landy, Leigh. 2001. From Algorithmic Jukeboxes to Zero-time Synthesis: A Potential A–Z of Music in Tomorrow's World. *Organised Sound* 6(2): 91–96.

Landy, Leigh. 2006a. The Intention/Reception Project. In Mary Simoni, ed., *Analytical Methods of Electroacoustic Music.* New York: Routledge: 29–53.

Landy, Leigh. 2006b. La Zététique: Musique mixte créée en collaboration. In Marc Battier, Bruno Bossis, and Anne Veitl, eds., *Musique, instruments, machines*, 69–79. Paris: OMF/Université de Paris IV-Sorbonne.

Landy, Leigh, and Evelyn, Jamieson. 2000. *Devising Dance and Music: Idée Fixe—Experimental Sound and Movement Theatre*. Sunderland: Sunderland University Press. Now available at: www.mti.dmu.ac.uk/~llandy/dance.html/.

Lagrost, Jean-François. 2001. Matières, espace, lumière et évolution: quatre manières de percevoir le début de Sud. *Portraits Polychromes* (on Jean-Claude Risset). Paris: INA-GRM/CDMC. Http://www.ina.fr/grm/acousmaline/polychromes/index.fr.html/.

Licata, Thomas, ed. 2002. *Electroacoustic Music: Analytical Perspectives*. Westport, Conn.: Greenwood Press.

Link, Stan. 2001. The Work of Reproduction in the Mechanical Aging of an Art: Listening to Noise. *Computer Music Journal* 25(1): 34–47.

Lippe, Cort. 1994. Real-time Granular Sampling Using the IRCAM Signal Processing Workstation. *Contemporary Music Review* 10(2): 149–155.

Lochhead, Judy. 1989. Temporal Structure in Music. In F. Joseph Smith, ed., *Understanding the Musical Experience*, 121–165. New York: Gordon and Breach.

López, Francisco. 2004. Profound Listeening and Environment Sound Behaviour. In Christoph Cox and Daniel Warner, eds., *Audio Culture: Readings in Modern Music*, 82–87. New York: Continuum. (Originally published as "Blind Listening" in David Rothenburg and Marta Ulvaeus, eds., *The Book of Music and Nature*. Middletown, Conn.: Wesleyan University Press, 1997.)

Lotis, Theodoros. 2003. The Creations and Projection of Ambiophonic and Geometrical Sonic Spaces with Reference to Denis Smalley's Base Metals. *Organised Sound* 8(3): 257–267.

Lucier, Alvin. 1995. *Reflections: Interviews, Scores, Writings*. Cologne: MusikTexte.

Malloch, Stephen. 2000. Timbre and Technology: An Analytical Partnership. *Contemporary Music Review* 19(2): 155–172.

Manning, Peter D. 1999. The Evolution of Interactive Graphical Control Interfaces for Musical Applications. *Organised Sound* 4(1): 45–59.

Manning, Peter D. 2003. The Influence of Recording Technologies on the Early Development of Electroacoustic Music. *Leonardo Music Journal* 13: 5–10.

Manoury, Phillipe. 1984a. The Arrow of Time. *Contemporary Music Review* 1(1): 131–145.

Manoury, Phillipe. 1984b. The Role of the Conscious. *Contemporary Music Review* 1(1): 147–156.

McAdams, Stephen, and Emmanuel, Bigend, eds., 1993. *Thinking in Sound: The Cognitive Psychology of Human Audition*. Oxford: Oxford University Press.

McCartney, Andra. 1995. Inventing Images: Constructing and Contesting Gender in Thinking about Electroacoustic Music. *Leonardo Music Journal 5*: 57–66.

McCartney, Andra. 1999. Sounding Places: Situated Conversations through the Soundscape Compositions of Hildegard Westerkamp. PhD Dissertation, York University, Canada. Available at http://www.emf.org/artists/mccartney00/.

McCartney, Andra. 2003. In and Out of the Sound Studio. *Organised Sound* 8(1): 89–96.

McLaughlin, Neil. 2000. A Spatial Theory of Rhythmic Resolution. *Leonardo Music Journal* 10: 61–67.

McNutt, Elizabeth. 2003. Performing Electroacoustic Music: A Wider View of Interactivity. *Organised Sound* 8(3): 297–304.

Menezes, Flo. 1998. La spatialité dans la musique électroacoustique. Aspects historiques et proposition actuelle. In Jean-Marc Chouvel and Makis Solomos, eds., *L'Espace: Musique/Philosophie*, 351–364. Paris: L'Harmattan.

Menezes, Flo. 2002. For a Morphology of Interaction. *Organised Sound* 7(3): 305–311.

Merzbow (Masami Akita). 1999. The Beauty of Noise. (Merzbow interviewed by Chad Hensley.) *EsoTerra* 8. Http://www.esoterra.org/merzbow.htm.

Milicivic, Mladen. 1998. Deconstructing Musical Structure. *Organised Sound* 3(1): 27–34.

Miller, Paul (aka DJ Spooky that subliminal kid). 2004. *Rhythm Science*. Cambridge, Mass.: MIT Press.

Minard, Robin. 1991. La musique environnementale. In Francis Dhomont, ed., *L'espace du son?* (2), 23–27. Ohain, Belgium: Eds. Musiques et Recherches (Liens: Revue de l'aesthétique musicale).

Mion, Philippe, Jean-Jacques Nattiez, and Jean-Christophe Thomas. 1982. *Envers d'une oeuvre: De Natura Sonorum de Bernard Parmegiani*. Paris: Buchet/Chastel.

Miranda, Eduardo Reck. 1994. From Symbols to Sound: AI-based Investigation of Sound Synthesis. *Contemporary Music Review* 19(2): 211–232.

Miranda, Eduardo Reck, ed. 1999. *Música y nuevas tecnologías: Perspectivas para el siglo XXI*. Barcelona: L'Angelot.

Miranda, Eduardo Reck. 2000. *Readings in Music and Artificial Intelligence*. Chur: Harwood Academic Publishers.

Miranda, Eduardo Reck, James Correa, and Joe Wright. 2000. Categorising Complex Dynamic Sounds. *Organised Sound* 5(2): 95–102.

Misch, Imke, and Christoph von Blumröder, eds. 2003. *François Bayle—L'image de son/Klangbilder: Technique de mon écoute/Technik meines Hörens* (In French and German). Signale aus Köln-Musik der Zeit—series Komposition und Musikwissenschaft im Dialog IV. Münster: LIT Verlag.

Monroe, Alexei. 2003. Ice on the Circuits/Coldness as Crisis: The Resubordination of Laptop Sound. *Contemporary Music Review* 22(4): 35–43.

Moore, Adrian, Dave Moore, and James Mooney. 2004. M2 Diffusion: The Live Diffusion of Sound in Space. In *International Computer Music Conference Miami 2004 Proceedings*, 316–320.

Mountain, Rosemary. 2001. Caveats from a Dyed-in-the-Wool Futurist. *Organised Sound* 6(2): 97–102.

Mountain, Rosemary. 2004. Marketing Strategies for Electroacoustics and Computer Music. *Organised Sound* 9(3): 305–313.

Mulder, Alex. 2000. Towards a Choice of Gestural Constraints for Instrumental Performance. In Marcelo Wanderley and Marc Battier, eds., *Trends in Gestural Contol in Music*, 322–353. CD-ROM. Paris: Ircam.

Müller, Ulrich. 1999. Klangkörper. In Jörg Stelkens and Hans G. Tillman, eds., *KlangForschung '98*, 127–136. Saarbrücken: Pfau.

Nattiez, Jean-Jacques. 1990. *Music and Discourse: Toward a Semiology of Music*. Princeton: Princeton University Press.

Neill, Ben. 2002. Pleasure Beats: Rhythm and the Aesthetics of Current Electronic Music. *Leonardo Music Journal* 12: 3–6.

Norman, Katharine. 1996. Real-World Music as Composed Listening. *Contemporary Music Review* 15(1): 1–27.

Norman, Katharine. 2000. Stepping Outside for a Moment: Narrative Space in Two Works for Sound Alone Lansky—Things She Carried/1, Ferrari—Presque rien avec filles. In Simon Emmerson, ed., *Music, Electronic Media, and Culture*, 217–244. Aldershot: Ashgate.

Norman, Katharine. 2004. *Sounding Art: Eight Literary Excursions through Electronic Music*. Aldershot: Ashgate.

Normandeau, Robert. 2002. Qu'est-ce concert? *Circuit* 13(1): 43–50.

Norris, Michael. 1999. Reinstating Interpretation: The Status of Analysis in an Electroacoustic Context. In *Proceedings of the 1999 Australasian Computer Music Conference*, 63–66. Victoria: University of Wellington. Also available at http://farben.latrobe.edu.ac.mikropol/volume5/norris_m/norris_m.html/.

Norris, Michael, and John Young. 2001. Half-heard Sounds in the Summer Air: Electroacoustic Music in Wellington and the South Island of New Zealand. *Organised Sound* 6(1): 21–28.

Obst, Michael. 1996. We Need New Criteria for the Evaluation of Electroacoustic Music. In *Académie Bourges I—Aesthetics and Electroacoustic Music, 1995*, 74–78. Paris: Actéon—Mnémosyne.

Okkels, Ingeborg, and Anders Conrad. 2000. Bricoleur and Engineer in Computer Music. In *International Computer Music Conference 2000/Berlin Proceedings*, 8–11.

Orton, Richard. 1992. Musical, Cultural, and Educational Implications of Digital Technology. In John Paynter, Tim Howell, Richard Orton, and Peter Seymour, eds., *Companion to Contemporary Musical Thought*, vol. 1 (2 volumes), 319–328. London: Routledge.

Ostertag, Bob. 1996. Why Computer Music Sucks. Http://www.l-m-c.org.uk/texts/ostertag.html/. (Originally published in *Resonance Magazine* 5(1), 1996.)

Ostertag, Bob. 2002. Human Bodies, Computer Music. *Leonardo Music Journal* 12: 11–14.

Oswald, John. 2001. *Plunderphonics*. 2 CD set. Fony 069/96 (including a 50-page interview with Norman Igma).

Paine, Garth. 2002. Interactivity: Where to from Here? *Organised Sound* 7(3): 295–304.

Paine, Garth. 2003. Editorial. *Organised Sound* 8(2): 127–131. (Thematic issue on sound installations which he guest edited.)

Palombini, Carlos. 1998. Technology and Pierre Schaeffer: Pierre Schaeffer's Arts-Relais, Walter Benjamin's technische Reproduzierbarkeit, and Martin Heidigger's Ge-stell. *Organised Sound* 3(1): 35–43.

Pape, Gerard. 2002. Iannis Xenakis and the "Real" of Musical Composition. *Computer Music Journal* 26(1): 16–21.

Paynter, John, Tim Howell, Richard Orton, and Peter Seymour, eds. 1992. *Companion to Contemporary Musical Thought* (2 vols.). London: Routledge.

Pendergast, Mark. 2000. *The Ambient Century: From Mahler to Trance—The Evolution of Sound in the Electronic Age*. London: Bloomsbury.

Pennycook, Bruce. 1986. Language and Resources: A New Paradox. In Simon Emmerson, ed. *The Language of Electroacoustic Music*, 119–137. Basingstoke: Macmillan.

Pennycook, Bruce. 1992. Composers and Audiences: New Relationships in the Technological Age. In John Paynter, Tim Howell, Richard Orton, and Peter Seymour, eds., *Companion to Contemporary Musical Thought*, vol. 1 (2 volumes), 555–564. London: Routledge.

Petitot, Jean. 1989. Perception, Cognition, and Morphological Objectivity. *Contemporary Music Review* 4: 171–180.

Piché, Jean. 2003. De la musique et des images. *Circuit* 13(3): 41–49.

Pierret, Marc. 1969. *Entretiens avec Pierre Schaeffer*. Paris: Pierre Belfond.

Polansky, Larry. 1998. Singing Together, Hacking Together, Plundering Together: Sonic Intellectual Property in Cybertimes. Paper written for Humanities Research Institute 98, "The Tangled Web." Available at http://www.the-open-space.org/osonline/polansky/singing.html/.

Poli, Giovanni de. 1996. In Search of New Sound. *Computer Music Journal* 20(2): 39–43.

Polli, Andrea. 2004. Modelling Storms in Sound: The Atmospherics/Weather Works Project. *Organised Sound* 9(2): 175–180.

Pope, Stephen Travis. 1996. A Taxonomy of Computer Music. *Contemporary Music Review* 13(2): 137–145.

Pope, Stephen Travis. 1999. Web.La.Radia: Social, Economic, and Political Aspects of Music and Digital Media. *Computer Music Journal* 23(1): 49–56.

Popper, Frank. 1993. *Art of the Electronic Age*. London: Thames and Hudson.

Poss, Robert M. 1998. Distortion Is Truth. *Leonardo Music Journal* 8: 45–48.

Pouts-Lajus, Serge. 2003. Nouvelles pratiques musicales des amateurs. *Les Dossiers de L'ingénierie éducative: Des outils pour la musique* 43: 16.

Prendergast, Mark. 2000. *The Ambient Century*. London: Bloomsbury.

Pressing, Jeff. 1994. Novelty, Progress, and Research Method in Computer Music Composition. In *International Computer Music Conference Århus 1994 Proceedings*, 27–30.

Ramstrum, Momilani. 2004a. *From Kafka to K . . . : A Multimedia Exploration of Manoury's Opera K . . .* DVD-ROM. Paris: IRCAM, Opera National de Paris.

Ramstrum, Momilani. 2004b. From Kafka to K . . . : Documenting and Electronic Opera. In *International Computer Music Conference Miami 2004 Proceedings*, 350–353.

Reddell, Trace. 2003. Laptopia: The Spatial Poetics of Networked Laptop Performance. *Contemporary Music Review* 22(4): 11–22.

Rémus, Jacques. 2004. La sculpture sonore, pratique artistique en recherche de définition. In Robert Barbanti, Enrique Lynch, Carmen Pardo, and Makis Solomos, eds., *Musiques Arts Technlogies: Pour une approche critique*, 61–77. Paris: L'Harmattan.

Richard, Dominique M. 2000. Holzwege on Mount Fuji: A Doctrine of No-Aesthetics for Computer and Electroacoustic Music. *Organised Sound* 5(3): 127–133.

Richards, John. 2005. Getting Beyond the Medium. In *Proceedings of EMS05 Montreal*. Available at http://www.ems-network.org/article.php?id_article=117/.

Riddell, Alistair M. 1996. Music in the Chords of Eternity. *Contemporary Music Review* 15(1): 151–171.

Risset, Jean-Claude. 1996. A Few Remarks on Electroacoustic Music. *Académie Bourges I—Aesthetics and Electrtoacoustic Music, 1995*, 82–84. Paris: Actéon—Mnémosyne.

Risset, Jean-Claude. 1999. Composing in Real-time? *Contemporary Music Review* 18(3): 31–39.

Risset, Jean-Claude. 2002. Foreword to Thomas Licata, ed., *Electroacoustic Music: Analytical Perspectives*, xiii–xviii. Westport, Conn.: Greenwood Press.

Roads, Curtis. 1992. Composition with Machines. In John Paynter, Tim Howell, Richard Orton, and Peter Seymour, eds., *Companion to Contemporary Musical Thought*, vol. 1 (2 volumes), 399–425. London: Routledge.

Roads, Curtis. 1996a. *The Computer Music Tutorial*. Cambridge, Mass.: MIT Press.

Roads, Curtis. 1996b. The Golden Age. In *Académie Bourges I—Aesthetics and Electroacoustic Music, 1995*, 85–87. Paris: Actéon—Mnémosyne.

Roads, Curtis. 2000. The Time Domain. In *Académie Bourges: Actes V (1999/2000). Time in Electroacoustic Music*, 153–160. Paris: Eds. Mnémosyne.

Roads, Curtis. 2001. *Microsound*. Cambridge, Mass.: MIT Press.

Rocha Iturbide, Manuel. 1995. Unfolding the Natural Sound Object through Electroacoustic Composition. *Journal of New Music Research* 24(2): 384–391.

Rodgers, Tara. 2003. On the Process and Aesthetics of Sampling in Electronic Music Production. *Organised Sound* 8(3): 313–320.

Rowe, Robert. 1993. *Interactive Music Systems*. Cambridge, Mass.: MIT Press.

Rowe, Robert. 2001. *Machine Musicianship*. Cambridge, Mass.: MIT Press.

Roy, Stéphane. 1996. Form and Referential Citation in a Work by Francis Dhomont. *Organised Sound* 1(1): 29–41.

Roy, Stéphane. 1998. Functional and Implicative Analysis of Ombres Blanches. *Journal of New Music Research* 27(1–2): 165–184.

Roy, Stéphane. 2003a. L'utopie, contrée fertile de l'aventure électroacoustique. *Circuits* 13(3): 19–31.

Roy, Stéphane. 2003b. *L'analyse des musiques électroqcoustiques: Modèles et propositions*. Paris: L'Harmattan.

Rubin, Anna. 2000. Forêt Profonde by Francis Dhomont—Representation of the Unconscious. In *International Computer Music Conference 2000 Berlin Proceedings*, 28–31.

Rudy, Paul. 2004. Spectromorphology Hits Hollywood: Black Hawk Down—A Case Study. In *International Computer Music Conference 2004 Miami Proceedings*, 658–663.

Savouret, Alain. 2002. Électroacoustique et perspective phonoculturelle. *Circuit* 13(1): 9–19.

Schaeffer, Pierre. 1952. *À la recherche d'une musique concrète*. Paris: Seuil.

Schaeffer, Pierre. 1967. *La musique concrète*. Paris: Presses Universitaires de France.

Schaeffer, Pierre. 1970. *Machines à communiquer 1: Genèse des simulacres*. Paris: Seuil.

Schaeffer, Pierre. 1971. Music and Computers. In *Music and Technology: Stockholm Meeting: La Revue Musicale*, special issue: 57–92.

Schaeffer, Pierre. 1972. *Machines à communiquer 2: Pouvoir et communication.* Paris: Seuil.

Schaeffer, Pierre. 1977. *Traité des object musicaux: essai interdisciplines*, 2nd edition. Paris: Seuil. (Originally published in 1966.)

Schaeffer, Pierre. 2004. Acousmatics. Trans. Daniel W. Smith. In Christoph Cox and Daniel Warner, eds., *Audio Culture: Readings in modern music*, 76–81. New York: Continuum.

Schaeffer, Pierre, and Guy Reibel. 1998. Solfège de l'objet sonore. Paris: INA-GRM M0018241LP (3 CD set).

Schafer, R. Murray. 1976. *Creative Music Education.* New York: Schirmer.

Schafer, R. Murray. 1994. *Our Sonic Environment and the Soundscape: The Tuning of the World.* Rochester, Vermont: Destiny Books. (Originally published in 1977 as *The Tuning of the World.*)

Schedel, Margaret Anne. 2004. Alternative Venues for Computer Music: SoundGallery_Living Room_Art Ship. *Organised Sound* 9(3): 301–303.

Schloss, W. Andrew. 2003. Using Contemporary Technology in Live Performance: The Dilemma of the Performer. *Journal of New Music Research* 32(3): 239–242.

Schneider, Hans. 2000. *Lose Anweisungen für klare Klangkonstallationen.* Saarbrücken: Pfau.

Schulz, Bernd, ed. 2002. *Rezonanzen/Resonances: Aspekte der Klangkunst.* Heidelberg: Kehrer Verlag. (Bilingual, with an enclosed CD.)

Scipio, Agostino di. 1994. Micro-time Sonic Design and Timbre Formation. *Contemporary Music Review* 10(2): 135–148.

Scipio, Agostino di. 1995. Centrality of Téchne for an Aesthetic Approach to Electroacoustic Music. *Journal of New Music Research* 24(2): 369–383.

Scipio, Agostino di. 1997. The Problem of 2nd-order Sonorities in Xenakis' Electroacoustic Music. *Organised Sound* 2(3): 165–178.

Scipio, Agostino di. 1998. Compositional Models in Xenakis's Electroacoustic Music. *Perspectives of New Music* 36(2): 201–243.

Scipio, Agostino di. 2002. Systems of Embers, Dust, and Clouds: Observations after Xenakis and Brün. *Computer Music Journal* 26(1): 22–32.

Scipio, Agostino di. 2003. "Sound Is the Interface": From Interactive to Ecosystemic Signal Processing. *Organised Sound* 8(3): 269–277.

Serra, Xavier. 2003. Computer Music Research: Present Situation, Future Ideas. Talk given for the Digital Music Research Network—Queen Mary's/University of London. Available at http://www.elec.qmul.ac.uk/dmrn/events/dmrn03/index.html/.

Settel, Zack, and Cort Lippe. 1994. Real-time Timbral Transormation: FFT-based Resynthesis. *Contemporary Music Review* 10(2): 171–179.

Sherburne, Philip. 2001. 12k: Between Two Points. *Organised Sound* 6(3): 171–176.

Simoni, Mary, ed. 2006. *Analytical Methods of Electroacoustic Music*. New York: Routledge.

Simoni, Mary, Benjamin Broening, Christopher Rozell, Colin Meek, and Gregory H. Wakefield. 1999. A Theoretical Framework for Electro-acoustic Music. In *International Computer Music Conference 1999 Beijing Proceedings*, 333–336.

Small, Christopher. 1987. *Music of the Common Tongue: Survival and Celebration in Afro-American Music*. London: Calder.

Smalley, Denis. 1986. Spectro-morphology and Structuring Processes. In Simon Emmerson, ed., *The Language of Electroacoustic Music*, 61–93. Basingstoke: Macmillan.

Smalley, Denis. 1991. Spatial Experience in Electro-acoustic Music. In Francis Dhomont, ed., *L'espace du son?* (2), 121–124. Ohain, Belgium: Eds. Musiques et Recherches. (This publication belongs to the series "Liens: Revue de l'aesthétique musicale.")

Smalley, Denis. 1992a. Listening Imagination: Listening in the Electroacoustic Era. In John Paynter, Tim Howell, Richard Orton, and Peter Seymour, eds., *Contemporary Musical Thought*, vol. 1 (2 volumes), 514–554. London: Routledge.

Smalley, Denis. 1992b. Valley Flow. On *Impacts Intérieurs*. Montreal: Empreintes DIGTALes IMED-9209-CD.

Smalley, Denis. 1993. Defining Transformations. *Interface* 22(4): 279–300.

Smalley, Denis. 1994. Defining Timbre—Refining Timbre. *Conpemporary Music Review* 10(2): 35–48.

Smalley, Denis. 1995. La spectromorphology: une explication des formes du son. In Louise Poissant, ed., *Esthétique des arts médiatiques, Tome 2*, 125–164. Sainte-Foy: Presses de l'Université du Québec.

Smalley, Denis. 1996. La spettromorfologia: una spiegazione delle forme del suono. In *Musica/Realità* 50: 121–137; 51: 87–110.

Smalley, Denis. 1997. Spectromorphology: Explaining Sound Shapes. *Organised Sound* 2(2): 107–126.

Smalley, Denis. 1999. Établissement de cadres relationnels pour l'analyse de la musique postschaefférienne. In Denis Dufour and Jean-Christophe Thomas, eds., *Ouïr, entendre, écouter, comprendre après Schaeffer*, 177–213. Paris: INA/Buchet/Chastel.

Smalley, Denis. 2004. Spektromorphologie: Ein Zeichensystem zum Verständnis einer neuen Klangkunst. In Marianne Kubaczek, Wolfgang Pircher, and Eva Waniek, eds., *Kunst, Zeichen, Technik: Philosophie am Grund der Medien*, 157–200. Münster: Lit Verlag.

Smalley, Denis, and Lelio Camilleri. 1998. The Analysis of Electroacoustic Music: An Introduction. *Journal of New Music Research* 27(1–2): 3–12. (Themed issue on "The Analysis of Electroacoustic Music" that they edited.)

Smith, Sophy. 2000. Compositional Strategies of the Hip-Hip Turntablist. *Organised Sound* 5(2): 75–79.

Smith, Sophy. 2005. The Compositional Processes of Hip-Hop Turntable Teams. Ph.D. thesis, Leicester, De Montfort University.

Spiegel, Laurie. 1999. Music as Mirror of Mind. *Organised Sound* 4(3): 151–152.

Stelkens, Jörg. 1999. Vorwort zur KlangForschung '98. In Jörg Stelens and Hans G. Tillman, eds., *KlangForschung '98: Symposium zur elektronischen Musik*, 7–8. Saarbrücken: Pfau.

Stelkens, Jörg, and Hans G. Tillman, eds. 1999. *KlangForschung '98: Symposium zur elektronischen Musik*. Saarbrücken: Pfau.

Sterne, Jonathan. 2003. *The Audible Past: Cultural Origins of Sound Reproduction*. Durham, N.C.: Duke University Press.

Stiegler, Bernard. 2003. Bouillonnements organologiques et enseignement musical. *Les Dossiers de l'Ingénierie Éducative: Des outils pour la musique* 43: 11–15.

Stockhausen, Karlheinz. 1958. Actualia. *Die Reihe* 1: 45–51. (Original German edition published in 1955.)

Stockhausen, Karlheinz. 1959. . . . how the time passes . . . *Die Reihe* 3: 10–30. (Original German edition published in 1957.)

Stockhausen, Karlheinz. 1961. Two Lectures/1—Electronic and Instrumental Music. *Die Reihe* 5: 59–66. (Original German edition published in 1959.)

Stockhausen, Karlheinz. 1964. Music and Speech. *Die Reihe* 6: 40–64. (Original German edition published in 1960.)

Stockhausen, Karlheinz. 1996. Electroacoustic Performance Practice. *Perspectives of New Music* 34(1): 74–106.

Stroh, Wolfgang Martin. 1975. *Zur Soziologie der elektronischen Musik*. Zurich: Amadeus.

Stroppa, Marco. 1999. Live Electronics or . . . Live Music? Towards a Critique of Interaction. *Contemporary Music Review* 18(3): 41–77.

Stuart, Caleb. 2003a. Damaged Sound: Glitching and Skipping Compact Discs in the Audio of Yasunao Tone, Nicolas Collins, and Oval. *Leonardo Music Journal* 13: 47–51.

Stuart, Caleb. 2003b. The Object of Performance: Aural Performativity in Contemporary Laptop Music. *Contemporary Music Review* 22(4): 59–65.

Stuckenschmidt, H.-H. 1958. The Third Stage: Some Observations on the Aesthetics of Electronic Music. *Die Reihe* 1: 11–13. (Original German edition published in 1955.)

Subotnick, Morton. 1999. The Use of Computer Technology in an Interactive or Real Time Performance Environment. *Contemporary Music Review* 18(3): 113–117.

Supper, Martin. 1996. *Elektroakustische Musik und Computer Musik*. Darmstadt: Wolke.

Supper, Martin. 2001. A Few Remarks on Algorithmic Composition. *Computer Music Journal* 25(1): 48–53.

Tanzi, Dante. 2001. Music Negotiation: Routes in User-based Description of Music. *Organised Sound* 6(2): 111–115.

Tanzi, Dante. 2003. Musical Experience and Online Communication. *Crossings: eJournal of Art and Technology* 3(1). Http://crossings.tcd.ie/issues/3.1/Tanzi/.

Tanzi, Dante. 2004. Information Technology and Communication of Musical Experience: Categories, Conflicts, and Intersections. *Organised Sound* 9(1): 27–34.

Taylor, Timothy. 2001. *Strange Sounds: Music, Technology, and Culture*. New York: Routledge.

Teruggi, Daniel. 2004. Electroacoustic Preservation Projects: How to Move Forward. *Organised Sound* 9(1): 55–62.

Thaemlitz, Terre. No date. The Go Between—E-Mail Interview mit Terre Thaemlitz von Christoph Strunz: Notions of Betweenness. Available at http://www.comatonse.com/reviews/spex0101.html/.

Thaemlitz, Terre. 2001. Operating in Musical Economies of Compromise (or . . . When Do I Get Paid for Writing This?). *Organised Sound* 6(3): 177–184.

Théberge, Paul. 1997. *Any Sound You Can Imagine: Making Music/Consuming Technology*. Hanover, N.H.: Wesleyan University Press (Univ. Press of New England).

Thibault, Alain. 2002. Culture numérique et électroacoustique. *Circuit* 13(1): 51–55.

Thies, Wolfgang. 1982. *Grundlagen einer Typologie der Klänge*. Hamburg: Verlag der Musikalienhandlung Karl Dieter Wagner.

Thomas, Jean-Christophe. 1999. Introduction. In Denis Dufour and Jean-Christophe Thomas, eds., *Ouïr, entendre, écouter, comprendre après Schaeffer*, 11–49. INA/Buchet/Chastel.

Thomas, Jean-Christophe. 2003. Fragments pour Bayle. *Portraits Polychromes* (on François Bayle). Paris: INA-GRM/CDMC. Available at http://www.ina.fr/grm/acousmaline/polychromes/index.fr.html/.

Thome, Diane. 1995. Reflections on Collaborative Process and Compositional Revolution. *Leonardo Music Journal* 5: 29–32.

Thomson, Phil. 2004. Atoms and Errors: Towards a History and Aesthetics of Microsound. *Organised Sound* 9(2): 207–218.

Toop, Richard. 1997. *Ocean of Sound: Aether Talk, Ambient Sound, and Imaginary Worlds*. London: Serpent's Tail.

Truax, Barry. 1984. *Acoustic Communication*. Norwood, N.J.: Ablex. (Second edition published in 2001 by Greenwood Press.)

Truax, Barry. 1992a. Electroacoustic Music and the Soundscape: The Inner and Outer World. In John Paynter, Tim Howell, Richard Orton, and Peter Seymour, eds., *Companion to Contemporary Musical Thought*, vol. 1 (2 volumes), 374–398. London: Routledge.

Truax, Barry. 1992b. Musical Creativity and Complexity at the Threshold of the 21st Century. *Interface* 21: 29–42.

Truax, Barry. 1994. The Inner and Outer Complexity of Music. *Perspectives of New Music* 32(1): 176–193.

Truax, Barry. 1996a. Sounds and Sources in "Powers of Two": Towards a Contemporary Myth. *Organised Sound* 1(1): 13–21.

Truax, Barry. 1996b. Soundscape, Acoustic Communication, and Environmental Sound Composition. *Contemporary Music Review: Real-World Music as Composed Listening* 15(1): 49–65.

Truax, Barry. 1999. *Handbook for Acoustic Ecology, CD-ROM Edition.* Burnaby, B.C.: Cambridge Street Publishing. CSR–CDR 9901. Also available at http://www2.sfu.ca/sonic-studio/handbook/.

Truax, Barry. 2000. The Aesthetics of Computer Music: A Questionable Concept Reconsidered. *Organised Sound* 5(3): 119–126.

Truax, Barry. 2002. Genres and Techniques of Soundscape Composition as Developed at Simon Fraser University. *Organised Sound* 7(1): 5–14.

Tsang, Lee. 2002. Towards a Theory of Timbre for Music Analysis. *Musicae Scientiae* 6(1): 23–52.

Turner, Tad. 2003. The Resonance of the Cubicle: Laptop Performance in Post-digital Musics. *Contemporary Music Review* 22(4): 81–92.

Ungeheuer, Elena. 1994. From the Elements to the Continuum: Timbre Composition in Early Electronic Music. *Contemporary Music Review* 10(2): 25–33.

Ungeheuer, Elena. 1999. Musikalische Experimente in der musikwissenschaftlichen Forschung: Werner Meyer-Eppler und die elektronische Musik. In Jörg Stelkens and Hans G. Tillman, eds., *KlangForschung '98*, 37–50. Saarbrücken: Pfau.

Vaggione, Horacio. 1994. Timbre as Syntax: A Spectral Modelling Approach. *Contemporary Music Review* 10(2): 73–83.

Vaggione, Horacio. 1996. Articulating Microtime. *Computer Music Journal* 20(2): 33–38.

Vaggione, Horacio. 2001. Some Ontological Remarks about Music Composition Processes. *Computer Music Journal* 25(1): 54–61.

Välimäki, Vesa, and Tapio Takala. 1996. Virtual Musical Instruments—Natural Sound Using Physical Models. *Organised Sound* 1(2): 75–86.

Vanhanen, Janne. 2003. Virtual Sound: Examining Glitch and Production. *Contemporary Music Review* 22(4): 45–52.

Varèse, Edgard. 1940. Organised Sound for the Sound Film. *The Commonwealth*, 204–205. December 13.

Vaughan, Mike. 1994. The Human–Machine Interface in Electroacoustic Music Composition. *Contemporary Music Review* 10(2): 111–127.

Veitl, Anne. 2001. Les musiques électroacoustiques et la politique culturelle: repères historiques. In Sylvie Dallet and Anne Veitl, eds., *Du sonore au musical: Cinquante années de recherches concrètes (1948–1998)*. Paris: L'Harmattan.

Visell, Yon. 2004. Spontaneous Organisation, Pattern Models, and Music. *Organised Sound* 9(2): 151–1365.

Voegelin, Salomé. 2004. How Can You Hear It When You Don't Know What You Are Listening for?—The Need for a Critical Context of Listening. *Diffusion* 17-3-04. Available at http://www.sonicartsnetwork/org/diffusion/diffusion_17_03_04.htm/.

Voorvelt, Martijn. 1997. The Environmental Element in Barry Truax's Composition. *Journal of New Music Research* 26(1): 48–69.

Voorvelt, Martijn. 1998. British Post-punk Experimental Pop (1977–1983). Ph.D. thesis, The University of Leeds/Bretton Hall.

Voorvelt, Martijn. 2000. New Sounds, Old Technology. *Organised Sound* 5(2): 67–73.

Waisvisz, Michel. 1999. Riding the Sphinx—Lines about "Live." *Contemporary Music Review* 18(3): 119–126.

Wanderley, Marcelo, and Marc Battier, eds. 2000. *Trends in Gestural Control of Music*. CD-ROM. Paris: IRCAM.

Waters, Simon. 1994a. Timbre Composition: Ideology, Metaphor, and Social Process. *Contemporary Music Review* 10(2): 129–134.

Waters, Simon. 1994b. *Living without Boundaries: Challenging Conventional Art Form Constraints within Education*. Bath: Bath College of HE Press.

Waters, Simon. 2000a. The Musical Process in the Age of Digital Intervention. *ARiADA* 1. Http://www.ariada.uea.ac.uk/.

Waters, Simon. 2000b. Beyond the Acousmatic: Hybrid Tendencies in Electroacoustic Music. In Simon Emmerson, ed., *Music, Electronic Media and Culture*, 56–83. Aldershot: Ashgate.

Waters, Simon. 2003. H-H-H-H-Hybrids. *ARiADA* 3. Available at http://www.ariada.uea.ac.uk/.

Waters, Simon, and Tamas Ungvary. 1990. The Sonogram: A Tool for Visual Documentation of Musical Structure. In *International Computer Music Conference 1990 Glasgow Proceedings*, 159–162.

Watson, Ben. 1996. Frank Zappa as Dadaist: Recording Technology and the Power to Repeat. *Contemporary Music Review* 15(1): 109–137.

Weale, Rob. 2005. The Intention/Reception Project: Investigating the Relationship between Composer Intention and Listener Response in Electroacoustic Compositions. PhD Dissertation, Leicester, De Montfort University.

Weidenbaum, Marc. 1996. Popp Music: Oval, Microstoria, and the Man Behind Their Curtains. *Pulse!* (December 1996). Available at www.disquiet.com/popp.html/.

Weinberg, Gil. 2002a. Playpens, Fireflies, and Squeezables: New Musical Instruments for Bridging the Thoughtful and the Joyful. *Leonardo Music Journal* 12: 43–51.

Weinberg, Gil. 2002b. The Aesthetics, History, and Future Challenges of Interconnected Music Networks. In *International Computer Music Conference 2002 Göteborg Proceedings*, 349–356.

Weinberg, Gil. 2005. Interconnected Musical Networks: Toward a Theoretical Framework. *Computer Music Journal* 29(2): 23–39.

Westerkamp, Hildegard. 2002. Linking Soundscape Composition and Acoustic Ecology. *Organised Sound* 7(1): 51–56.

Winkler, Tod. 1999. *Composing Interactive Music: Techniques and Ideas Using Max*. Cambridge, Mass.: MIT Press.

Windsor, W. Luke. 1994. Using Auditory Information for Events in Electroacoustic Music. *Contemporary Music Review* 10(2): 85–93.

Windsor, W. Luke. 2000. Through and Around the Acousmatic: The Interpretation of Electroacoustic Sounds. In Simon Emmerson, ed., *Music, Electronic Media, and Culture*, 8–35. Aldershot: Ashgate.

Wishart, Trevor. 1978. *Red Bird: A Document*. York: University of York Music Press.

Wishart, Trevor. 1985. *On Sonic Art*. York: Imagineering Press. (Second edition, edited by Simon Emmerson, appeared in 1996, published by Harwood Academic Publishers, Amsterdam.)

Wishart, Trevor. 1986. Sound Symbols and Landscapes. In Simon Emmerson, ed., *The Language of Electroacoustic Music*, 41–60. Basingstoke: Macmillan.

Wishart, Trevor. 1992. Music and Technology: Problems and Possibilities. In John Paynter, Tim Howell, Richard Orton, and Peter Seymour, eds., *Companion to Contemporary Musical Thought*, vol. 1 (2 vols.), 565–582. London: Routledge.

Wishart, Trevor. 1993. From Architecture to Chemistry. *Interface* 22(4): 310–315.

Wishart, Trevor. 1994. *Audible Design: A Plain and Easy Introduction to Practical Sound Composition*. York: Orpheus the Pantomime.

Wörner, Karl H. 1973. *Stockhausen: Life and Work*. London: Faber and Faber.

Worby, Rob. 2000. Cacophony. In Simon Emmerson, ed. *Music, Electronic Media, and Culture*, 138–163. Aldershot: Ashgate.

Worrall, David. 1996. Studies in Metamusical Methods for Sound and Image Composition. *Organised Sound* 1(3): 183–194.

Young, John. 1996. Imagining the Source: The Interplay of Realism and Abstraction in E-A Music. *Contemporary Music Review* 15(1): 73–93.

Young, John. 2002. The Interaction of Sound Identities in Electroacoustic Music. In *International Computer Music Conference 2000 Göteborg Proceedings*, 342–348.

Young, John. 2004. Sound Morphology and the Articulation of Structure in Electroacoustic Music. *Organised Sound* 9(1): 7–14.

Index